LIFE
WORTH
LIVING

A Guide to What Matters Most

**MIROSLAV VOLF,
MATTHEW CROASMUN
and RYAN MᶜANNALLY-LINZ**

RIDER

1

Rider, an imprint of Ebury Publishing,
20 Vauxhall Bridge Road,
London SW1V 2SA

Rider is part of the Penguin Random House group of companies
whose addresses can be found at global.penguinrandomhouse.com

Penguin
Random House
UK

First published in Great Britain by Rider in 2023
Published in the United States by Viking in 2023
www.penguin.co.uk

A CIP catalogue record for this book is available from the British Library

Hardback ISBN 9781846047206
Trade Paperback ISBN 9781846047213

Printed and bound in Great Britain by Clays Ltd, Elcograf S.p.A.

The authorised representative in the EEA is Penguin Random House Ireland,
Morrison Chambers, 32 Nassau Street, Dublin D02 YH68

Penguin Random House is committed to a sustainable
future for our business, our readers and our planet. This book
is made from Forest Stewardship Council® certified paper.

THE OPEN FIELD

Dear Reader,

Years ago, these words attributed to Rumi found a place in my heart:

> *Out beyond ideas of*
> *wrongdoing and rightdoing,*
> *there is a field. I'll meet you there.*

Ever since, I've cultivated an image of what I call the "Open Field"—a place out beyond fear and shame, beyond judgment, loneliness, and expectation. A place that hosts the reunion of all creation. It's the hope of my soul to find my way there—and whenever I hear an insight or a practice that helps me on the path, I love nothing more than to share it with others.

That's why I've created The Open Field. My hope is to publish books that honor the most unifying truth in human life: We are all seeking the same things. We're all seeking dignity. We're all seeking joy. We're all seeking love and acceptance, seeking to be seen, to be safe. And there is no competition for these things we seek—because they are not material goods; they are spiritual gifts!

We can all give each other these gifts if we share what we know—what has lifted us up and moved us forward. That is our duty to one another—to help each other toward acceptance, toward peace, toward happiness—and my promise to you is that the books published under this imprint will be maps to the Open Field, written by guides who know the path and want to share it.

Each title will offer insights, inspiration, and guidance for moving beyond the fears, the judgments, and the masks we all wear. And when we take off the masks, guess what? We will see that we are the opposite of what we thought—we are each other.

We are all on our way to the Open Field. We are all helping one another along the path. I'll meet you there.

Love,
Maria Shriver

To our Life Worth Living students, at Yale and beyond:
This book is dedicated to you. We hope it bears witness
to what we have learned together.

To our readers: Your life is worth living.
We hope this book helps you more profoundly appreciate
the worthiness of our shared humanity.

CONTENTS

Part 4: Facing the Limits

Part 5: Back to the Surface

This Book Might Wreck Your Life

Before he became the Buddha, Siddhartha Gautama's life was going quite well by the usual standards. He was a prince, after all, and enjoyed the luxuries and privileges of royalty. He lived in an opulent palace, ate delicacies, dressed in fine clothes. His father cared for him and was grooming him to rule the kingdom. He had married a princess. They were expecting their first child.

Wealth, power, and familial bliss were his. Every day, he tasted the fruit of the good life. Until it all turned to ashes in his mouth.

One day, while riding through the royal park, Siddhartha saw a feeble old man and was struck by the tragic decay of age. The next day, in the same park, he came upon a sick man. And the day after that, a rotting corpse. Thoroughly shaken by the suffering that seemed to pervade existence, he returned once more to the park, on the day of his son's birth. This time, he met a wandering monk and was overtaken by the impulse to renounce his royal life.

That very night, Siddhartha left everything to seek enlightenment. He didn't stop to say goodbye to his wife and newborn son, for fear that his courage would fail. His life was now a quest. He had seen the truth of suffering and would not stop seeking until he had found the way to overcome it. He began to fast and to discipline his body, trying to attain release through spiritual exertion. All to no avail. So he searched elsewhere.

Several years after leaving home, Siddhartha sat motionless at the foot of a fig tree. For seven weeks he meditated, until at last he reached the insight he had been seeking: suffering comes from craving, so the one free from craving will be freed from suffering. He dedicated the rest of his life to communicating this insight, delivering the gift of enlightenment to anyone who would receive it. Nearly twenty-five hundred years later, his teachings shape the lives of millions of Buddhists and countless others who have found value in his way of life.

BEFORE HE BECAME KNOWN as the first pope, Simon was an ordinary man. He lived in a small house in a small town by a small lake in a small fiefdom at the edge of a very large empire. He had married a woman from the same town and lived near his in-laws. Like many of his neighbors, he made his living as a fisherman. He spent many of his nights out on the lake with his brother, Andrew, plying their trade, looking for a catch. On the seventh day of the week, as the law of God commanded, he rested and attended services at the local synagogue.

A stable trade, a family, a community. Not a flashy life, but a respectable one filled with ordinary goodness. Until two words turned the whole thing upside down.

"Follow me." Jesus, the new teacher from Nazareth, stood on the shore and called to Simon and Andrew. Ordinarily, this would be crazy talk. Who walks up to two guys at work and tells them to drop everything and follow him around? But Jesus spoke with surprising authority. Word around town was that his preaching rang true, that his words carried power, that amazing things happened when he was there.

For some unknown reason, Simon followed. For three years, he listened and tried to understand. Awestruck, he watched miracle after miracle. He learned to call this man not merely "teacher," but "Lord." And this lord, in turn, gave him a new name: Peter, which means "rock." But time and again, Peter failed to live up to his name. He misunderstood, he got overzealous, and when it counted most, he lost his nerve: when the authorities arrested Jesus, Peter denied even knowing him. He watched helplessly as imperial soldiers crucified his Lord. Everything would have been lost, all of his following come to nothing. Except that on the third day, astonishingly, he encountered his Lord, raised from the dead.

From then on Peter's whole life was devoted to living as Jesus directed and spreading the good news about him. For years, he led the growing community of followers. Not many fishermen got farther away from home than a hundred-mile pilgrimage to Jerusalem. Peter's mission led him to Syria and Greece and even the imperial capital, Rome. Eventually, it led to his death. According to Christian tradition, Peter was crucified in Rome. He is said to have insisted that he be hung upside down, because he was not worthy of the honor of dying in the same way as his Lord.

BEFORE SHE WAS the hero of the anti-lynching movement and an icon of Black and women's liberation, Ida B. Wells was a young woman building a life in the midst of difficult circumstances. Born into slavery in Mississippi and freed as a child by the Emancipation Proclamation, Wells lost her parents and her infant brother to a yellow fever epidemic when she was sixteen. To support herself and her surviving siblings, she took a job as a schoolteacher. By her twenties, she had saved enough money to purchase a one-third share in an upstart newspaper, the *Free Speech,* and start a journalistic career. Things were looking up. Until a horrifying but all-too-predictable injustice changed everything.

On March 9, 1892, Thomas Moss, Calvin McDowell, and William "Henry" Stewart were lynched just outside the Memphis city limits. The crime was personal for Wells: she was godmother to Moss's daughter, Maurine.

The experience led Wells to see that she had been fed a lie: "Like many another person who had read of lynching in the South, I had accepted the idea meant to be conveyed—that although lynching was irregular and contrary to law and order, unreasoning anger over the terrible crime of rape led to the lynching; that perhaps the brute deserved death anyhow and the mob was justified in taking his life." But Wells knew Moss and McDowell and Stewart. They "had committed no crime against white women." Suddenly, she saw that lynching was really "an excuse to get rid of Negroes who were acquiring wealth and property and thus keep the race terrorized." Few others in her time would speak this truth so clearly.

When Wells said it plainly in print, "a committee of leading citizens" (i.e., a mob of White vigilantes) ransacked the offices of the *Free Speech* and left a note "saying that anyone trying to publish the paper again would be punished with death." Wells lost her paper, but she stood firm in her vocation to tell the truth about lynching to a world that often didn't want to listen.

She carefully researched lynchings throughout the United States and published her findings in widely circulated pamphlets. She spoke throughout the American North and in Britain. She influenced the founding of the National Association for the Advancement of Colored People (NAACP). Wells also worked tirelessly for women's rights, helping build the Alpha Suffrage Club and the

National Association of Colored Women's Clubs (NACWC). In 2020, Wells was posthumously honored with a Pulitzer Prize special citation. Millions have benefited from her tireless work and unfailing commitment to truth.

The Question

Gautama Buddha: the privileged prince who became the venerable founder of one of the world's great traditions. Simon Peter: the fallible follower of Jesus who became the rock on which the Christian church was built. Ida B. Wells: the stable schoolteacher who became the truth-telling icon of Black and women's liberation. Three very different people with very different lives. What their stories share is an experience that put the shape of their lives into question. What had been normal and assumed became questionable. Something—maybe everything—had to change.

Implicit in these experiences was a fundamental, hard-to-articulate question. There are countless ways to try to express it: What matters most? What is a good life? What is the shape of flourishing life? What kind of life is worthy of our humanity? What is true life? What is right and true and good?

None of these phrasings captures it completely. The question they try to articulate always exceeds them. It always escapes full definition. But that doesn't make it any less real or any less important. Hard as it is to pin down, it is the Question of our lives. The Question is about worth, value, good and bad and evil, meaning, purpose, final aims and ends, beauty, truth, justice, what we owe one another, what the world is and who we are and how we live. It is about the success of our lives or their failure.

However it gets to us, when the Question comes, it threatens (or promises?) to reshape everything. Nothing was ever the same for Siddhartha after his renunciation or Simon after his call or Wells after she took up her vocation in response to the murder of her friends. From one perspective, their lives were wrecked. From their own new perspectives, however, their lives had been reoriented. True, they gave up a lot. (In Wells's case, the loss was double. What she gave up came on top of what the lynch mob had taken from her.) But what they gained—transformation, a radically new orientation toward the world and their place in it, a driving impulse for their lives—was qualitatively more important. Indeed, it was more important to them than their very lives.

This book is about the Question.

We're going to chart out the topography of that Question, point out some landmarks, draw a few boundaries. And we're going to equip you with some habits of reflection specifically suited for engaging this most consequential (and slippery) of questions, so that whenever it comes for you, you'll have the ears to hear it and the resources you need to respond to it well. Think of this as an atlas and a tool kit.

Admittedly, reading this book probably won't do the dramatic work that a major life experience does. Losing friends to White supremacist violence, encountering a teacher who seems to embody the power and truth of God, suddenly seeing the depth of suffering in the world—these are the kinds of shocks to the system that can't be planned or predicted or manufactured by a book.

But the Question is unpredictable. When truth and worth are on the table, even a book can lead to serious change. Frederick Douglass (1818–1895) read *The Columbian Orator* as an enslaved youth and found not only an education in rhetoric but a vision of freedom and human rights. The Question can show up when we least expect it. It lurks behind the seemingly ordinary moments of our lives, ever ready to turn things upside down and put us on surprising new paths.

Maybe all this sounds daunting. Overwhelming, even. Maybe you have a little knot twisting in the pit of your stomach. That's OK. In fact, it's good. If all this feels a little above your pay grade, it just means you understand the stakes. The good news is you're not alone.

Finding Some Friends

The Christian thinker and novelist C. S. Lewis (1898–1963) distinguishes between mere *companions* and true *friends*. With our companions, we share some common activity, whether it's a religion, a profession, an area of study, or just a favorite pastime. This is all well and good, but it is not *friendship* in Lewis's sense of the term. Friendship requires something more: a shared *question*. The one "who agrees with us that some question, little regarded by others, is of great importance," he says, "can be our Friend. [They] need not agree with us about the answer."

The Question is too much for each of us to handle on our own. We *need* friends who will pursue it with us. So here's an invitation: for the purposes of this book, let's be friends. The Question is of great importance to us. We care deeply about it. And we invite you to do the same. We don't need to agree on an answer.

Now, one of the great things about friends is that they often introduce you to other people—people who start out as their friends, but over time become your friends too.

Since 2014, the three of us have been teaching a class at Yale College called Life Worth Living. Over the years, more than a dozen colleagues have taught with us and hundreds of students have participated. We gather small groups of fifteen or so students around seminar tables, and we devote our time together to the Question. For each class, we read texts by a handful of people from major religious and philosophical traditions to help us orient our conversation. We've facilitated similar conversations with groups of mid- and late-career adults and a group of men incarcerated in a federal prison. In each context, we treat Life Worth Living as one long conversation among present-day friends, with help from extraordinarily insightful friends from the past.

That's what we'll do in the coming pages. As opportunity arises, we'll bring to the table some of the people from across the globe and throughout history who have thought deeply about the Question. We'll let them speak up, and we'll see what they can teach us about what matters most and why.

We'll hear from the Buddha again and from other major figures from religious and philosophical traditions (Abraham, Confucius, Jesus, and the like), but also from some lesser-known people who followed one of these traditions, and even from some of our contemporaries. Think of this book as a seminar table that breaks the rules of time and space. And somehow we've all gotten a seat with the whiz kids. As we tell our Yale students, the more focus you put into listening to what your friends around the table say, the more you'll get out of the experience.

Before we move on, let's make four quick caveats. Otherwise, the seminar table approach might lead to some rather serious misunderstandings.

1. Most of the time in this book, we'll be describing what other people think. When we do that, we'll try to do it well. We'll try to make those perspectives as convincing as we can. But they won't be *our* perspectives. Not everything we say here is something we ourselves believe. As you read, pay attention to whether we're representing our own views or describing what someone else thinks. Not only will that cut down on misunderstandings; it will also help you appreciate the dynamic conversation between diverse perspectives that we're trying to facilitate.

   Having said that, it's important for you to know that we're not some sort of neutral Good Life tour guides. Nobody addresses the Question from nowhere. We're all situated and all have our own commitments. So, as we do right off the bat in our classroom, let us tell you briefly where we're coming from. All three of us are Christians. More specifically, we're Christian theologians (that means it's our job to think about Christian faith) who live and work in the United States. We've tried our best (for specifically Christian reasons) to be evenhanded in our treatment of all the voices around the table. We've tried not to slyly stack the deck. But it would be sneaky not to at least tell you where we're coming from and let you do what you will with that information.

2. When we bring folks to the table, we're not supposing that they can speak on behalf of whole religions or philosophical schools. There's no way to sum up or boil down what is often thousands of years of beautiful tradition in a few pages. Or even a few books. We don't intend for you to come away from

this book thinking that you now understand Confucianism or utilitarianism or Judaism. Instead, we hope you come away thinking you've encountered a few key things that particular people in those traditions have said and done. And if one or more of the friends around the table really interest you, go find out more about them. (We say the same thing to our Yale students on the first day of class.)

3. Don't assume that everyone we've brought to the table basically agrees with one another on the really important stuff. It may be tempting to think so, especially for those of us who worry that religious and ideological disagreements drive the social, cultural, and political conflicts of our day. A universal core that everyone agrees on seems to offer a way out. But no such thing exists. Here, the seminar table metaphor is helpful. Humanities teachers don't go into their classrooms assuming that the students all already think the same thing. Or that they'll think the same thing at the end of the class, for that matter. Enduring disagreement is baked into the format.

4. Also baked into the format of the seminar is that someone will inevitably make the last comment in a given conversation—but that doesn't mean they've decided the question. It just means class is over. So, too, with our imagined seminar table. Somebody has to go last, but that doesn't mean they've given the best or final answer. Just because we end a chapter with one particular view doesn't mean it's the right one, or even the one we think is right.

OK. Enough throat-clearing. Let's get going.

Pre-pos-ter-ous

It just so happens that each of us authors has a daughter. When Ryan's was six years old, she was learning how to read and had gotten to the point where she was trying big words. Words like *preposterous*.

Now, when her little six-year-old eyes looked at PREPOSTEROUS, they saw an unpronounceable, unreadable, effectively never-ending string of letters. Everything in her told her to throw in the towel. Except, when you're the big person reading *The Book with No Pictures* to your little brother, you don't just give up and hand the book to Dad. This is serious business, after all.

The trick, she learned, is to take that big, scary string of letters and break it down into more manageable pieces: PRE-POS-TER-OUS. Now, *that's* a phonetic mountain you can climb.

The Question, we've said, is dauntingly big. It's preposterously big. It's the kind of question that can tempt you to throw in the towel. Except, when you're the big person responsible for the shape of your life, you can't just give up and hand your life to somebody else. This is truly serious business.

We'd like to suggest the same trick here that Ryan's daughter used with *preposterous*: take the big, scary Question and break it down into at least somewhat more manageable pieces. As with phonics, so with life-shaping reflection about what matters most— more or less. The more manageable pieces in this case aren't syllables. They're somewhat smaller, more focused sub-questions that address individual aspects of the one preposterously big Question.

This is the approach we've taken with our Life Worth Living class. It works. Students come in not knowing how to start asking the Question or even not really knowing there's a Question to ask. They certainly don't know how to *answer* it. They leave with a set of tools that help them go back to it again and again with more confidence and a better chance of coming to some good answers.

We'll use the same approach here. In each chapter of the book we take on one of the sub-questions. We introduce the particular sub-question, see who raises their hand to offer an answer, and then lay out the stakes of answering in different ways.

What these chapters won't do is answer the sub-questions for you. That's your job. While it's important to have friends alongside you in the quest, when it comes down to it, only you can actually respond to the Question, or even its more manageable sub-questions, for yourself.

Only You

How free are we to shape our lives? And how much responsibility do we have for them?

At the start of the card game war, you are dealt a random hand of cards. So is everyone else at the table. You don't know what your cards are, and you can't see the other players' either. Each player flips over the top card on their deck. Whoever flips the highest card takes all the cards that have been flipped and puts them at the bottom of their deck. If two or more players tie for the highest card, they each flip another . . . and another . . . and another . . . until one of them shows a higher card.

The game goes on—inexorably, mercilessly—until one player has all the cards.

There are no decisions in war. There's only a procedure. Any machine that could recognize which cards were higher and lower could play the game just as well as a human. Nobody is responsible for how the game turns out.

At the start of a round of poker, just like in war, you are dealt a random hand of cards. And so is everyone else at the table. You can't see the other players' hands. But in this game, you *can* see your own. As play proceeds, players make bets and cards are turned over for all the players to combine with the cards in their hands. You're hoping to build the strongest hand of five cards.

There are rules that say which hands are the strongest. And there are rules about how you can respond at each point in the round. There might be limits on how much or how often you can bet. You certainly can't flip over other players' cards. Or reshuffle the deck at random. That sort of thing.

When you play poker, you're not in complete control. You don't pick your cards. Or your opponents' cards. Or how your opponents bet. Or how they respond to your bets. Or the rules of the game. Most of it is out of your control.

Even so, you're responsible for how you play your hand. You can't determine the outcome. That always depends on both chance and how other players act. But you're not uninvolved in the outcome either. How things turn out depends in part on what you do with the situations you're given. You're a participant. And you answer for how you participate.

It seems like war and poker stand in stark contrast. In war, you appear to have no choices and no responsibility, whereas in poker you have some constrained choices and some real responsibility. But here's the thing: even when you play war, you have a certain kind of responsibility. You're not even partly responsible for the outcome, of course. But you are responsible for how you play. Will you be gracious to the toddler who's having the time of her life across the table from you? Or will you resent her for dragging you into this deterministic hell? Will you play by the rules? Or will you sneakily change seats to get the better hand while your opponent is getting a snack? (One of us tried this as a four-year-old. It did not work.)

Is life more like poker or more like war? How much maneuvering room do the "rules" of life give us? It's hard to say. There are serious arguments on both sides. But regardless of where on the poker-to-war spectrum the truth falls, two points are important. First, you have *some* responsibility for the shape of your life. (The shape of your life includes both your wins and losses and how you play the game.) Second, that responsibility is not unlimited. It's constrained. You didn't get to say where you were born. An enormous, stupefyingly complicated world is always shaping the situations you find yourself in. And you don't get to determine the outcomes. (Elbow grease and pluck won't guarantee you success. That's an American fiction. And a harmful one, at that.)

Not even *who* you are is fully up to you. Everyone goes through things that shape them in ways they wouldn't want if they'd had the choice. In really important ways, we simply find ourselves being who we are.

You are not an omnipotent dictator. You don't call all the shots. That's clear enough.

But to go back to the first point, you are also not a rock. A rock doesn't respond if someone picks it up, chisels it a bit, and lays it down as part of a garden path. You do respond, in limited but nevertheless very real ways, to what happens to and around you. You play your hand.

You're not a hamster either. A hamster does respond if someone picks it up. There might even be a sense in which it decides how to respond. But a hamster can't ask how it *ought* to respond. You can. And because you can, you're responsible for whether or not you do.

Even here, there are constraints. Ancient Mayans couldn't just decide that enlightenment or following Jesus or seeking racial justice was what life is really about, what they should be seeking. Those weren't even truly thinkable possibilities for them. But the responsibility here is real nonetheless. Just because there's a normal path to follow doesn't mean you're not responsible for whether you follow it or not. Just because there's a standard vision of the good life for someone like you doesn't mean you're not responsible for whether or not you make it your own.

This is the most fundamental form of that constrained responsibility that characterizes your life. It's the responsibility to discern, as best you can, what kind of life would be truly worth seeking— the responsibility to see the Question and respond to it.

It's as Bad as You Think It Is (and That's a Good Thing)

Without a doubt, the most beloved saying of Jesus of Nazareth in our day is "Do not judge, lest you be judged," not least because some contemporary Christians are distressingly eager to judge others. We recoil at judgment—especially judgment of our whole lives. Our biggest fear when someone judges some part of our lives is that they're actually judging the whole.

This book claims that our greatest fears are true. Our lives— not just one or another aspect, but the whole of them—are subject to judgment. Who gets to judge and by what standards—these are important questions. We'll touch on them in the pages that follow.

But we begin with the idea that our lives as a whole can succeed or fail. Some of the things we do and leave undone indicate successes and failures not just in one or another aspect of life, but of our humanity itself.

But this book also claims that it's actually a good thing that our lives have these sorts of stakes. The meaning and richness of life as we know it and live it, here and now, comes in part from its seriousness. A championship game means more than an unplanned pickup game because more is on the line. Even more fundamentally, the weight of our lives comes from their irreplaceability. By most accounts, we have only one life to live. By most accounts, there is nothing more precious than life. To succeed or fail with respect to the whole of our lives is the weightiest thing we can do.

Above All an Architect

Albert Speer (1905–1981) was an intelligent young man and a brilliant architect. When Hitler offered him the role of chief architect for the Nazi Party, he was less than thirty years old. He found the offer impossible to pass up. He was, as he put it, "above all an architect." And Hitler offered him the opportunity to "design buildings the like of which had not been seen for two thousand years. One would have had to be morally very stoical to reject the proposal," he wrote years later. "But I was not at all like that."

So he said yes. And then he participated (more than he ever admitted) in some of the most egregious crimes in history. He served the German war effort, made use of slave labor, facilitated the Holocaust. And meanwhile, he did, indeed, design spectacular buildings.

There is a certain greatness to Albert Speer. It lies in the fact that he was "above all an architect." That singular devotion to his career made him an exceptionally *good* architect. But that greatness also contains the monstrosity of his life because that same singular devotion also made him an exceptionally *bad* human being.

It is possible to succeed in our highest aspirations and yet fail as human beings.

Part of the beauty of our humanity is that we are able to ask the Question and to enact responses to it in our lives. This ability makes possible both the goodness and the corruption of our humanity, both the truth and falsity of our lives.

Perhaps very few of us will ever face the kind of catastrophic failure that Speer exemplifies. Perhaps we will not be confronted with the question of whether achieving our personal ambitions is worth collaborating in crimes against humanity. And perhaps we will therefore escape Speer's dreadful affirmative answer. Or perhaps we will fall short of our humanity simply by not aspiring to anything of particular note. But each of us has to answer for the shape of our lives one way or another. Is it enough to bet that if we fail to live a life worthy of our humanity, the failure will at least be modest? Or might we instead embrace the Question, devote ourselves to answering it as well as we can, and seek to become people who could honestly say not "I was above all an architect" but "I was above all a human being"?

How to Read This Book

We hope you're convinced that it's worthwhile to invest serious time and energy in wrestling with the Question. Stakes as high as the shape of our lives call for serious reflection. That said, it's important to make a distinction: wrestling seriously with the Question is one thing, and doing that through reading, writing, and dedicated reflection time is another. We recognize that not everyone has the opportunity to reflect on the Question in the specific way we're inviting you to. Systemic inequalities and existing conditions can make it impossible. Most people throughout history have asked what matters and why, what it means to flourish, what kind of life is deeply worth living. And most of them have done so without relying on reading books and writing down their thoughts. Many have done so in the midst of toil and hardship. Millions still do today.

There are also millions of us who are unable to wrestle with the Question cognitively due to intellectual disabilities and other limitations. Indeed, all of us were unable to do so when we were very young. And many of us will see our capacity for this sort of reflection radically transformed by dementia. There is no bigger human question than the Question, but that doesn't mean you're only human if you're able to wrestle with it.

All of this *does* mean that there's a certain privilege in the fact that you're here reading these pages: at this moment you have abilities and opportunities that not everyone has. We encourage you to take this privilege seriously and use it well. Here are some recommendations for how you might do that while reading this book:

1. Read the chapters in order. The five parts of the book follow a progression, and the individual chapters build on one another. You'll likely get the most out of the experience if you follow this path, rather than jumping forward and backward based on which questions interest you the most. We've broken

the Question down into somewhat more manageable pieces, but that doesn't mean it's just a grab bag.

2. Find a pace that works for you. It may be that you'll benefit from going slowly. But it's also possible that you'll find a groove and want to read one chapter after the next in quick succession. Either approach could be great! Our one caution would be that there's not much to be gained by just racing from start to finish and then leaving it behind. The Question isn't an item on a to-do list. We can't just cross it off and move on. So, whatever pace you settle into, give yourself some space to sit with the questions and claims you encounter. There's no shame in reading a paragraph, a page, or a chapter twice.

3. Consider writing as you read. It will help you engage actively with the questions and voices we'll be considering. It doesn't really matter where you write. Write all over the book if you want (unless it's a library copy, of course). We'd be honored. Academics that we are, we're big fans of underlining, highlighting, and writing notes in the margins. Or you may want to grab a notebook or journal to have more space to express your thoughts.

4. We've offered a section at the end of each chapter called "Your Turn." You'll find prompts and questions there to help you organize your reflection. These provide opportunities for you to work out your own reactions, thoughts, and convictions. But they could also be seeds for enriching conversations with others. Which brings us to another recommendation. . . .

5. Talk with people about the thoughts that come up as you read. The Question is best considered in dialogue, both with people who you agree with and those you don't. To be clear: the point isn't to talk about this book. The point is to talk about the questions and ideas (and ultimately ways of living) that the book discusses. That said, it can be truly wonderful to have a consistent community of people reflecting on the same questions for a specific period of time. If that sounds appealing to you, think about forming a book group and meeting (online or in person) for regular conversations. We've created some resources for book discussion groups. You can find them at lifeworthlivingbook.com.

6. Finally, cut yourself some slack. We've emphasized the stakes and weightiness of the Question. Those are real and true, and it's important to emphasize them because it's all too easy to miss the Question entirely. But it's also important not to put too much pressure on ourselves. Reading one book won't "answer" the Question for us. That's not what reading this book (or writing it, for that matter) is for. It's meant instead as part of a lifelong process. (As authors, each of us found that our responses to the Question have been challenged and refined yet again in the process of writing.) We hope this book offers you something more durable than an answer. We hope it helps you get a better understanding of the Question and the sub-questions along the way. If you come away able to ask and wrestle with more precise, richer, and deeper forms of these questions, that's plenty. The reason it's enough is that we're seeking to build habits of reflection together, along with skills and abilities that make the serious work of wrestling with the

Question more doable. Lastly, we hope you come away with some basic raw material that, over time, you might work into a sturdier, more compelling response to the Question. So to reiterate: the goal isn't to finish thinking about the Question. The truly important thing is to get started. Let's do that.

....

Your Turn

We invite you to start this process by taking stock. The questions below will serve as a life inventory of where you stand now—a glimpse of how you're implicitly responding to the Question as you live your life. Future exercises will refer back to these answers, so feel free to take a bit of time with them. (Fear not. Future exercises will also be shorter!)

As you answer the questions, notice (but don't judge) what answers immediately come to mind, and what thoughts surface after several minutes of reflection. Write down your observations, ideally in a notebook or journal. They can take the form of notes, keywords and phrases, full sentences, or longer reflections—whatever you find helpful.

To start, check in with yourself. What's going on with you *right now*? Ask yourself:

* How is my body?
* What are my dominant emotions?
* What thoughts have been occupying my mind?

Next, take stock of some key aspects of your life: how you invest your time, money, and attention. Maybe even go straight to the sources—flip through your calendar, look through your recent expenses, or scroll through your newsfeed. Consider the following aspects of your life:

* Time
  * What is your daily schedule like?

* What events regularly appear on a weekly, monthly, and yearly basis?
* How much time is unscheduled? What time do you give yourself for rest? Social connection? Spiritual practice?

* Money
  * What are your largest regular expenses?
  * Who do you spend money on?
  * What do you splurge on?
  * To what sorts of organizations do you donate?

* Attention
  * What's the first thing you listen to, read, or consider when you wake up? What websites do you frequent?
  * Which apps on your phone do you use most frequently?
  * Whose voices and opinions are most present to you? (Consider newspaper columnists; TV, podcast, or radio hosts; the people you follow on social media.) What are they saying?
  * What's the last thing you listen to, read, or consider before you go to bed?

For each of these, notice without judgment what comes to mind. Write down your observations, large or small, consequential or seemingly insignificant. Simply gather the facts.

Now do the same thing for your orienting emotions (how you

feel not just right now, but from day to day in the regular course of your life).

* What are your greatest hopes for yourself? For your community? For the world?
* What are your greatest fears?
* What brings you joy?
* What are your sources of peace?
* What memories trigger responses of regret or disappointment? What memories trigger responses of satisfaction or delight?
* What tends to make you feel embarrassed?

OK, now step back. If someone looked at this inventory (not that anyone needs to, unless you want them to) and they tried to summarize your life, how might that person finish the sentence, "Above all, they (i.e., *you*) were _____"?

How would you feel about that answer? How would you *want* them to finish the sentence?

If there's a gap there, don't worry. We're at the beginning of our journey, and while it might be uncomfortable, admitting a certain degree of "hypocrisy" can be really helpful at this point. The easiest way not to be a hypocrite is to lower your standards to match your life. It takes moral courage to hold on to standards and at the same time admit that we are falling short of them.

If you're reading this book with a trusted friend or group (our sense is that all the questions we're tackling are best tackled together in truth-seeking communities), consider sharing what surfaced for you.

Part 1

....

DIVING IN

ONE

What's Worth Wanting?

It can be surprisingly difficult to keep the Question clear. For a moment, it seems we've got it. A moment later, it's slipped through our fingers. A conversation about what sort of life is truly worthy of our humanity becomes a conversation about tips and tricks to help us live a long, happy, healthy life. A question about the truth of flourishing life can suddenly become one about what sort of life we happen to want.

Of all the communities where we've had these conversations, one stands out as most naturally able to keep the Question clear. Within the cinder block walls of Danbury Federal Correctional Institution, incarcerated Life Worth Living students have no problem tracking the distinction between "what I want" on the one hand and "what's truly worth wanting" on the other. They know themselves, in some sense, as "criminals." (Matt once accidentally [and red-facedly] referred to them as such, and to a man [the course was taught in a men's facility], they owned the label entirely.) That means they begin with the assumption that for a substantial period of their lives, they were wholeheartedly pursuing a mistaken vision of life. It was more or less exactly what they wanted, but it was not in fact worth wanting. This gave the men of Danbury FCI a serious leg up on just about all of their fellow Life Worth Living students on the "outside."

As we take up the challenge of responding to the Question, we want to help you distinguish the various related but, importantly, different questions that will naturally present themselves as we attempt to home in on the Question that so easily slips through our fingers.

To do so, we'll describe four different modes of being in the world, each with its own characteristic kind of question. Sorting them out will help orient you among the questions we'll be wrestling with. One mode is *reflexive*—a spontaneous, embodied state of activity. We'll call it "autopilot." The three other modes of being in the world are *reflective*. We'll call them "effectiveness," "self-awareness," and "self-transcendence." Each of these modes has its own corresponding question, so there are four modes and four questions. No mode is bad in and of itself. All four need each other.

We experience these four modes as "layers," so we can imagine our interaction with them as a little like a deep-sea dive. There's a surface layer, and then there are different zones underwater, each with its own characteristics. As in a dive, we generally move between adjacent layers, rather than jump over them. As we enter into deeper reflection—and we must!—we move into deeper layers. When we move toward action—and we must!—we move into higher layers.

Each layer depends on the answers given to the questions asked at the layers below—even, or especially, when those questions haven't been answered explicitly. If we haven't answered one of these questions—perhaps it hasn't even occurred to us—everything we do, say, and think nevertheless shows evidence of some answer to it. We live answers to the deep questions of life even if we couldn't give those same answers if we were asked for them point-blank. All the more reason to dive in and get used to the deep water.

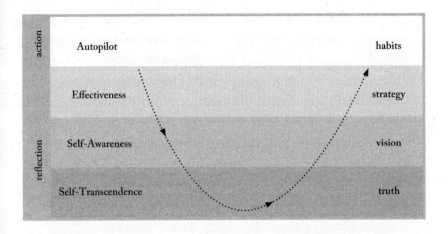

It would be rude, however, to just push you off the boat without first telling you what to expect, so this chapter offers an orientation to the four layers.

Life on the Surface: Autopilot

The surface layer is what we'll call "autopilot." When we're living only in this layer, we're not even aware of *why* we do what we do. We simply do what we do because that's what we do. This layer is a matter of spontaneous, embodied practice: reflex and habit. Life here is lived out of the sort of knowledge that dwells in our muscles and our bones. The machinery of our lives—individually and collectively—just keeps churning and we do not think to ask how or *why*.

Much of life is lived up at the surface. And that's as it should be. When life at the surface is humming along, we're in a state of "flow" and living lives worthy of our shared humanity. We're locked in and operating smoothly, absorbed in our activity and doing it well. In the best-case scenario, what we do reflexively is finely tuned to give us the results we really want, and what we really want is worth wanting. In this case, our reflexive life reflects our deepest values—and, indeed, what is true independent of our values. If so, we are the sort of people the Greek philosopher Aristotle (384–322 BCE) would call wise. We have practical wisdom of the sort an excellent woodworker has. In our case, however, we know how to build not a chair but a life.

But a state of virtuous flow isn't the only time when we do what we do simply because that's what we do. We live by reflex whenever we aren't reflective about our actions. This is Socrates's infamous "unexamined life," which he said "is not worth living." So this layer can also be the one in which, in our collective lives—say, at a company we work for—our daily routine has no deeper justification than "that's the way we've always done it." And it doesn't take groupthink to operate this way. We can just as well live on autopilot all on our own. Cut off from deeper modes of reflection, reflexiveness is just mindless routine. The machine keeps churning, but we have no idea why—which can (or should) be deeply troubling.

Just Below the Surface: Effectiveness

We have probably all experienced the unhelpful form of autopilot and the way it can make us feel stuck and compel us to take a step back and reassess our habits. We also may know that feeling of relief when, at last, someone bursts into the room and asks, "But is what we do getting us what we want?" or "How can we get more of what we want?" Whichever form it takes, this is the effectiveness question. It's the heart of the "design thinking" that's so in vogue these days.

When autopilot isn't working, the effectiveness question *does* come as a great relief. We're able to step back and reflect on our actions and consider whether they're really getting us where we want to go. For organizations and for individuals, this can be a watershed moment that re-centers our daily routines and tunes them around our goals.

There's also a helpful ruthlessness to reflection in this layer. "That's how we've always done it" no longer cuts it. New processes are designed. New practices are cultivated. If we're doing it right, reflection at this layer streamlines our daily routines and directs our energies. As a team, we say we're now all "pulling in the same direction." After a season invested in reflection in this layer, we can return to reflexive life with the knowledge that our new habits will yield the results we're after.

The disadvantage of this layer of reflection, however, is that it is ends-agnostic. There's no concern for whether the goals we have are the right ones—or even really ours. An efficient system gets you more of what you want—*whatever* that is. And that can actually be dangerous if you haven't thought all that hard about what you really want. An effective strategy for homing in exclusively on your professional goals and neglecting the most meaningful relationships in your life is actually worse for your life than an ineffective strategy. If the ends are bad, then better means are hardly the solution.

The example of allowing one's professional life to overrun one's relationships may sound a little ridiculous, but often we don't venture deeper than these top two layers. The effectiveness question strikes many people today as the most insightful question there is. Under its spell, we marvel at those who are able to master it. Silicon Valley captivates the imagination because its firms churn out products and services that can do anything. They are masters of effectiveness. And so they appear to be masters of what really matters.

Let's be clear, though: there are matters deeper than effectiveness. One great lie of the twenty-first century is that the effectiveness question is the most profound question we can ask. The truth is closer to this: these days, the effectiveness question is the most profound question many of us know how to answer.

Deeper Still: Self-Awareness

Most of us, however, have experienced the hollowness of effectiveness. We realize in such moments that there must be a deeper question. It's all well and good to know how to get more of what we want, but it's even more important to ask, What do we *really* want? What are we really after? Where are we really trying to go?

This is the self-awareness question. It invites us to a process of introspection. From the hustle and bustle of autopilot and the cold-blooded calculus of strategic reflection, we enter a private space. We look inward. We stop being distracted by what's most easily accomplished and instead ask what it is that, deep down, we desire. We take stock of what it is we genuinely value most.

The self-awareness question can get recursive really fast. "What do I want? More authority at work. Well, why do I want that?

What do I really want when I want it? A sense of efficacy, maybe, and the knowledge that people I respect respect me. Well, what am I seeking out of efficacy and respect?" And so on. The deeper we probe here, the more we come to realize that what we want isn't a set of discrete things or outcomes or feelings or even character traits. What we really want is more holistic than that. What drives us is an entire vision of a good life—a comprehensive response to the Question. Somewhere, deep down, we have a vision of the life that we want for ourselves, for our communities—perhaps most clearly of all, for our children or young people we care about. This kind of vision is capacious. By "a vision of a good life," we don't mean a list that specifies every little detail of a life. We mean the broad strokes: what we see when we imagine a life led well, a life going well, and a life feeling as it should.

But even at the level of broad strokes, this vision of life involves some *specificity*. Perhaps what we want is a life lived with courage. Or maybe it's a life that, most of all, leaves room for others. Perhaps we treasure a life of abundant provision. Or maybe one that has just enough. Do we want a life of ecstatic joy or peaceful serenity? Do we prize a life of independence or *inter*dependence? Choices abound. And the choices are ours.

The self-awareness layer can be a lonely place. As we probe the depths of our own intuitions and preferences, there is no escaping the fact that these visions of a good life—and our reasons for preferring them—are just ours. Even if we do this sort of reflection as a group, we come to realize that our collective vision is inescapably ours. It may not be compelling, or even understandable, to those outside the group.

If we want to live with integrity, we will need to orient the rest of life—our effective strategies and our reflexive habits—around this vision of life that we've found through greater reflection. That is, the task we are presented with in the self-awareness level is to explicitly and intentionally orient our lives around that which our hearts have always been called to (both automatically and implicitly).

Bedrock: Self-Transcendence

A life intentionally oriented toward the deep desires of one's heart sounds pretty good. Getting to that self-awareness and integrity would be a serious accomplishment. But even if we get to substantially actualized self-awareness, we may still feel a nagging, unsettling dissatisfaction. There are two different versions of this experience.

On the one hand, there's the "success" scenario. We've managed to orient our lives around getting us what we really do want. And, in large part, we're actually getting it. And yet . . . there's still something missing. Admittedly, this is a privileged problem. It's the stuff of mid- and quarter-life crises for those "fortunate" enough to stumble into them. Many spend their entire lives climbing a ladder only to find at the top that the ladder has been leaning against the wrong wall.

But the ladder of success isn't the only path to this insight. There are also those moments when the frustration of being shut out of what we've always been told is "the good life" raises an analogous concern: sometimes, with our nose pressed up against the glass, we start to wonder whether that shiny object in the store window of life is worth all we've invested in getting it. Ta-Nehisi

Coates expresses something like this insight when, from his standpoint as a Black American who grew up on its margins, he questions the value of the American Dream that holds so many under its sway.

Whether it comes from "success" or frustration, whenever we discover we've built our lives around a vision that rings hollow no matter how much we actually want it, we find ourselves in moments of crisis. Asking the effectiveness question doesn't help. In fact, our ruthless pursuit of what we want—of the vision of a good life we've chosen to orient our lives around—seems to be part of the problem.

And the self-awareness question won't really help either. We can try to meet the crisis by recursively applying the lesson we learned at the self-awareness level, but that quickly becomes a never-ending loop of introspective navel-gazing. The answer, sadly, is not within, because we really do *want* the very things we have now found *wanting*; we wouldn't be where we are if we didn't really want them.

No, the only question suited to these moments—the question we ought to get to know sooner rather than later, lest we maroon our lives on the reef of successful self-actualization or waste them chasing after visions of life unworthy of our humanity—is not "What do we want?" but rather "What is worth wanting?"

As we said above, what we really want is not simply a set of things or experiences or even character traits, but rather a whole vision of life. The same goes here. We might ask and attempt to answer the question "What is worth wanting?" with respect to various particulars in our lives: What's worth wanting when it comes to where I live and with whom? Or what's worth wanting when it comes to a meaningful career? Or what's worth wanting in the sphere of economics, ecology, or government? But when it comes to what is worth wanting, the worthiness we seek is not, first of all, in one or another component of our lives. It is to be found, rather, in the holistic unity of flourishing life. When we answer the question "What is worth wanting?" in any of the particulars of our lives, our answers depend on some larger answer to the biggest version of this question. Something like: What is the shape of flourishing life? It's what we've called the Question.

action	Autopilot	We do what we do because that's what we do.
	Effectiveness	Is what we do getting us what we want?
reflection	Self-Awareness	What do we really want?
	Self-Transcendence	What is worth wanting?

The effectiveness question pushed you to find reliable strategies to get wherever you happened to be going. The self-awareness question pointed you to your orienting vision of a good life, your compass. The self-transcendence question, in contrast, asks you about the *validity* of that vision. Is your vision of a good life—that vision of the life you want for yourself, your community, and your world—true? Is what you see as a good life in fact true life? Does your compass point to true north—or is it leading you astray?

In other words: Is the life you're after really worth pursuing? How could you know? On what basis could you make such a determination? What or who is so worth pursuing that it makes plain the worthiness of all else in a life organized around pursuing it?

When we reach this layer, the self is no longer at the center of our quest. Our desires are no longer the criteria for what matters. *We* are no longer the heart of the matter. In fact, quite the opposite: this question aims to push us out of the center. It invites—maybe even demands—self-transcendence.

At these depths, we can easily begin to lose our bearings. Here, the question is no longer about our intuitions or desires. Here, the question is about truth. This is unfamiliar territory for most of us. Indeed, the effectiveness and self-awareness questions often pose as strategies for no longer having to wrestle with questions of truth. They suggest that we instead ask whether we are effectively getting what we really want and then be done with it.

But then that nagging question comes back to us again: Is what we want worth wanting?

In dealing with questions of *truth*, we need a different set of skills, a different set of mental habits. Here, the name of the game is *normative inquiry*: careful reflection about how we and the world ought to be.

The good news is that while the self-awareness layer is prone to isolation, in the self-transcendence layer we find that we are not so alone after all. Others come back into view, because the questions have to do with them as well. To be honest, we may find these others troublesome. The claims we make about worth and value and truth in this layer aren't comfortably private. They impinge on others. To claim with the Buddha that craving is the cause of suffering, with St. Peter that Jesus is Lord, or with Ida B. Wells that lynching is a betrayal of our humanity, is to make a claim about what is true for everyone. The truth of our shared humanity is a shared truth. And so we have to contend with one another about any claims we make to truth, keeping in mind that we won't all come to the same conclusions.

It's not just our contemporaries who come into view at this level. The ancients reappear as well. They've been down here in the depths waiting for us. When we begin to ask questions about the good life, we find that while we're in uncharted territory for ourselves, we're actually right in the thick of conversations that the world's great traditions have been having for thousands of years. Moses, Plato, Confucius, the Buddha, Jesus, Muhammad—to say nothing of more recent thinkers, from Mary Wollstonecraft to Friedrich Nietzsche to Martha Nussbaum—all were asking this question long before we stumbled upon it. Their answers probably cannot simply be our answers without contextualization. That would ignore the question of self-awareness, which we'll still have to attend to on our way back to the surface. But their answers can help us—the way they posed the question perhaps even more so.

In their—and one another's—presence, we will find that the question of the truth of the good life can be asked. And that, with all humility, we can answer it.

The Return Journey

It's a long dive to get from autopilot to the deep and extraordinarily rich space where self-transcendence takes us. It's no easy task.

Even so, after we have plumbed the depths, we still need to get back to the surface. Apprehending the truth of the matter does us no good if we do not embrace this truth as our own. The truth learned on the journey of self-transcendence has to become our own vision. And any work we do at these deeper levels remains esoteric knowledge unless we have effective strategies to live out what we've learned. There's a limit to how intentionally we can live our daily lives, so we'll need to have practices that can give expression to these insights we've found. What we've learned with our minds needs to be knit into our bodies. Indeed, the relationship between minds and bodies is not so simple. This process, like most processes, is one we'll need to return to again and again. And during some dives, what we'll need to consider down below is whether our practices might be smarter than our ideas.

Returning to the surface will often feel just like that: a return to where we can breathe! To the place where what we've gained below receives life. Here visions of the good life become, bit by bit, actual good lives. If it would be foolish never to probe the depths, it would be equally foolish to try to live our whole lives below the waterline. Such endless reflection (were such a thing possible) would be suffocating.

But if we learn to take these dives with some regularity, we may indeed find our way into flourishing life.

The Course Ahead

The rest of this book is designed as a guided tour down to the depths. Chapters 2 to 12 each take one slice of the self-transcendence question and introduce you to some fellow questioners who can help you respond to it for yourself. After that, we'll turn to the return journey with three chapters that equip you to chart your course from self-transcendence through self-awareness and practices toward a life you believe is deeply worth living. But first we have to take stock of some common answers we maybe haven't thought very hard about.

Your Turn

1. Think back nonjudgmentally over the last few days. What questions have been on your mind? Write down your observations.

   Read over your list of questions. Not every one of them will fit into the categories from this chapter (*Where did I put my keys? Why is it called a platypus?*). Of the ones that do (*How can I spend less time replying to emails? Why did I get so angry at so-and-so the other day? Should I stop eating meat?*), mark them as effectiveness, self-awareness, or self-transcendence questions. Where has the weight been falling for you? Which ones are you most interested and invested in?

2. Stepping back, at what layer do you feel most comfortable? Where do you like to spend your time? Do any of the layers of reflection make you afraid?

3. How does the idea that there might be a *true* answer to the Question sit with you? Are you more prone to assuming that your answers are the true ones or to thinking that every answer must be equally right?

TWO

Where Are We Starting From?

An adult student once came to Matt with a confession. Her teenage daughter had come to her looking for advice: Should she serve as the manager of one of the school's sports teams?

"Well, what would look best on your college applications?" the mother responded.

The daughter, a bit underwhelmed, quickly ended the conversation and went to see the school's guidance counselor. He had a different question: "What would make you happiest?"

As we said, the woman told this story as a confession. She was crestfallen as she reported the guidance counselor's advice. "What's wrong with me? I've tried to live a meaningful life. I've gone to church all my life. But when my daughter comes looking for wisdom, I have none to offer."

We readily recognize why the mother felt chastened. Surely the guidance counselor's advice to consider happiness was better for the daughter than her mother's austere career strategy. The guidance counselor's "wisdom" seems to come from a deeper, more holistic vision of a good life. And not just any vision of a good life, but one that's especially popular today. In the face of crass careerism, materialism, and desire for fame, it appears deep, unpretentious, and humane. But what sort of wisdom is this?

At the Corner of Happy and Healthy

Call it the "Walgreens vision."

Maybe you remember the old slogan: "Walgreens—at the corner of happy and healthy." Many of us would say that's where the good life is found. Whatever else it might be, the good life is happy and healthy.

And long too. Long is important. After all, if the experience of happiness is good, then a longer experience of happiness is better. In some ways, *healthy* is insurance against a "be careful what you wish for" fulfillment of our desire for a long life. We want a long life only if it's also healthy—and happy. You need all three.

Long, happy, healthy: it's the slogan for a peculiarly modern vision of a life worth living.

The world's great traditions don't endorse a "long, happy, healthy" life without qualification. Neither do billions of followers of Buddha, Jesus, the Hindu sages, or the prophet Muhammad around the world today. In fact, these traditions problematize many components of the Walgreens vision. Why, then, is it so popular?

For one thing, "long, happy, healthy" is pitched to us incessantly. It comes to us from doctors, from well-meaning friends, from profit-seeking advertisers—perhaps most of all from psychologists. It's the vision commended in the pages of *The New York Times* and championed by the burgeoning "wellness" industry (now estimated to be worth $1.5 *trillion* globally). Read the latest wellness listicle online, or consult the most recent psychological study, and there it is, lurking without ever being articulated: the long, happy, healthy life. This is the vision that counts as wisdom in comparison to the unreflective impulses that dominate so much of our culture.

We're not sure we know how to get this life. But that's where psychology, behavioral economics, life hacks, and countless consumer goods come in. The "long, happy, healthy" industry doesn't just help us find our way to its vision of the good life. It also keeps us from considering whether this is the life worth wanting for ourselves, our communities, and the world. It's difficult to pause and consider the *merits* of this vision when we're so busy chasing after it.

Then again, it's not a hard sell. After all, who *wouldn't* want a long, happy, and healthy life? Who exactly is repping short, sad, and sickly?

The Walgreens vision is the grass-fed organic burger on the good life menu. By default, it comes with a side salad, but you know you can swap in fries for that (and add bacon and cheese—isn't virtue fun!). The fact is, it's indulgent—and yet you still get to order something with a leaf icon next to it. Compared to the lifestyles of the rich and famous, it's so sensible. You're not asking for anything extravagant. No helicopters or yachts or fifty million Instagram followers. The server praises your selection, giving you a look that lets you know that your virtue signaling has not gone unnoticed. Then again, the server was going to praise your choice regardless. After all, at the Good Life Bistro, all choices, we assure one another, are excellent ones.

This is how "long, happy, healthy" has become so dominant. It's the result of a feedback loop of our desires, our expectation that they'll always be praised, and a marketing industry wise enough to offer us just the right amount of "virtue" to thrill us without turning us off. In the final accounting, it's not a product we've been force-fed. It's a bill of goods we've sold ourselves. In any case, it may be time to ask for our money back.

Happiness Is King

The slogan may be "long, happy, healthy," but it's not hard to see which bit reigns supreme: happiness. It can be difficult to shake the intuition that what's most valuable in life is feeling the way we want to feel. And why would we possibly want to feel anything other than happy? The French philosopher and mathematician Blaise Pascal (1623–1662) perhaps said it most strikingly: "All men are in search of happiness. . . . This is the motive for men's every action, even those who are going to hang themselves." After all, if you thought something *else* would make you happier, you'd do *that*. It can seem, well, obvious. We do what we do because—whatever our reasoning—we prefer it, and we prefer things because we think they'll make us happier. In chapter 4, we'll look more carefully at just how important it is to feel good and whether feeling good is the same as feeling happy. For now, suffice it to say that the Walgreens vision makes it hard for us to shake the intuition that making ourselves happy is what we're really after.

But this creates a problem. (Actually, a number of problems—but we'll stick with just this one for now.) How on earth do you make yourself feel a certain way? Even worse, suppose you feel responsible for helping someone else find the good life or that you owe someone else happiness. How on earth do you make *them* feel a certain way?

Well, it seems likely that we don't just feel happy for no reason. Maybe it's possible. Maybe we could invent a pill that would make us happy. But for now at least, it's not in the cards. We have to do things a bit more indirectly: arranging the world so that it makes us happy. If we want to be happy, we need the world to be a certain way for us. If we want someone else to be happy, we need the world to be a certain way for them. If we want to maximize happiness for all, we need the world to be a certain way that will make everyone happy.

And so the most important thing to do is make the world that certain way that makes people happy. In this way, the "pursuit of happiness," to borrow from Thomas Jefferson, gives order to the entirety of our lives—or, more than that, to the entirety of life itself. The goal of life is to feel happy. The ideal state of the world is the one that allows people to feel happy. How, then, should we live? Work hard to bring about the world that makes us and the people we care about happy.

The Good Life Tangle

The triple promise of "long, healthy, and above all happy" forms the core of what we tend to assume is worth wanting in life. The core, however, isn't everything. Much of the power of the Walgreens vision is that it builds a whole life around longevity, happiness, and health: a fulfilling career, daily rhythms of work and rest, a good diet and exercise, meaningful relationships, emotional regulation, resiliency, even virtue and character of a sort. Long, happy, and healthy aren't all there is to this vision of the good life. They're more like the little knot at the center of a tangled ball of yarn. Everything else wraps around them.

Talk to a positive psychologist and you'll get no argument for why we ought to prefer a long, happy, and healthy life. Research psychologists are scientists, after all. Strictly speaking, science is about what is, not what ought to be. Philosophy and theology deal with questions of ought. Modern science is primarily about what correlates with what. Dropping a stone correlates with the stone falling. Hydrogen and oxygen in the presence of heat correlates with a loud bang. Getting seven hours of sleep every night correlates with greater rates of self-reported happiness. So does practicing gratitude—and doing yoga. Those same things also correlate with better health outcomes and greater longevity. It's a tangle of correlations, a web of things that tend to happen together.

At base, the psychologist has no reason that you ought to prefer to be in *this* tangle of correlated outcomes rather than some other. They're just building a cloud of correlations. But who would look at this tangle of health, happiness, longevity, gratitude, yoga, and ample nocturnal rest and want to opt out?

Besides, there are great benefits to thinking about the good life as a tangle or a cloud of correlations. For one, because all you're trying to do is get inside the "good life tangle," you don't have to be all that thoughtful about where to start. You can start anywhere. Eat healthier. Keep a gratitude journal. Start doing yoga. Volunteer with the homeless. Get more sleep. Watch a random TED Talk and do what it says. Develop a few close relationships. Start with any one thread from the good life tangle, and eventually you'll find your way into *all* these good things. Because they're all tangled up with one another.

Second, the good life tangle implies that there are no trade-offs. Every single thing worth having correlates with everything else worth having. Being happy will make you healthier and help you live longer. Being healthier will yield happiness and longevity. Even being a good person will make you happier and healthier and help you live longer! According to the strictest version of the Walgreens vision, this is *why* you should care about being a good person. Do the right thing because it will make you happy. Perhaps even: you know it's the right thing to do if it ultimately makes you happy. After all, how could doing the right thing not make you happy? It should all be part of the good life tangle. There are no trade-offs.

Now, it might be that we live in a universe where there are no trade-offs between doing well, doing good, and feeling good. But consider what a stroke of luck that would be. Granted, from time to time, we find that good things we want all seem to come together. For example, the more we invest in significant relationships, the more emotionally resilient we seem to become. But quite often in life, we find that there are in fact trade-offs. The more time we invest in our professional vocation, the less time we have for our families. And even the positive feedback loops that we stumble upon often entail serious costs. For example, the emotional resilience we glean from significant relationships is often tested precisely in the deep conflicts we have to navigate in those same significant relationships.

At any rate, most human beings who have inhabited this planet haven't assumed that we live in a utopian universe without serious trade-offs. Most have assumed that life involves some tough choices. Many have found that if you stand up for what's right, you won't necessarily be praised for it. In fact, you could end up suffering for it. For all the buzz at the beginning of this millennium around "doing well by doing good," many throughout humanity's history have found just the opposite. Doing good can hurt your chances of doing well. They have found that the good life isn't always long, happy, and healthy. Many of the lives we most admire aren't the sort of lives we're actually pursuing.

Not Long

Martin Luther King Jr. (1929–1968) was thirty-nine when he was murdered. He had come to Memphis, Tennessee, to support sanitation workers striking for safe working conditions and fair pay. It was the latest in a string of unpopular moves since he received the Nobel Peace Prize in 1964. He had moved from protesting the Jim Crow South to opposing segregation in northern cities like Chicago. He had vehemently criticized the Vietnam War. He had launched the Poor People's Campaign to advocate for economic justice. None of these stances had majority public support, and King's public profile was in the tank. One poll found that 75 percent of respondents had an unfavorable view of him. And yet there he was in Memphis, still working.

The night before he was killed, King delivered a speech to his fellow protesters. He recounted how, years before, he had been stabbed in the chest and had come within a hair's breadth of dying. He said how happy he was that he had survived. It had allowed him to participate in the following decade of fighting for civil rights for African Americans. He told the audience that he was well aware that his life was still in danger. Then he said this:

> Like anybody, I would like to live a long life—longevity has its place. But I'm not concerned about that now. I just want to do God's will. And He's allowed me to go

up to the mountain. And I've looked over, and I've seen
the Promised Land. I may not get there with you. But I
want you to know tonight, that we, as a people, will get
to the Promised Land!

King didn't *want* a short life. But he didn't make the decision to
pursue a long one. He could have admitted that his views were
unpopular, left public life, and likely lived for many more years.
But he saw that something else mattered more than the length of
his life.

Not Happy

Abraham Lincoln (1809–1865) suffered from crushing, persistent
melancholy. From at least the time of his mother's death when he
was nine, he would go through periods of deep depression. His
friends worried that he might harm himself. By the time he was
president, a profound sense of sadness had impressed itself on his
whole character. One acquaintance remarked that "the melancholy
seemed to roll from [Lincoln's] shoulders and drip from the ends
of his fingers."

As president, Lincoln led the United States through the dreadful violence and death of the Civil War. The burden only intensified his unhappiness. "If there is a worse place than hell, I am in it,"
he lamented. And yet Lincoln chose that place. He took the burden
on himself.

Of course, it's possible that it wasn't in Lincoln's power to feel
happy. Maybe he was inescapably predisposed to a depression that
nineteenth-century techniques couldn't treat. But it's certain that

Lincoln could have spent more of his energy and immense talents trying to feel happy. It's also certain that he didn't. True, Lincoln didn't seek out sadness. But he didn't run from it either, and he didn't let fear of it keep him from doing what he saw as his duty.

What's more, Lincoln's sadness likely contributed to what was most admirable in his character. Knowing and feeling the tragedy of death, wrestling with a sadness that would never go away for good—all this equipped Lincoln to lead with gravity, persistence, and significant (if nevertheless imperfect) compassion and honesty.

Not Healthy

Chronic rheumatism had left Lady Constance Lytton's heart weak. Physically speaking, she was ill suited for the extreme ordeal of a hunger strike. But Lytton (1869–1923) was wholly devoted to the cause of winning women the right to vote in the United Kingdom. And she knew that her high status in society would draw added attention if she joined other activists, known as suffragettes, in rejecting food while imprisoned for their activism.

So when she was arrested at a protest in Newcastle on October 8, 1909, Lytton immediately refused food and drink. The authorities used her weak heart as an excuse to release her quickly and avoid the potential scandal of force-feeding an aristocrat whose brother sat in the House of Lords. The less privileged suffragettes who had been arrested along with Lytton got no such treatment. Their mouths were forced open by steel braces. Tubes were shoved down their throats. And liquefied food was pumped directly into their stomachs as they gagged and choked.

Lytton was incensed. She wanted to expose the unjust favoritism for what it was. So she disguised herself as a poor seamstress named Jane Warton, joined a protest in Liverpool, was arrested again, and began another hunger strike. As Jane Warton, she was repeatedly force-fed.

When Lytton's identity was discovered, it caused a scandal of the sort she had been hoping for. The government denied wrong-doing. But press coverage increased the pressure for a changed policy. Winston Churchill (not yet prime minister) instituted a new rule giving suffragette prisoners the privileges afforded to political dissidents. Lytton's brother chaired a new committee in search of a legislative compromise on suffrage. In response to the change in treatment, hunger strikes subsided for several years.

Lytton never quite recovered from the trauma of her second hunger strike. She toured the country over the next year, giving speeches and protesting. But she suffered from increasingly fre-quent "heart seizures" and bouts of illness. She never again had the strength for the kind of vigorous activism she wanted.

It wasn't until 1928 that all British women over twenty-one won the right to vote. (Property-owning women over thirty had gained the vote in 1918.) When the victory came, it was well after Lytton's most important contributions. She was by no means the central hero of the story. But it is hard to look at Lytton's life and not find something inspiring in her willingness to risk her health for the sake of one of the twentieth century's great justice movements.

Short, Sad, and Sickly?

King, Lincoln, and Lytton weren't superhuman heroes. They weren't perfect. But they didn't have to be perfect for their lives to make us stop and think. Maybe the Walgreens vision isn't as obvious an answer to the Question as it seems to be. And maybe things aren't quite as convenient as the good life tangle would have it. These people (and countless others like them) have paid real, concrete costs in their efforts to live out answers to the Question. That fact should make us skeptical of the ideas that (a) we can know what it means to do good by figuring out what feels good or helps us do well, or that (b) doing good will automatically make us feel good and do well. The good life tangle is a falsifiable hypothesis, not a self-validating axiom. And at first glance, there's some pretty strong evidence to suggest that it is false.

Now, to be clear, we aren't advocating for short, sad, and sickly. As far as we know, none of the world's great religious and philosophical traditions do either. Confucius lived to a ripe old age. Socrates had a cheerful demeanor and lived a joyful life, even in the face of his execution by the Athenian state. The Buddha was renowned for his excellent health. Jesus healed people left and right. Even the famously austere Stoics said that—all else being equal— long, happy, and healthy are preferable to short, sad, and sickly.

But these traditions—like King's, Lincoln's, and Lytton's lives— suggest that there are other things worth living for, even if they cost you your health, your happiness, or your life. They (often passionately) disagree about what those things are and how to pursue them, but that doesn't change the fact that they give the lie to the Walgreens vision's supposed self-evidence.

The Walgreens vision isn't natural and inevitable. Maybe at some level everybody wants a long, happy, healthy life. But that doesn't mean it's anywhere close to the top of the list of things worth wanting. Plenty of the people who will show up in these pages think otherwise.

The Walgreens vision isn't neutral either. It doesn't just translate into plain language what everyone has always dressed up in fancy religious myths and philosophical terminology. It is one answer to the Question among many. And it needs to be interrogated, tested, wrestled with just like the others.

So as we explore the Question together, pay attention to the ways the Walgreens vision might influence your discernment. If you find yourself reflexively leaning in that direction, take note, and do your best to be open to alternatives. That way, if you come out of the process convinced that long, happy, and healthy isn't just what you want but what's worth the best of your energies and effort because it is the measure of everything that is truly worth wanting, you'll be more confident that your vision can stand up under pressure.

If, on the other hand, you realize you need to loosen the grip the Walgreens vision has on you—well, welcome to the struggle.

Your Turn

We're still in the exploratory stage here, trying to uncover more about your own implicit answer to the Question. It's often easiest to illuminate our aspirations, our values, and the like by thinking about how we view other people. Especially the people we think are living (or have lived) flourishing lives.

Think about one or two people you deeply admire. They could be people you know or ones you've heard or read a lot about. Go ahead and jot down their names.

* What do you admire about them? Is it their achievements? Their character? Their good fortune? Their happiness?
* As far as you can tell, does "long, happy, healthy" describe their lives?
* As far as you can tell, does "long, happy, healthy" describe their answer to the Question?

Think about one or two people you envy. Again, they could be people you know or just ones you know about. (It's OK to be honest. Envy might not be pretty, but it can tell us a lot about our desires and dreams.)

* What do you envy about them?
* As far as you can tell, does "long, happy, healthy" describe their lives?

* As far as you can tell, does "long, happy, healthy" describe their answer to the Question?

Since the Walgreens vision is so prevalent today, it will be helpful to take stock of what you think of it before going on to more clearly discern your vision of flourishing.

* What, if anything, do you find attractive about the "long, happy, healthy" view of the good life?
* What, if anything, do you find to be lacking from it? Where does it leave you wanting something deeper, richer, or fuller?
* What might you value more than a long, happy, healthy life?

Part 2

....

THE DEPTHS

THREE

Who Do We Answer To?

In the introduction we suggested that our lives might, much to our dismay, be subject to judgment. This whole book is driven by the thought that we might live more or less *worthy* lives—that one can in fact fail or succeed at being human.

In this chapter, we want to know: Who has standing to render this sort of judgment? Who do we answer to?

When we first started teaching Life Worth Living, it didn't occur to us that this question needed to be on the table. But then, in the middle of that first semester, one of Miroslav and Ryan's students—Leah Sarna, a young Jewish woman who would go on to become one of the first women ordained as an orthodox rabbi—showed us how much it matters. We were sitting in a house on the Connecticut shoreline at an off-site retreat for the class on a crystal-clear winter day. Leah listened attentively as one of her fellow students described his approach to life. When he finished, she looked at him and asked, "Who are you responsible to?"

Her colleague was dumbfounded. He wasn't sure he even understood the question. Undeterred, Leah shared that for her, as a Jew (and as the particular sort of Jew she is), following or not following the Torah isn't just a matter of personal preference. She considers herself responsible to her whole community and to the

God who gave the Torah to that community. In principle, her failure to observe Shabbat or keep kosher would be a failure to hold up her responsibility to her community and God. It would let them all down. And it's that responsibility, she insisted, that changes everything. Without some sense of responsibility—to someone or something—for living our lives a certain way, the whole quest lacks urgency. It becomes a matter of preference. And when it comes to lives that are worth living, preference is dangerously close to whim. She was adamant. Before we can get serious about the question of flourishing life, we need to ask about responsibility.

But not just any sort of responsibility.

Smokey Responsibility

It turns out that *responsibility* is one of those words we use to mean a bunch of different things—in this case, at least three. And while each of these three senses of responsibility is important to our quest, it's helpful to keep them distinct. So before we get started, we need to clarify the question a bit.

To help us out, we'll turn to Smokey Bear, America's iconic forest fire prevention representative. For those who aren't familiar with him, Smokey Bear is a cartoon character created by the United States Forest Service for their public service campaigns to prevent wildfires. Since 1944, he has appeared, clad in jeans and a round-brimmed hat, on road signs, in print ads, and in television public service announcements in the middle of Saturday morning cartoons. Until 2001, his signature line was "Only you can prevent forest fires." (It's now "Only you can prevent wildfires." Grasslands matter too!)

Three distinct senses of responsibility are captured in this single ursine admonition.

First, there's the "only you." This is the *agent* of responsibility, the responsible self. Now, Smokey's not trying to say that you are literally the only one on the planet who can prevent forest fires. What he means is something like the sort of responsibility for your life that we talked about in the introduction. You have an inalienable responsibility for your life, choices, and actions. Including, as it turns out, whether or not you properly extinguish your campfire. Even if you tried to give this responsibility away, that would still be a way of exercising it. (Only you, after all, could try to give away the unique responsibility for your life that only you have.)

Then there's the bit about the forest. This is the *scope* of your responsibility. It's often the sort of responsibility we think of first: what we're responsible for, what we have to do, whose well-being we need to take into consideration. To get a full understanding of our responsibilities, we have to ask, How big is our forest? Maybe we're responsible for acting virtuously. Maybe we're responsible for the happiness of every sentient being, present and future. The scope of our responsibility is a crucial question. It's one of the key features of any answer we give to a question we'll come to in chapter 6: How should we live? We'll save "forest" responsibility for that chapter.

But then there's the guy with his finger in our chests: Smokey Bear. He represents the *authoritative source* of our responsibility to prevent forest fires. He represents the one *to whom* we are responsible. He defines the rules that put us under the obligation to handle fires responsibly. He assesses whether we are, in fact, doing what we can and should to prevent forest fires. And he calls us to account when we fall short, holding us to the relevant forest fire prevention standards. Smokey is lawgiver, judge, and law enforcement official in one. (We don't need to quibble about precisely *how* he represents the authoritative source of responsibility or why the source is authoritative. That's what the rest of this chapter is for.) This is the kind of responsibility this chapter is about: "Smokey" responsibility. We'll focus especially on the question, Where does our responsibility to live a certain kind of life come from?

Maybe *You* Are the Bear

Many of us don't spend a lot of time thinking about Smokey responsibility. There's something unsettling about someone or something outside ourselves that can set the standards for our lives. Often we try to avoid the idea entirely.

Maybe, we think, we can be our own Smokeys. If all responsibility comes down to "only you" responsibility, the source of our responsibility is simply our own choices and whims. After all, we're free. We're independent—or at least we imagine so. We may commit ourselves to various people or causes, but we suppose that *we* do that of our own free will and for our own reasons, whatever those happen to be.

The problem is that if we answer *only* to ourselves for living whatever sort of life we ourselves deem worthy, it's all too easy for our lives to feel arbitrary. If we're both playing the card game and deciding what counts as a winning hand, the game loses the tension that makes it fun to play. If we both sing the song and decide by ourselves what counts *as* a beautiful song, perhaps we're less likely to fail—but we can hardly be said to have succeeded either. The problem isn't just that we may be easy judges (if we're perfectionists, perhaps we'll be the hardest judges of all). More profoundly, the danger is that if we take ourselves to be not just the arbiters but the *sources* of our responsibilities, we may be free to pursue our every whim but we won't be able to rescue our lives from the sneaking suspicion that they are simply products of those whims. The biggest choices of our lives—what career to pursue, whether to start a family, what to do in our retirement—can seem impossible to make. And not so much because it's hard to thread the needle of various cross-pressures, but because there are too many options that seem valid, appealing, and effectively interchangeable.

We may well have a profound responsibility to ourselves. There are thoughtful ways of approaching the Question that center on certain sorts of responsibilities to the self. We'll consider one later in this chapter ("The Law Within") and another in chapter 6 (the ethic of authenticity). But if we want to avoid the sense that the pivotal moments of our lives are merely preferred selections off the menu of life, we'll need to come to terms with the fact that our choices alone can't be the ultimate source of our responsibility. We each have a conscience—and we no doubt ought to pay good attention to it. But to really do its job, this conscience must be an internalized impression of some nonarbitrary (and quite possibly external) source of responsibility. Otherwise, it's hard to tell conscience apart from neuroses we ought to seek to overcome (or not—maybe we like our neuroses; it's up to us—and that's the problem).

If we want our choices to be *meaningful,* there's no escaping the bear. We need some ultimate source of our responsibilities beyond our choices. Better to get familiar with that source sooner rather than later.

Don't Forget Where You Come From

You could imagine it like Westeros, the mythical world of George R. R. Martin's *A Song of Ice and Fire* novels and HBO's *Game of Thrones*: a weakened central power, under pressure from external forces, giving rise to a tangled mess of vassal lords who then dared to call themselves kings. Such was the world of Master Kong (Chinese: *Kongzi*), known in the West as Confucius (551–479 BCE).

The Zhou Dynasty, established five hundred years earlier by the Duke of Zhou, had been a remarkable achievement: the unification not just of a nation but of a *civilization* into a single feudal order. But by the time Confucius arrived on the scene, the Zhou world was falling to pieces. With seemingly every cut-rate lord vying for and claiming one's allegiance, our question—Who do I answer to?—was literal and practical. But behind the immediate question of political allegiance lay a host of more fundamental puzzles: What holds the social fabric together? What form of life is right, regardless of the political winds? When everything else seems up for grabs, to whom are we accountable for living our lives the way we should?

Confucius's followers collected stories about him and sayings of his into a book known as the *Analects*. Right at its beginning, we find the key to Confucius's vision of life:

> A man who respects his parents and his elders would hardly be inclined to defy his superiors. A man who is not inclined to defy his superiors will never foment a rebellion. A gentleman works at the root. Once the root

is secured, the Way [*Dao*] unfolds. To respect parents and elders is the root of humanity.

Try not to get tripped up on the word *gentleman*. This is the Confucian word for the well-cultivated, flourishing human being. While the ancient word was gendered (like the chauvinism built into our word *virtue*, from the Latin *vir*, meaning "male"), we needn't read it that way. The point is that if you want a life worth living—if you want to pursue the Way—you will want to work at the root of what makes a human being truly *humane*. You will want to begin with your responsibility to your parents and elders.

That's precisely how Confucius presents himself. While we may think of him as the founder of Confucianism, he insists, "I transmit rather than innovate; I trust in and love the ancient ways." Even his commitment to honoring the past is built on the model of sages who have gone before: "I might thus humbly compare myself to Old Peng." He declares, "I simply love antiquity, and diligently look there for knowledge."

Why this passionate love for and accountability to those who came before us? It's not just nostalgia for an imagined golden age. Here's the claim:

The traditions into which we are born aren't mere *options* we can pick up or lay down at our discretion. We ourselves came to exist and continue to live in and through these relationships. Our very bodies were generated by and within our biological parents' bodies. We were sustained through infancy and early childhood by those who cared for us.

The language we speak—this, too, is a tradition. We didn't invent it. There's no way we *could* invent it. We can only receive a language and then, through our creative use of it, contribute to the language that others then receive. Everything we say, every question we ask, even every assertion of our alleged modern "individualism," is woven from and back into a tapestry of ever-evolving language received from generations gone by.

In short, we are hardly so independent as modern Westerners sometimes imagine us to be. Rather, we are constituted by the traditions we live in and by the relationships that gave (and give) us life. Therefore, how we live is not arbitrary at all. We answer for the shape of our lives to those from whom we received them and the whole cultural world that provides the means to render our lives significant. We live under responsibility to those who gave us life. They mediate to us, to use Confucius's term, the very Way of heaven, the cosmic order of things. Everything else follows from this responsibility to those who have come before us. It is the root of flourishing humanity. It is the root of the dignity of the self, the peace of one's neighbors, the peace of all. This is how the self is cultivated. This is how community flourishes. This is how political order is established and sustained.

But what happens if something breaks the connection between root and branch, if the root itself becomes rotten? History is littered with examples of loyalty to family leading to theft, murder, and even the kind of rebellion and social breakdown Confucius feared. And there's no reason to think that only families might go astray. Governments do so as well. Who is to guarantee that our entire civilization may not lose the Way? For Confucius, these local sources of responsibility only mediate and can never supplant the ultimate source of responsibility: the Way of heaven itself.

But if heaven is what really counts, might it not be best to cut out the go-betweens and let heaven speak for itself?

The Most Important Promise You Don't Remember Making

Muhammad's revelations began with dreams in the night—but not just any dreams. During the day, what he had dreamed about would come to pass. Odd, to say the least. Then, more and more, he wanted to be alone. He'd leave his wife and go out to the wilderness for days at a time to worship God. And then, on one of these retreats, it happened. In the cave of Hira, an angel appeared and commanded him three times: "Recite!" Like many humble prophets before him, Muhammad demurred, refusing twice. The third time, he was overwhelmed. The revelation began to come: "Recite in the Name of thy Lord Who created, created man from a blood clot."

Leaving the cave, Muhammad was shaken and doubtful. "What is wrong with me?" he asked his wife. Khadijah assured him that he was a good man; God would not put him to shame. She brought him to her cousin, who also encouraged him. The revelations continued. His life was no longer his own. Maybe it never had been to begin with.

The Quran—the book that, we are told, comes from the divine encounters Muhammad had over a period of years—contains a striking story about Smokey responsibility. At the very beginning, when God created human beings, before any of them entered the world, God asked them, "Am I not your Lord?" Every single one answered yes. And God took note so that no one who disregarded God's commands in their earthly life could plead ignorance.

Before we entered this life, Muhammad's visions led him to believe, we recognized God's lordship and committed before God to live by God's commands. You may not remember it, but the

Quran's claim is that it happened. And—whether or not you remember—the responsibility that results is real. There's no getting out of it. That's the point of the story. Come Judgment Day, there's no claiming that you didn't know.

We're *not* sovereign agents, the Quran claims. We can't just do whatever we please. We're accountable to a Judge who has authority over us by virtue of having created us, an authority we've already acknowledged. What's more, according to much mainstream Muslim interpretation of the Quran, you *do* in some sense remember it. At least faintly. Your conscience? That niggling sense of right and wrong? That's the faint echo of the forgotten commitment you made and of your subsequent responsibility to do as God says. Deep down, you know who you answer to. This is a stark, bracing claim. What are we to make of it?

If our responsibility for living our lives a certain way feels like a commitment we don't remember making, then we've probably just reached a crucial insight. This is a basic feature of Smokey responsibility. It comes to us from somewhere other than our own choices. It comes whether we ask for it or not. It comes whether we welcome it or not. It is simply part of what it means to be human.

So many of us, as we discussed above, live our lives on the presumption that when the chips are down, we answer to ourselves. We imagine ourselves to be masters of our own destinies—at least in terms of our aspirations, if not their realization. And whether or not we actually each made a vow to God before entering this life, if taking the possibility seriously offends our sense of "sovereignty," then it has done some important work on us.

Every time we teach Life Worth Living, we make sure to lead our students in an encounter with this story. And we don't present it as just a story. We encourage them—and we encourage you—to consider, What if it were true? What if it *is* true? What if, ultimately, you answer to *God* for the shape of your life? How would your life have to change? Taking this stance toward new and different views can be hard, but our experience teaching Life Worth Living suggests that it's worth it. So we invite you to receive not just this one claim from the Quran but each perspective we present in this book with this same spirit. We invite you to pose the question for yourself again and again: If this were true, how would my life have to change?

The Law Within

Confucius says we're responsible to the traditions we live through. Muhammad says we're responsible to the God who created us. Both save us from the threat of arbitrariness by finding a Smokey outside of us. But couldn't there be some way of being responsible to yourself without falling into arbitrariness? Isn't there something reliable inside us—not something that came from our parents or from God, but something sturdy that is ours as human beings— that could hold us accountable?

Immanuel Kant (1724–1804) thinks so. He thinks reason is our defining quality as humans. And that in the end, we answer to the reason inside us. A moral life is one that heeds the commands of reason. And since Kant thinks reason is universal, the responsibility here is consistent across all people. There's no room for arbitrariness.

As Kant sees it, reason stands distinct from, and above, your feelings and inclinations and desires. But it's not outside you. You are, fundamentally, a rational being. Reason is yours. And that means that when reason commands something—"Tell the truth!" or "Keep your promise!"—it's really you who's giving the command to yourself. In Kant's terminology, you're "autonomous." You give yourself (from the Greek *autos*) the law (from the Greek *nomos*).

Kant's view of moral autonomy has been incredibly influential in the modern era. Unsurprisingly, however, there are significant challenges to it. For one thing, insisting that humans are essentially rational beings and that human dignity comes from our rationality seems to deny dignity to people with limited cognitive capacities. For another, Kant's supposedly universal reason can look suspiciously parochial, like the habits and inclinations of a highly educated, well-off European man.

If you find something like Kant's idea of responsibility compelling, you're on the hook to find some sturdy responses to these challenges. But that's true for any answer to the question of who we answer to. We've already seen, for example, that Confucius's proposal faces the problem of twisted traditions. And those who accept the Quran's account of responsibility need to address the possibility that we don't remember making a primordial promise to God simply because it never happened.

Embracing the Bear

Sorting out Smokey responsibility is serious—and for many of us, seriously unfamiliar—business. It can be tempting to try to avoid it altogether, but if we really *are* responsible to someone or something, we're responsible whether or not we realize it. That's just how responsibility works.

Without a sense of Smokey responsibility, we are left with the threat of arbitrariness. We're "free" to do as we like, but what we do may not matter. If you feel the sting of that threat, then you've already got a taste for the Question. You might not ever be convinced that there's a real source of responsibility, in which case the Question for you is whether there is meaning to be found nonetheless. Alternatively, you might find that you have a deep sense that what matters most can't be arbitrary. In that case, you'll need to come to terms with the idea of a source of responsibility. That source will be something each of us will have to embrace for ourselves ("only you"). But embracing it means recognizing that it makes an ultimate claim on us—a claim that would stand even if we ignored it. Just what we think that source is may have a lot to do with our sense of the really big picture of things: who we are, who God is (or isn't), where we came from, where we're headed (see chapter 8). So we may need to return to the question of accountability again as that sense becomes clearer. In the meantime, some provisional answer to the question of who we answer to will ground all the questions we're about to ask.

After all, it's our sense of Smokey responsibility that grounds the possible gap between the life we want and the life worth living. Without it, all we have is our desires. Questions of worth—of value—appear only when we have to take seriously the possibility that we answer to someone or something beyond our desires— whether family, God, reason, or something else entirely. It's Smokey responsibility that gives teeth to the "oughts" of the questions we're about to ask.

So as we begin to ask the question of the good life in all earnestness, take some time and consider: Who *do* you answer to?

Your Turn

1. Return to the "life inventory" you took on pages xxxii–xxxiv. To whom does the person you see there answer? It may take some digging underneath the data you gathered in the inventory to get a sense of this, but what sources of responsibility (in the Smokey sense) seem to lie behind your life as you currently live it?

2. Who *should* we answer to? To whom or to what are you ultimately responsible? When you think about not just one or another choice, but about the shape of your life as a whole, whose perspective (or perspectives) ultimately counts in assessing whether you're living a life worthy of our shared humanity?

3. How do your answers to questions 1 and 2 line up? Are you living in light of the responsibility you recognize? If not, how would your life be different if you were? Be careful. It's all too easy for this kind of question to lead us into making New Year's–style resolutions. That's not the point here. As we'll see in chapter 15, resolutions are doomed to fall short if we try to use them to live into our deepest insights about the Question. So the point here isn't to make a to-do list. It's to get a glimpse of the kind of life you hope to be living.

FOUR

How Does a Good Life Feel?

It's kind of a silly question, right? A good life feels *good*. Maybe there's some value in occasional pain or in going through an emotional struggle now and then. But what we're all after is a life that feels good.

Let's suppose that's right. So what does it mean to feel good? Again, it seems like a silly question. The difference between feeling good and feeling bad is like the difference between daylight and pitch black. It's obvious. Supreme Court Justice Potter Stewart famously said of pornography, "I know it when I see it." Well, when it comes to feeling good, we know it when we *feel* it. If your feeling feels good to you, that's what counts. Who else could possibly be the judge of that?

Even so, it would be helpful to have a shorthand for "the quality of a feeling that makes it feel good." Let's call it "pleasure." And let's call its opposite "pain."

So, it would seem, the good life has lots of pleasure and as little pain as possible. But we probably don't want to have our pleasure all at once and then live out the rest of our lives in dull monotony. We want lives that are happy for a long time. If there's a common-sense answer to the question of what a good life feels like, this is it. And as it turns out, this answer has some serious philosophical advocates.

Push-Pins and Poetry

It was the summer of 1822, and Jeremy Bentham (1748–1832) wanted the enlightened governments of the world to know he was available. If anyone was looking to adopt the most cutting-edge, logically coherent, philosophically robust constitution known to humankind, he was their guy. And he had the letters of recommendation to prove it.

To get the word out, Bentham wrote the delightfully titled "Codification Proposal, Addressed by Jeremy Bentham to All Nations Professing Liberal Opinions; or, Idea of a Proposed All-Comprehensive Body of Law, with an Accompaniment of Reasons." That might sound like the title of a crackpot's collection of ravings, but Bentham was one of the most highly respected intellectuals of his day—a serious thinker with a serious project.

By the time he published "Codification Proposal" at age seventy-four, he had gained a reputation as a leading social reformer (anti-slavery, anti–death penalty, for the legal equality of women) and had laid out his views in a number of highly regarded books and articles.

Bentham's philosophy is known as *utilitarianism*. It gained a massive following, especially in the English-speaking world, and it remains deeply influential today. They may not know it, but just about every TV pundit talking about the economy simply assumes that utilitarianism is true. It's the philosophy behind their whole growth-maximizing agenda. It's the philosophy that gives some weighty intellectual credentials to our popular take on how the good life feels.

A simple principle is at the heart of Bentham's utilitarianism: "Good is pleasure or exemption from pain. . . . Evil is pain or loss of pleasure." Translating out of his nineteenth-century English: Pleasure is good. So things that lead to pleasure are good. And things that cause us to lose it are bad. Also, pain is bad. So things that lead to pain are bad. And things that cause us to avoid it are good. Nothing else is good. Nothing else is bad.

Moreover, pleasure is just pleasure. This idea opposed a well-worn cultural prejudice of Bentham's day. He came from a wealthy family in a notoriously snobby culture. Most of his peers considered it obvious that some pleasures were "higher" than others. Poetry, orchestral music, painting, ornamental gardening (really)—all these more "intellectual" and "refined" arts—were considered better than the vulgar delights of the masses. Bentham cried foul. "Prejudice apart," he said, "the game of push-pin is of equal value with the arts and sciences of music and poetry." If anything, silly bar games like push-pin have probably made more people happier than poetry ever has. This was like telling a film connoisseur that *Batman v Superman: Dawn of Justice* (Rotten Tomatoes audience score 63% and critic score 29%; $874 million box-office draw worldwide) is more valuable than the Coen brothers' *Hail, Caesar!* (Rotten Tomatoes audience score 44% and critic score 86%; $64 million box-office draw worldwide). Critics' assessments don't matter. What matters is the total amount of pleasure all the viewers combined get from watching a movie. For Bentham, a pleasure is a pleasure is a pleasure. Call this the "push-pin principle."

This all tracks closely with the common view we discussed above. What makes a feeling good? The experience of pleasure. Who is the judge? Whoever is having the experience. Bentham even has his own version of the "as much as possible for as long as possible" principle. He offers a simple calculus for determining how good an action would be: the more intense and long-lasting the pleasure it gives, the better the action. He throws in bonus points for actions that yield pleasure sooner rather than later, that are more certain to yield the pleasure they promise, that are likely to produce future pleasures after their immediate effect, and that are unlikely to produce future pains.

The basic utilitarian approach is elegantly simple. It reduces all possible goods to one: the experience of pleasure. What matters is how much of this you can get. The question of the good life is one of arithmetic. All goods can be added together, and all bads subtracted. The whole trick, whether you're an individual or a whole country looking for a new constitution, is then to set things up so that you maximize the sum. Bentham called this the "greatest happiness principle": do whatever leads to the most happiness.

How does the good life feel? For Bentham, as for many people today, it feels good. It's a life of pleasure, with a minimum of pain. Where the pleasure comes from is different for different people.

As straightforward as this answer might seem, however, only a few of those who have seriously thought about the question agree.

Subha's Eye

It is said that long ago, in the time of the Buddha, a nun named Subha was on her way into the forest to study and meditate when a man with untoward intentions stopped her. She rebuked him, and he proceeded to spout a painful series of the ancient South Asian equivalent of terrible pickup lines. He talked about the blooming flowers and the jewelry he would get her, about the dangers of the forest and the luxury of the palace they would live in together, about how nice his bed smelled (!), and about how the life of a nun would be a waste of a body as beautiful as hers. It was . . . not persuasive. A particularly cringeworthy example: "The trees are covered in flowers like body-hairs standing on end, they seem to moan in pleasure when the breeze blows."

The heart of his overwrought proposition was, *You would get a lot more pleasure with me than you would living a nun's life in the forest.* ("What delights of love will there be for you if you go into the forest all by yourself?") *With me, though* . . . [wink, wink]

Unimpressed, Subha chided the would-be seducer by reminding him that beautiful bodies are just a collection of parts that will all eventually die and fall apart.

Joining a long line of sexual harassers who ignore a very clear rejection, the man tried another approach: complimenting Subha's eyes. (It seems this was already trite 2,500 years ago.)

Subha was still far from convinced. It wasn't just that she didn't find *him* appealing. It was that everything he thought enticing, she found uninviting. "I am happy that I have gone to a deserted place," she told him. The reason was that she wasn't seeking pleasure, but equanimity, a state of consciousness that would remain calm like the ocean's depths regardless of what was happening on the surface: "My mindfulness stands firm in the middle of scolding and praising, happiness and suffering." Meanwhile, she said, you're laughably infatuated with my eyes—which are just gross, watery collections of matter that ooze "milky mucous"!

To demonstrate her own detachment from bodily pain and pleasure, as well as the ridiculousness of the man's fixation on her beauty, Subha then—seriously, this is how the story goes—gouged out her own eye and gave it to him, saying, in effect, "If you like it so much, you can have it." The man immediately repented and asked her forgiveness. Subha went on to the Buddha, and when she saw him with her one remaining eye, the lost eye was restored.

Subha's story comes down to us in a collection of poems about the earliest Buddhist women known as the *Therīgāthā* (or *Poems of the Women Elders*). The poems recount the tales and experiences of women who gained enlightenment through the teachings of the Buddha. A common theme is their rejection of a worldly kind of happiness based on the "as much pleasure as possible for as long as possible" principle. Tempted with sex, wealth, security, and love, the women often respond, "What you take as pleasures are not for me."

The women see that there is a different, higher form of feeling: the contentment that comes from enlightenment, the state of release from the cycle of desire. This is not just a greater amount of pleasure, but a different kind of feeling altogether. The pleasure of getting what you want is hot, burning, passionate. The contentment of enlightenment is cool, calm, peaceful.

Indeed, enlightenment's contentment is experienced at a wholly different level of consciousness than desire's pleasure and pain. It's a calmness that transcends immediate feelings. An experience of not being attached to those immediate feelings, not being invested in them. So it's not that Subha doesn't feel the pain of plucking out her eye. It's that the pain doesn't disturb her at a deep level. And the trouble with pleasure isn't that it feels good. It's that we get invested in it feeling good. It draws our attention away from what really matters. It drives us to have exaggerated concern for ourselves and for what will satisfy our cravings. It might even drive us, like it drives Subha's assailant, to view another person as nothing more than a tool for satisfying our cravings.

Crucially—and we can hardly emphasize this enough—what

Subha and the other women of the *Therīgāthā* are saying is not that they simply prefer a different kind of good feeling to the one their suitors, families, and sleazy seducers are offering. Rather, they are saying that the feeling of enlightenment is better than that of pleasure because it is a more appropriate response to the human condition.

According to the Buddha's teaching, the whole cycle of desiring, seeking, getting what you desire, and then desiring again is "unease" or "suffering" (*duhkha*). It's a bad deal. Even worse, it's embedded in the process of karma. Actions elicit recompense, good for good and bad for bad. When we die, we are reborn in a state befitting our karmic balance: as an animal or a prince, as a god or a ghost, or even in hell. We then die again and are reborn again. The cycle continues on and on with no end. This whole thing is *duhkha*, says the Buddha. Following the Buddha's path and achieving enlightenment is the only way to overcome the problem, and to do so once and for all. Sure, we can and do feel good (even great!) at certain times within the cycle, but it never lasts. So for the women of the *Therīgāthā*, the contentment that comes from following that path and, above all, achieving enlightenment is how a good life feels.

Something More Wonderful

On February 18, 1895, John Sholto Douglas, the Marquess of Queensberry, stormed into the Albemarle Club in London and demanded to see Oscar Wilde. Upon being refused, he left a calling card that read, "For Oscar Wilde, posing Somdomite [*sic*]." Since so-called sodomy was a felony in England at the time, the card amounted to a public accusation of a crime. Hence, either Wilde was guilty of the crime or Queensberry was guilty of libel.

Incensed, Wilde had Queensberry prosecuted. The trouble was, Queensberry's defense was able to compile ample evidence that Wilde had in fact engaged in the alleged behavior. Several trials later, Wilde was convicted of the misdemeanor charge of "acts of gross indecency" and was sentenced to two years of hard labor. One of the most famous writers in Europe suddenly found himself in prison alongside ordinary convicts. The only thing that distinguished him from them is that everyone in England knew that he was there—and why.

The whole affair had begun because of Wilde's relationship with Queensberry's son, Lord Alfred Douglas. On the cold bench of his cell in Reading Jail, Wilde wrote a long, meandering text. It was framed as a letter to Douglas, but Wilde may have intended parts of it for broader publication. It was in fact published after Wilde's death with the title *De Profundis* (Latin for "from the depths").

Looking back on his relationship with Douglas, Wilde chided himself for letting himself get caught up in senseless pleasure. (A character in one of Wilde's plays says of himself, "I can resist everything except temptation." One gets the sense that Wilde's will-power was similarly flawed.) They had wasted away their days with three-hour meals and endless bottles of champagne and concerts and witty banter.

All this fit quite well with Wilde's pre-prison philosophy. He was a hedonist, pure and simple. He lived for pleasure. "I wanted to eat of the fruit of all the trees in the garden of the world," he says. "I filled my life to the very brim with pleasure, as one might fill a cup to the very brim with wine."

It might seem like Wilde is setting us up for a big turnaround. *Once I was devoted to pleasure, but now I see that was wrong! I forsake it all—every last drop!* But Wilde *doesn't* reject the pleasures of the high life. He doesn't deny that they were good in their own way. "I don't regret for a single moment having lived for pleasure," he says. "I did it to the full, as one should do everything that one does."

That said, when Wilde looks forward to life after prison, he doesn't plan to go back to extravagant days and wild nights. Those pleasures had their day. But that day is past. From now on, he will be perfectly happy with no more than his freedom, good books, and the beauty of nature. He can't contain his excitement at the thought that the lilacs will be in bloom when he is released.

These are quieter, more muted, but *deeper* pleasures. Wilde now sees that not all pleasures are equal. Some are "senseless." They flit along on a whim. And while there may be a time and place for them, they aren't the heart of what a good life feels like. The happiness Wilde seeks after prison is one that has "sense" to it. It is the joyful resonance of his being with the tension-filled order of life. Push-pin, he insists, is not equal to poetry. And no matter how much of it there is, fame's pleasure just can't live up to flowers in the fields.

Wilde pushes it further, though. Popular culture, Bentham, and Subha all agree that whatever the good life feels like, it feels good in some sense. To the extent that it feels bad, it's not good. Wilde disagrees.

Sorrow, he says, is "the supreme emotion" humans are capable of. The problem with his all-out pursuit of pleasure wasn't the pleasure part. It was that he ignored sorrow. He cut himself off from this supreme emotion.

Wilde's easy, successful life had come crashing down. When he surveyed the wreckage from his prison cell, he saw something surprising. He saw a deep suffering running through things: "The secret of life is suffering. It is what is hidden behind everything." Life is shot through with disappointments, failures, broken relationships, unintended injuries. And Wilde is convinced that you can't get rid of all this suffering. It's baked into the world. The appropriate response to this secret is sorrow. Sorrow is holy, because it's in touch with the suffering that courses through the world.

In other words, sorrow is true. It echoes inwardly the very reality of life. And truth is the heart of beauty. Which means sorrow is beautiful. And that's what makes it central to the good life in Wilde's new understanding of things.

The last lines of Wilde's letter to Douglas read, "You came to me to learn the pleasure of life and the pleasure of art. Perhaps I am chosen to teach you something much more wonderful—the meaning of sorrow and its beauty."

Wilde never says that sorrow is pleasant. It doesn't feel good. But it is *wonderful*. And a good life must include a sizable dose of its pain. That's because Wilde's answer to the question of what the good life feels like is, *Whatever is true to life in all its splendor, all its suffering, and everything in between.*

So How *Does* It Feel?

Bentham, Subha, and Wilde give us three very different answers to the question of what the good life feels like. It looks like the question isn't so silly after all. It demands your serious attention.

We can't answer this question for you. We can't answer *any* of these questions for you. (Remember the whole responsibility thing?

"Only you . . .") But we can offer some advice on how to go about answering them. There are certain things you should take into account or else you'll miss an important part of the picture.

Here's what we can learn from Subha and Wilde. They both deny that our feelings straightforwardly tell us what the good life feels like. They deny that the satisfaction of our desires is enough. How a good life feels has to do with getting in sync with something deep about the world—not just with getting what we want.

That means that it's at least imaginable that so-called negative emotions might be part of the good life. Consider the possibility. Maybe sometimes it's not just OK but *good* to be sad. Because maybe what matters most isn't feeling a certain way but being rightly attuned to the world—like choosing to mourn with a friend who has lost a loved one.

Now, you can disagree. By all means, go ahead. Again, it's up to you. You can cast your lot with Bentham. You can say that all that matters is how good the feeling feels. Lots of smart people have. But if you do, know what you're giving up. You would have to decide that it would be better for any meaningful experience of sorrow to have never happened in your life. In fact, if sorrow is simply bad, all causes of sorrow are bad, which might well mean that you have a serious responsibility to prevent all potential causes of sorrow. As we'll see in the following chapters, that can be a powerful driver of a demanding vision of moral life. However, your ideal emotional life—indeed, everyone's ideal emotional life—will be available only if and when the world is perfect.

Or maybe not. The strong version of the push-pin principle says it doesn't matter at all what the pleasure is about. It doesn't matter if it's even *about* anything at all. If there were a drug that could make you feel amazingly, astonishingly great for no reason, without any negative consequences, that would be just as good as the joy of meeting your child for the first time. Or let's say the drug could reliably make you feel good over the long haul, no matter what. So regardless of whether you lose your job or your friends betray your deepest trust or your child is never going to speak to you again or a dear friend loses a loved one, you feel splendid. You feel precisely how the good life feels. If you really buy the push-pin principle, you can't object.

So take a good hard look at pleasure and ask if that's really what you're after. Is the good feeling alone what's worth wanting? Or are the really worthwhile good feelings ones that are *about* something good? Would a perfectly chemically engineered high really equal the rush of a long-awaited first kiss, the satisfaction of having completed an important mission, or the quiet joy of cradling a sleeping infant?

Your Turn

1. Return to the "life inventory" you took on pages xxxii–xxxiv.
   * What kinds of connections can you discern between circumstances (in the world and in your life) and your orienting emotions?
   * Where do you hope to see your emotional responses change?
   * What emotions do you desire to feel more often or more deeply?

2. What feelings do you think characterize a genuinely good life?
   * Do you think we can measure all our feelings according to how much pleasure or pain they include? Why or why not?
   * How much does it matter that your feelings connect with something true about the world?

FIVE

What Should We Hope For?

Several years before coming to work with us at Yale, a colleague of ours taught a college class called The Good Life. The class read texts by great moral philosophers. They reflected on personal vocation. They asked about what's right and wrong, and what's important and incidental, in a human life.

At the end of the semester, our colleague perused the course evaluations. Like any dedicated teacher, she was looking for lessons on how she might improve the class. One student's (joking?) comment brought her up short: "I thought there would have been a lot more in this class about yachts."

Our popular imagination often equates the good life with the high life. When you ask about the good life, you're in yacht territory: fabulous homes (plural!), unforgettable vacations, and very fancy boats. Put that way, it sounds silly. But bear with us. There are some deep questions here if we look closely.

The student's comment points to the fact that most of us care about our material conditions. There's some way we want the world to be for us. There's something (maybe a lot of somethings) that we want to have. Now, whenever we have desires like this, we can push down to the level of self-transcendence and ask about genuine worth. What circumstances are worth wanting? What does it mean for life to truly go well? And because we're in the territory of things that happen to us or that we might try to bring about in the world—things that aren't entirely under our control—this is the territory of hope. So we might put the question like this: What should we hope for?

It turns out quite a lot of things we're inclined to value go in the circumstances bucket. Indeed, everything except how you feel (chapter 4) and your own agency (chapter 6) belongs here.

Take money, for example. In 2017, 82.5 percent of students surveyed by the American Freshman Survey said it was "essential" or "very important" to be "very well off financially." No other question got that strong a positive response.

Money is such a big deal because it's a nearly universal means. It's the resource you can exchange for just about any circumstance. There's not much that money can't buy. The sociologist Hartmut Rosa points out that we modern folks *really* like things like money, things that are effective means to just about anything. We may not be so sure how to answer the Question, but we're pretty sure that whatever substantive answer we might someday come to, money will help.

You want delicious food? You can pay for that. You want a good education? Money will hire tutors and build a prestigious résumé too. You want to be healthy? Health care certainly isn't free. A beautiful body? Money will get you cosmetic surgery and a personal trainer. You actually do want a yacht? You'll have to pay—and if you have to ask what it costs, you don't have enough.

Power—or, to use a less aggressive word, *influence*—is similarly appealing. It's also a quintessential means to any end. (Indeed, money is just a form of influence. Pieces of paper and little plastic rectangles don't actually get you anything in themselves. They induce other people to give you things or do things for you.) Millions of people are building Instagram and TikTok followings in the hope of becoming influencers, in great part because of the doors that influence can open for them. The same goes, in different ways, for businesspeople and political leaders looking to build their networks. It's good, they think, to be able to pull strings, call in favors, exert pressure. It gets things done.

A similar impulse underlies a lot of current thinking about education. At its crassest, education becomes simply another way to amass money and power. In 2019, thirty-three well-to-do parents were charged with fraud and bribery for paying to get their children admitted to top universities. They were, it seems, anxious to guarantee their kids the kinds of opportunities such an elite education supposedly opens up, in terms of both future earnings and connections and social influence. (And let's be honest, it's not exactly bad for a parent's reputation for their kid to go to one of those schools.)

Less crudely, education can be seen as a matter of acquiring a set of skills that will prove useful later in life. But even in this case, education isn't seen as an end in itself. It's a means to (ideally) a whole host of possible ends.

So what should we hope for? This common view says: pure efficacy. The ability to get whatever it is you're trying to get. Your response to the Question might change, but if you have influence and money and the like, at least your ability to achieve the life you're seeking will stay the same. Rosa calls this the "Triple-A vision" of life going well because it focuses on things being available, accessible, and attainable. But what does this vision actually get us?

A life almost entirely consumed with securing means. Means, it turns out, have a propensity for dressing themselves up as ends.

Like the view that a good life feels good, the Triple-A vision has some (decidedly limited) affinities with at least one of the great religious and philosophical traditions. But—this won't surprise you by now—other notable answers call it into serious doubt.

The Luster of Blessedness

As a teenager, Aristotle had left his home in the small town of Stagira to travel to the great city of Athens in search of wisdom. He sought out the school of the renowned Plato and studied there for twenty years. It was a time of seismic political and cultural changes. Various city-states fought for influence, wealth, and prestige. Systems of government were in flux. In the north, not far from Aristotle's hometown, a new, militaristic power was rising in Macedon.

By the time Aristotle gathered his mature thoughts on the good life into the book we know as the *Nicomachean Ethics*, Macedon had subjugated all of Greece. Old ways of life in the cities were now in question. Alexander the Great, who had been Aristotle's pupil as a boy, was leading massive campaigns to conquer the Persian Empire to the east. The closer-than-ever encounter of Greek culture with the civilizations of western Asia and Egypt added to the sense of uncertainty and fluidity.

The Question was as pressing as ever.

Aristotle, like most Greek philosophers at the time, thought the most straightforward answer could be given in a single Greek word: *eudaimonia* (you-die-mo-NEE-uh), which is probably best translated into English as "flourishing." Of course, such a concise answer immediately raises the question, What's that? The *Nicomachean Ethics* is one long answer to this question. It's an extended attempt to tell us just what flourishing is. At its heart, Aristotle claims, *eudaimonia* is a particular form of activity. Flourishing is fundamentally something that a person does.

But Aristotle doesn't think we've said enough about flourishing if we've identified it only as a kind of activity. He says something more is needed: namely, "external goods." Some circumstances make it a lot easier to act well, after all. Things like friendships and money and political influence are "the proper equipment" for flourishing action. Even Rafael Nadal would have trouble winning a tennis match without a decent racket and shoes. And even the most virtuous person would find it hard to act well without the right resources. If it's worth seeking the end, it's worth hoping for the means to get there. So friendship, money, and influence are indeed worth wanting, as Aristotle sees it.

That's where Aristotle lines up with Triple-A: good circumstances are ones that open up possibilities. But he departs from Triple-A in two ways. First, he thinks there's a very specific kind of activity that it's good to be able to do: virtuous activity. Aristotle is not advocating piling up means without a clear sense of the end to which they should be deployed—or, even worse, getting so obsessed with acquiring means that we never bother to think about the ends for which we're accumulating these means. (That's what *we* tend to do.) Second, Aristotle doesn't stop with circumstances as *means* to flourishing.

Aristotle thinks some circumstances add to flourishing directly. They're not merely means to virtuous action. They take flourishing and add some polish to it, giving it "the luster of blessedness." As examples, Aristotle mentions a well-off, respected family, children you can be proud of, and personal beauty. Without these things, he says, someone is hardly flourishing. The ugly, solitary man (for Aristotle, it's definitely a man—more on that shortly) from a disreputable family won't necessarily be wretched. He can still make the best of his circumstances and act well. But there's a ceiling to his flourishing. His *eudaimonia* will always be crushed and maimed by his unfortunate circumstances.

Aristotle's list of external goods is pretty recognizable. What's worth hoping for, Aristotle thinks, are those things that sensible people in a functioning society value. Ordinary, moderate human goods. The kinds of things that might come to mind when you ask what life you hope your children or nieces and nephews will have. Maybe not yachts, but a comfortable house, enough money that you're the one helping out your friends and neighbors (rather than the other way around), a healthy family, a good reputation, plenty of leisure time, and so on.

These things are so ordinary that it's hard to imagine objecting to them. The Buddha, however, did just that.

"An Impediment Has Come into Being"

The Buddha's perspective on life's circumstances changed over time. When he first started seeking enlightenment, he thought literally everything on Aristotle's list was an impediment to what truly mattered. In finding enlightenment, he came to realize that this was an exaggeration. But he still saw things like wealth and power as distractions from what really matters. To see how his mind changed and where he wound up, it's helpful to look at the story of the Buddha's relationship to his son.

On the day Siddhartha Gautama resolved to renounce his princely life and seek enlightenment, messengers came to him with a joyful announcement from his father, the king: Siddhartha's son was born. On hearing the message, Siddhartha remarked, "An impediment (*rāhula*) has come into being. A bond has arisen." When the king heard what his son had said, he took it upon himself to give his grandson a name: Prince Rāhula, the impediment.

You see, Siddhartha couldn't see his newborn son as a *good* circumstance in his life. His newfound mission was to break the bonds of excessive attachment and to achieve enlightenment. Children literally cry out for attachment. To pursue his vision of the good, Siddhartha felt compelled to leave Rāhula behind. Even to stop and give the child a kiss might break his resolve and endanger his mission.

Six years later, Siddhartha was the Buddha. He had attained enlightenment. Now he offered his teaching to all who would listen.

His father, the king, heard of the momentous achievement with the interest you might expect from a loving father. He sent word to his son, urging him to return and visit the city he had left. Actually, he sent word twelve times. The first eleven messengers heard the Buddha's teaching, saw the true nature of reality, experienced enlightenment, and declined to deliver the king's message. When the invitation finally reached the Buddha, he accepted.

On the seventh day of the Buddha's stay in the city, his wife, Yasodharā, sent Rāhula to see him and to ask for the sizable inheritance he had abandoned, which would rightly belong to his only child. Just because Siddhartha had left behind wealth and power didn't mean his family should have to do the same, after all.

Prince Rāhula dutifully went to the Buddha and followed him through the city, asking for his inheritance. The Buddha reflected on his young son's request. It was perfectly reasonable. The wealth belonged by right to Rāhula's father, so it was indeed the boy's inheritance. But the Buddha also saw that this wealth would drive his son into craving and suffering. To give it to Rāhula would be to burden him with a true impediment. So instead the Buddha resolved, "I will make him the heir to the transcendental inheritance": enlightenment. He had Prince Rāhula ordained as a monk.

From his departure to his return, Siddhartha's perspective shifts. He no longer sees Rāhula as an impediment to his mission. In fact, it's precisely because he didn't yet understand the enlightenment he was seeking that he could see his son as an impediment at all. From the standpoint of enlightenment, Rāhula appears as he really is: another human in need of insight and release from the cycle of suffering.

Wealth and power, though? Still obstacles. Still impediments. To have them is bad for your life. To give them to your child would be bad for your child's life. These things are not worth having, much less hoping for or seeking after. Like a carton of rotten eggs, the best you can do with them is throw them away.

But the Buddha doesn't just say what kinds of circumstances are bad to have. He *does* give an inheritance to Rāhula, just not the one Rāhula asks for. Instead of wealth and power, the boy receives a place in the monastery. Concretely, that means access to truth (the Buddha and his teachings), a community of others seeking to understand and live that truth, and enough food, shelter, and clothing to live. A bowl, a robe, a roof. True friends. True teaching. These are the truly good circumstances for a truly good life.

Siddhartha starts by thinking about what circumstances will promote his own achievement of enlightenment. He ends up concerned with the circumstances not only of Rāhula but of everyone he encounters. That raises an important question: Just whose circumstances are we talking about when we ask what we should hope for?

What About the Galley Crew?

The somewhat well-known writer Frank Conroy was once paid by a cruise company to write a glowing review of one of their cruises. The review appeared as a little stand-apart essay in the brochure for Celebrity Cruises in the mid-1990s. In one passage he wrote:

> I realized it had been a week since I'd washed a dish, cooked a meal, gone to the market, done an errand or, in fact, anything at all requiring a minimum of effort and thought. My toughest decisions had been whether to catch the afternoon showing of *Mrs. Doubtfire* or play bingo.

Note what Conroy portrays here as appealing about the cruise experience: no work, no chores, no effort, no thought. Think for a second about what's required to give the cruise passenger that experience. It's not like dishes had not been washed, meals prepared, supplies bought, errands done, effort expended, and painstaking thought applied to Conroy's week. And where such things are being done, there is someone doing them. It's just not the passengers.

The hundreds of employees on a cruise ship generally work seven days a week for months on end. A typical workday lasts ten to twelve hours. The median employee made less than $20,000 a year in 2018.

Cruises aren't everyone's cup of tea. They have their downsides, and as 2020 underscored, they are nearly perfect vectors for contagious viruses. All that granted, the depiction of Conroy's cruise passenger nicely distills a certain set of purportedly good circumstances, the kind that only some people can have.

Many of Aristotle's "external goods" fall into this bucket. It's not accidental that Aristotle imagined a free, property-owning man when he pictured a flourishing life. He accepted and even explicitly justified that a life of leisure required the labor of many others; that in his society the production of wealth for some produced poverty for many; that if everyone receives honor, then nobody does—in short, that for some to have flourishing circumstances, others must lack them.

Pushed to its limit, building scarcity into the very structure of good circumstances can lead to the outright glorification of hierarchy, exclusion, and competition. Take the philosopher Friedrich Nietzsche (pronounced NEE-chuh; 1844–1900) as an example. As a young man, he wrote an essay as a birthday gift for his friend Cosima Wagner, wife of the famous composer Richard Wagner. In the essay, Nietzsche argued that the highest aim in life is the development of artistic genius. But that requires ample time not spent worrying about the everyday necessities of life.

So Nietzsche concluded, "In order for there to be a broad, deep, fertile soil for the development of art, the overwhelming majority has to be slavishly subjected to life's necessity in the service of the minority.... At their expense, through their extra work, that privileged class is to be removed from the struggle for existence, in order to produce and satisfy a new world of necessities," namely the creative necessities of culture.

Even if we don't go as far as Nietzsche and see it as a good thing that not everyone's circumstances can be good, accepting the essentially competitive, scarce character of good circumstances might still seem sober and realistic. The world is how it is, we might find ourselves saying. There's no good in pretending otherwise. To face the facts is clear-sighted and courageous. To deny them is, at best, to set yourself up to land at the bottom of the pyramid.

But what if all this is merely ideology? What if it is a convenient way to let ourselves off the hook, so we don't have to care about how our own good circumstances arose or about what happens to everyone else? And what if we're setting our hopes too low when we aim for good circumstances only for ourselves (and our loved ones, and maybe people like us)? What if we ought to be hoping not just for good personal circumstances but for a good *world*?

The Horizon of Our Hopes

Saul of Tarsus (first century CE) is in the running for having the most famous life-changing religious experience in history. He doesn't say much about it himself. But the Acts of the Apostles, a book that tells part of his life story, says that Jesus appeared to Saul in a blinding light that knocked him from his horse. Saul went from persecuting the early followers of Jesus to being one of them. He became known by the nickname Paul (which means "short" or "little") and is widely regarded as the most important figure in early Christianity. His letters make up between one-sixth and one-fourth of the New Testament, the part of the Bible that Christians added to the Jewish scriptures.

Paul was absolutely convinced that God had graciously forgiven his sins, united him with Jesus, given him a new life, and sent him on a mission to spread the gospel across the Roman Empire. While his new life involved plenty of trouble and difficulty, he looked forward to his own resurrection and life "with Christ."

It seems like it would have been easy enough for Paul to simply fulfill his mission and rest assured in his own coming salvation. To reduce Jesus to his "personal Lord and Savior," as some Christians these days put it. But two things kept him from doing that.

For one thing, Paul, like most of the early followers of Jesus, was a Jew. He loved his people. And he worried about how few of them saw Jesus the same way he did. Did it mean that their God had given up on them or left them behind? And if so, what good would it be for him to enjoy salvation and new life if they did not? "I could wish that I myself were accursed and cut off from Christ for the sake of my own people," he wrote.

For another thing, when Paul looked around, he saw not only people in need of redemption, but the whole world broken and suffering, out of joint like a dislocated limb and longing for transformation. Where there should have been peace and flourishing life, there was violence, conflict, and death. What was needed was not just the transferal of individuals into new, good lives, but the transformation of the world into a new creation and the kingdom of God, where "righteousness, peace, and joy" would characterize everything.

Paul didn't think it was in his power to solve these two problems. God's faithfulness to the Jewish people and theirs to God were not for him to sort out. The healing of the fractured, decaying world was not something he could bring about. But these problems still *mattered* to him. Something vital would be missing from Paul's own good circumstances—indeed, they would be tainted, even rotten—if they weren't set within a horizon that addressed these problems.

Paul and the many Christians who agree with him are far from alone in thinking that truly good circumstances can exist only in a truly good world, an order where everyone's (indeed, *every living thing's*) life is going well.

There have been revolutionaries and reformers hoping for a just social order: Marx's vision of communism as "the genuine solution of the antagonism between man and nature and between man and man . . . between existence and essence, between objectification and self-affirmation, between freedom and necessity, between individual and species." Or US president Harry Truman's vision of "a world in which all nations and all peoples are free to govern themselves as they see fit, and to achieve a decent and satisfying life."

There have been ecological thinkers and activists hoping to bring the thriving of humans and the flourishing of the planet into harmony.

There have been Confucians hoping that the Way would once again govern human affairs.

There have been utilitarians dreaming of a world optimized for the happiness of all.

And there have been many, many others, each launching their hopes beyond the island of their own lives and toward the horizon of a changed, improved, renewed, or transformed world. These perspectives challenge us—challenge *you*—to consider whether we've been too narrow in our hopes, whether it is possible for any of us to flourish without all living things flourishing at the same time.

So What *Should* We Hope For?

Aristotle and the Buddha give us dramatically different accounts of what it would mean for our circumstances to be good. The Buddha's claim in particular turns a lot of our reasonable intuitions on their heads. You thought it was good for you to have a lot of money or power or social recognition? Think again. There's nothing there for you but chains. "The things you own end up owning you," as the *very* non-Buddhist Tyler Durden says in *Fight Club*.

Don't dodge the seriousness of this challenge. Whether you're well-off and well-known, right in the midst of scrapping your way up the income slope or the fame ladder, or just struggling to make ends meet, ask yourself whether the kinds of circumstances you have or are hoping for are really the kind that make for flourishing life.

Once you've answered that question, there's still the issue of the scope of your hopes. Can everyone enjoy the kinds of circumstances you've settled on as good, or is there bound to be competition? (If you're after fame or influence, for example, you're aiming at something that is by nature competitive.) Does your vision amount to a cruise with Frank Conroy, blissfully but callously ignoring the grueling work of the galley crew? If so, are you OK with that? Or ought you to hope for something wider? If so, just how wide is wide enough? And if you're hoping for a whole world transformed—especially if the transformation is one you can't bring about—what should you hope for in the meantime?

Your Turn

1. Return to the "life inventory" you took on pages xxxii–xxxiv.
   * How many of the activities you invest your time in are aimed at acquiring money, power, or skills that you can use to achieve whatever your goals turn out to be?
   * What kinds of circumstantial goods do your purchases suggest you prioritize?

2. What *should* we hope for? What are genuinely good circumstances? How much is enough when it comes to these circumstances?

3. Where *should* we set the horizon of our hopes? In other words, how universal do good circumstances need to be in order to be fully good?
   * If you're committed to a wide horizon, where are you depending on others lacking good circumstances in order to supply yours? How might your vision of what we should hope for change to accommodate your wide horizon?
   * If you think it's acceptable or even important that some people wind up losing out on flourishing circumstances while others accumulate large amounts of them, what reasons can you give to support your view?

SIX

How Should We Live?

Before he saw his brother-in-law in the refugee camp, Mohamad Hafez's life had a clear direction: up. Like towering-above-the-Houston-skyline-on-the-sixty-fifth-floor-of-a-skyscraper-you-designed-yourself. That kind of up. Born in Syria, raised mostly in Saudi Arabia, educated in the United States, hired by a top architectural firm, and entrusted with massive projects for giant corporate clients, Hafez had so far enjoyed a life of stunning success.

While Hafez had been flying comfortably from meeting to meeting, however, millions of his fellow Syrians had been fleeing what remained of their homes as bombs fell from the sky. The civil war in Syria had escalated just as Hafez's career took off. An ache of grief for his home country haunted his growing success. Then came the camp. Unbeknownst to Hafez, his brother-in-law, a fellow architect, had left home in desperation to seek a better future for his family, not knowing where he would go. He wound up in a refugee camp in Sweden. Once Hafez learned of this and came to visit him, it turned everything upside down. Suddenly, the fragility of life snapped into focus. The threads that had carried him across the Atlantic and away from Syria well before the war looked tenuous. Any one of a thousand things could have gone differently and landed him right here, a refugee like his loved one. That all of those things had gone the way they did—that he had the life he had—seemed like a blessing, but also a responsibility, a task, even a test.

Hafez had always been a Muslim. He had always believed in God. He had always practiced the religion. But his practice had been mechanical. It hadn't sunk down to the core. It hadn't animated his whole life.

After this moment, it came alive. Islam teaches that there will be a day of judgment when God will call everyone to account for how they have lived. Hafez imagined himself standing before God on that day. He imagined God asking him, "I gave you all these things—security, education, talent. What did you do with them? What did you do when Syria was burning?" And he imagined the answer he would have to give: "I built some shiny buildings for some very rich corporations." It sounded laughable.

He knew everything needed to change. He understood that professional success couldn't determine his life anymore. He had to do something that would meaningfully benefit others, especially those in dire need. He started to cut back on his hours at work and poured more and more of his time into producing meticulous scale models of scenes from Syria. Some preserve the stunning beauty of the old city of Damascus: mosaics, ancient porticos, intricately carved doors. Others capture the devastation of the war: bombed-out buildings, rubble, shattered glass. Just enough of the beauty remains to underscore the tragedy of the city's destruction. He also started giving workshops and lectures (including to our Life Worth Living class) and sharing refugee stories with predominantly Western audiences. And Islam became central to his days, the driving force behind his new mission.

Hafez is still an architect. But he is not the architect of his life anymore. He thinks of himself as a servant, a tool for the one who is the Architect. And so even what has stayed the same has changed completely. His life has a whole new direction and a completely new shape.

This chapter is not about what you can do to be happy. There are no tips here. And no snazzy studies showing that sleeping eight hours a night and feeling good about your life are correlated. "What will make me happy?" is a question of means. It asks how to get to an already-given end, namely happiness. "How should I live my life?" is a question of purpose. It asks what ends you *ought* to pursue. If you jump straight to the means question, you answer the purpose one by default (i.e., "I should live in whatever way makes me happy").

This chapter is also not about how to solve moral dilemmas. There are no trolleys barreling toward pedestrians or leaky lifeboats here. Focusing only on the tough calls distracts us from the bigger picture. Life isn't a series of crises calling for Heroic Moral Deeds. Most of the time, it's a series of small, seemingly insignificant decisions and nondecisions. It's made up of habits and assumptions and incremental changes. The shape of who we are and how we live isn't like Stonehenge. It's not made by stacking a few massive rocks on top of one another. It's built up over time, brick by brick.

This chapter is also not about your life plan. What career you should pursue. Or when and where you should retire. Or whether you should have kids. Those are all important questions. They really are. But they make sense only as part of a broader picture of the kind of life worth planning. And besides, they're too particular—too much about the details of *your* life—for a book like this to take them on directly. They don't have a one-size-fits-all answer.

Instead, this chapter is about the direction and shape of our lives. This is what we're after when we really, seriously ask, "How should I live my life?" We're asking about the highest ideals, the deepest values, and the way they work themselves out in the little details. We're asking about our visions of a life that is led well, a life led as it ought to be led. We're asking about the proper orientation of all our activity—our true north. And we're asking about the heart of all that we do—what the novelist and essayist James Baldwin (1924–1987) called our "moral center."

This is where "only you" gets its real traction. This is what your Smokey is asking you about when they stick their finger in your chest. It is among the biggest of the big questions. It's too big for a book chapter, that's for sure. Too big for a book. Probably too big for a library. It's roughly the right size for a life. As long as you can act and reflect on your actions, this question—the question of how you ought to act—will be with you. You're never going to finish answering it. But you have to start somewhere.

Ready?

Moral Alchemy

James Madison (1751–1836) had a problem. A decade had passed since the thirteen British colonies in North America had declared their independence and four years since they had won the ensuing war. Their first attempt at a new government was failing, and an alternative was needed. So Madison joined fifty-four other delegates in Philadelphia to come up with a proposal.

The problem was this: How could you form a good society out of not especially good people? Americans weren't angels. Madison was under no such illusion. They were just as unreliable as other people, just as prone to lie and cheat and hurt each other. (This was plain even to a man like Madison, who was morally blind enough to hold slaves.) In fact, Americans couldn't even agree on what it would *mean* to be good to their fellow human beings. (Again, see slaveholding.)

After almost four months of debate, the convention in Philadelphia had drafted a new constitution for the United States, which tried to meet this problem head-on with "checks and balances."

You wouldn't need angels to make the system work. Ordinary, selfish humans would do. Indeed, the system would *rely* on their selfishness. Ambition would counteract ambition. Congress would defend its privileges and keep the president from going off the rails. Each different region of the country would keep the others from hijacking the national interest. Voters would keep an eye on representatives to make sure there wasn't too much funny business. In short, "opposite and rival interests" would do the work that Madison couldn't count on good character to do. Everyone would just play their roles and the whole thing would work itself out.

As modern folks, we love this kind of solution. It promises a sort of "moral alchemy." Take the base stuff of human self-interest and turn it into the gold of a functional—maybe even a "just"— society.

You can see this kind of move all over the place. Take the problem of value, for example. It would be overwhelming if we had to figure out and agree on what things are *really* worth. How would we even get started? Markets, we're told, solve the problem for us. Money translates countless different forms of value—comfort,

usefulness, safety, nutrition, beauty—into a single, eminently count-
able measure, and the intricate workings of supply and demand
yield prices. Everything can be compared. The question shifts
from "What is this worth?" to "How much does this cost?" None of
us needs to know what anything is really worth. All any of us has to
do is buy what suits our preferences and our pocketbooks. Out of
the mess of market interactions comes a price—which isn't really
the same as the value of a thing, but it'll do.

Moral alchemy is built into our legal system too. A defense lawyer's job isn't to seek the truth, but to represent their client's interest, even if that client is guilty. They aren't directly responsible for
discerning the truth. The *process* is supposed to suss out the truth—
at least often enough that we can feel OK about it.

The same impulse is behind interest group politics. Your job as
a voter isn't to discern what's right and just for your society and the
world. It's to represent your interests. Elected officials, in turn, are
there to fight for what their districts want. And the process is supposed to sort it out into something like fairness and justice.

It's easy to see why procedural moral alchemy is so appealing.
"Only you" responsibility can be daunting. How can we be expected to discern the good (value, truth, justice) over and over
again as life throws us into the daily grind, not to mention the
crises and conundrums and dilemmas that crop up more often than
we'd like?

The problem is that our trust in moral alchemy may be un-
founded, and depending on it may leave us unable to do what we
need to when systems fail. These days, there are plenty of reasons
to doubt that democratic systems and free markets can produce
virtue despite the nefarious actions of vicious participants. A Western world once confident that the line between good and evil ran

between democracy and autocracy now worries about democratically elected autocrats. Increasingly, we see that discerning the truth by letting opposing views argue it out doesn't work if both sides don't actually have some sort of basic commitment to truth-seeking. And free markets regularly seem to miss crucial components of the value equation, like the CO_2 emissions that are destroying the planet. Unfortunately, the longer we lean on moral alchemy, the more dependent on it we become. Our moral discernment muscles atrophy. And precisely at the moment we need to discern what is just or true or to assess value for ourselves, we find ourselves and our societies unable to do so.

Trusting in moral alchemy is a decision. It's an exercise of your responsibility. Are you sure it's a good one? Isn't it worth the effort at least to ask: What shape would a well-led life take? What's worthy of your (constrained, dependent, but nevertheless real) agency?

Leave No Trace

A Life Worth Living student at Yale once came to Matt to talk about his final paper. Tasked with articulating his own vision of a life worth living, the student had hit upon a pithy, inspiring slogan to encapsulate it all: "Leave no trace."

The mantra came from the United States Forest Service. If your aim is to keep wildlands wild, "leave no trace" makes a lot of sense. Don't drive ATVs on fragile sand dunes. Don't overfish a lake until its stock of bass collapses. And so on. The student wanted to apply this ethos to all of life.

Humans, his thinking went, are gigantic resource sinks. We mine over 2.5 billion tons of iron ore and fell 15 billion trees each year. We have driven unknown thousands of species to extinction. We level whole ecosystems for our cities and farms. In our interactions with each other, we compete and betray, we cause deprivation and pain and trauma. We do a lot of harm.

Friedrich Nietzsche said that "to live and to be unjust is one and the same thing." He meant that life inherently depends on the destruction of other life. Little fish eat plankton. Big fish eat little fish. Seals eat big fish. Great whites eat seals. And bacteria feed on the carcasses of all of them. If wheat is going to thrive in a field, there can't be trees there. Competition and conquest are everywhere.

Nietzsche thought we ought to accept—even embrace—this "injurious, violent, exploitative and destructive" character of life.

Our student thought otherwise. He wanted out. He looked around, saw all the harm he might do, and thought the best way to live his life would be to keep it to a minimum.

He was giving voice to an increasingly common intuition. What gives any of us the right to barrel through the world taking and taking and taking? What makes us so special, after all? Agency is dangerous. It tends to harm. So maybe we ought to limit our agency, or at least its effects. Maybe the best thing we can do with our lives is let others be.

Such was the calculus of Arjuna, the warrior at the center of the Bhagavad Gita, a Hindu text composed in the first millennium BCE. The Gita is largely a philosophical dialogue between Arjuna and the deity Krishna. But the dialogue is set within a dramatic narrative scene. Arjuna is about to charge into battle for the fate of the world, Avengers style. He is fighting on the side of good against the forces of evil. This is a just war if ever there was one.

But it's still war. And as he surveys the battlefield, Arjuna sees members of his own family on the other side. To win the battle, he would have to kill his own cousins. And so he despairs of acting rightly.

Krishna, disguised as Arjuna's charioteer, pulls no punches: "Why this cowardice in time of crisis, Arjuna?" Krishna's counsel begins with a simple but daunting invitation: "Look to your own duty." Further questions abound (and animate the following seventeen teachings of the Gita). But for now, Krishna's simple response challenges us: duty demands that we find the courage to act even when the world is messy and outcomes are unclear.

"Leave no trace" has a certain logic. But it would be a startling discovery to find that the life worth living is one that, at least in terms of impact, comes as close as possible to never having lived at all. Arjuna learns to act in accordance with duty. Ultimately, Matt's student went in a different direction with his paper. If we, too, wind up unsatisfied with "leave no trace," we'll need to respond to two questions. First, how can we exercise our agency rightly? And second, who should we take into account as we do so? We'll tackle each of these questions in order.

Of Consequences, Commands, and Character

Jeremy Bentham (remember him?) has a rather straightforward way to answer the question of how we can exercise our agency rightly. He claims that pleasure and the absence of pain are the only things that are good in themselves. If that's true, a well-led life is just one that increases pleasure and decreases pain.

The logic is pretty simple. Humans act in order to make things happen. Good human actions make good things happen. There's one thing that's good in itself (pleasure). The more of it, the better—no matter whose it is. There's no such thing as too much of this good thing. So human agency is good to the extent that it increases pleasure for as many people as possible. Act so that you maximize the world's pleasure and minimize its pain and, voilà, you're living a moral life.

One key feature of this approach to the question of how to live is that it focuses on results. What matters is how much pleasure and how little pain you cause. When the chips are down, that's what counts. Philosophers call this kind of ethics "consequentialist" because it's concerned with the consequences of our actions.

There's something really appealing about consequentialism. It has no time for your self-justification. You don't get credit for your good intentions. You get credit for the actual good you bring about. And you have to accept blame for the pain you cause.

One problem with consequentialism is that in a world as complex as ours, consequences are not so easily connected to causes. Even after the fact, it can be difficult to parse out which factor caused a particular result (good or bad). In advance, it can be nearly impossible to know what the consequences of your actions will be. Paralysis by analysis is a real threat.

Even worse, in the consequentialist view, you're responsible for the consequences of your analysis-induced paralysis. The time you spent trying desperately to figure out how to maximize your contribution to the overall pleasure in the world could have been spent doing something—anything—that would actually have increased the pleasure in the world. But, then, what should you have spent that time doing? It can get dizzying pretty fast.

If these difficulties hit home, we might want to find an approach to exercising agency that sets us free from having to weigh the consequences of our actions in advance. Unsurprisingly, there are some options on offer. We'll consider two: (1) doing what the God of Abraham says, and (2) becoming virtuous.

JUST LIKE THIS, the story of the Jewish people begins: "The LORD said to Abram, 'Go forth from your native land and from your father's house to the land that I will show you.' . . . Abram went forth, as the LORD had commanded him."

A word from God (a command) and a corresponding action from a human (obedience). God does follow the command with a promise: of blessing, a renowned name, and many descendants. But there is no explanation.

Over and over again in the story of Abraham (God changes Abram's name along the way), God instructs and Abraham listens, God leads and Abraham follows.

Several hundred years later, as the Bible tells it, Abraham's descendants were camped at the foot of a mountain in the desert. God had liberated them from slavery in Egypt, and now their leader, Moses, was high up on the mountain, shrouded in dark, thundering clouds and listening to the voice of God. What he heard was a law, a set of commandments (traditionally counted at 613 in total) for the whole people. From then on, a well-lived life for them would be a life in conformity with these commands, in fidelity to God.

This messes with the way many of us understand religion. If God's commands touch on everything from what to eat, to what to wear, to how to treat your enemy's donkey, then religion can't be one sphere of life, where you check off some boxes and then get on with other things. It encompasses the whole of life. Everything should be shaped by obedience. "Give Him what is His, for you and yours are His," says the ancient Jewish rabbi Eleazar of Bartota (first and second centuries CE). (There's a resonance here with the story from the Quran about God's lordship and authority that we discussed in chapter 3.) No circumstance and no human project could take priority over God and God's instructions.

Obedience is required "whether all things are smiling around us, or dark clouds obscure us beneath their shades," reflects the English Jewish novelist Grace Aguilar (1816–1847). In a certain sense, the obedience itself takes priority even over the content of the action. It is said that one who is commanded to do a righteous deed and does it is greater than one who does it without having been commanded.

Many Christians have also placed a lot of weight on living in response to God's command or will. (Christianity began as a marginal Jewish movement. Jesus was a Jew. So were all of his first followers.) Paul, one of the first to try to convert non-Jews to the way of Jesus, wrote to a group of Greek Christians: "Obeying the commandments of God is everything."

Why would anyone want a life like this?

For one, you don't have to figure out in advance what the consequences of your actions will be. You can be a "non-consequentialist." You don't have to figure out what will yield the best results. (Whew! What a relief!) Your job is to follow and leave the rest to God.

As odd as it might sound to many modern folk, living under God's command can yield a deep sense of freedom. The commandments given to Moses were said to have been engraved on stone tablets. Because in ancient Hebrew texts only the consonants were written out, the word for "engraved" (*charut*) looked exactly the same on the page as the word for "freedom" (*cherut*). Playing on this linguistic quirk, Rabbi Joshua ben Levi (third century CE) said that we should read the text to mean "freedom" because nobody is truly free except one who studies God's law—and obeys it.

This isn't the freedom of being allowed to do whatever you want. Instead, it's freedom *from* the threat of arbitrariness, the nagging sense that you just decided on a whim what is good to do. It's not all up to you. God, the creator of all that is, set the terms. And it's freedom *to* live as you're meant to live, as you were created to live. So not only might God's command relieve the impossible burden of calculating the consequences of our actions; it might also give our actions more weight than our own arbitrary choice ever could.

This isn't an easy way to live. It comes at the (potential) cost of your own desires. Consider the paradigmatic Christian example. On the night before he was killed, just before he was arrested, Jesus prayed. He knew what was coming. He sensed that faithfulness to God would lead to death. But he didn't want to die. So he prayed. "Father, for you all things are possible; remove this cup from me; yet, not what I want, but what you want." Everything—even the intense, good, totally understandable desire to survive—is subordinate to heeding God's will.

And what's more, this way of living is risky. One of the more troubling stories in the Bible starts with another sudden command to Abraham. "Take your son, your favored one, Isaac, whom you love, and go to the land of Moriah, and offer him there as a burnt offering on one of the heights that I will point out to you." Just to be clear, God told Abraham to *kill his son*.

Isaac was the son God had promised. Abraham had done what God commanded and received what God had promised. And now God was saying, "Give him back." What's really incredible is that Abraham goes to Moriah. He gets to the point of literally raising the knife before an angel intervenes and shows him a sheep to sacrifice instead.

Now, this story raises all kinds of questions. Can God just decide that it's good to sacrifice a child? Do God's commands supersede otherwise reliable moral rules? Do God's new commands supersede previous ones? (There's already a divine command not to kill at this point in the story.) Was Abraham really right to obey? If so, why?

For our purposes, the key point is the risk inherent in this way of living. What if Abraham had done it, and it turned out he was wrong, that God had given no such command? The thought is horrific.

What the risk of misunderstanding God's command underscores is how central discernment will be to any way of life that puts God's commands front and center. We'll need practices that attune us to God and God's commands. Almost certainly, they will be communal. It will be a matter of how to discern together, as a church community or a synagogue or a small group of devoted friends or a whole people.

Not even reliance on a fixed set of commands, like the 613 from the mountain, can get rid of the risk of discernment. There's always a need for interpretation. No set of laws can address every situation in advance, after all. In a sense, the last two thousand years of Jewish tradition are one long, rich exercise in that interpretation. There's study and debate and then study of the debates and debate about the debates. All in search of understanding the commands of God and what they mean for life in a given place and time.

So for many who belong to the Jewish and Christian traditions (and Islam, which also traces its roots to Abraham), the core of a life led well is one of discerning the will of God and then doing it.

. . .

WHEN THE GREAT Confucian sage Mencius (Chinese: Mengzi; ca. 372–289 BCE) looked at a human being, he saw a fertile field. Four sprouts peeked up out of the soil. If all went well, they would grow into thriving, sturdy trees. The person would become a flourishing garden.

Mencius's sprouts represented four feelings he thought all humans have innately:

1. The feeling of compassion. If you see a child about to fall into a well, you feel distress. The child's plight calls forth something in you. That's compassion.

2. The feeling of shame and aversion. As a young kid, one of us (we won't say who) lost his TV privileges on the day of the week when *Teenage Mutant Ninja Turtles* was on. When the dreaded half hour of deprivation arrived, he had a brilliant insight. If he turned on the TV and his mom called him on it, he could just say he forgot. If she didn't call him on it, he could watch some sweet anthropomorphic reptilian martial arts. The TV went on. Cowabunga, dude. Mom said nothing—until later that afternoon, when she calmly asked why he had thought it OK to behave that way. It sucked the air right out of him. That feeling of not having lived up to who he should have been is something like what Mencius means by shame and aversion.

3. The feeling of modesty and respect. This names our tendency to defer to those we recognize as having authority or status.

Little kids look up to big ones. We let the doctor ask most of the questions during an exam. That sort of thing.

4. The sense of right and wrong. We all have a basic sense of "should" and "should not." Try taking a toddler's stuffed animal away in front of his four-year-old sister. You'll be on the receiving end of a passionate, indignant, exceedingly loud sisterly complaint. That's the sense of right and wrong in action.

Mencius thinks each of these feelings grows into a corresponding virtue (quality of character). Compassion becomes *humaneness*, or attentiveness to the well-being of those we're responsible for. Shame and aversion produce *righteousness*, which is the disposition to actions that fit with the situation. Modesty and respect mature into *propriety*, which is the appropriate way of performing social interactions. And the sense of right and wrong blossoms as *wisdom*, correct discernment about what really is humane and right and proprietous about our own and others' character.

Compassion → Humaneness

Shame and aversion → Righteousness

Modesty and respect → Propriety

Right and wrong → Wisdom

According to Mencius, it is the nature of humans to have all four sprouts. But there's no guarantee that the sprouts will reach maturity. (Look around. Is everyone humane, righteous, marked by propriety, and wise? Didn't think so.) If you expose a sprout to too much sun or let weeds grow over it or don't give it enough water, it will wither and die. Same here, says Mencius. If we don't attend to our sprouts—if we don't nurture them and give them what they need to grow—they won't become virtues.

What the sprouts need most of all is attention. We need to notice these feelings and reinforce them. We need to look around and see how they apply in new and surprising places. We need to think through their implications. If instead we just flit about doing what we want, the sprouts will shrivel.

A life led well is thus one that cultivates the sprouts into virtues. It's a life that seeks, establishes, and then lives out a certain kind of character. The point isn't to minimize the harmful impact of your agency. We oughtn't try to leave no trace. Nor do we have to know in advance what the consequences of our actions will be. Rather, the goal is to become the kind of person whose agency can be trusted, who can be counted on to act well.

Mencius focuses especially on virtues that he thinks support good social relationships. Every human being is who they are in relation to a whole host of others. Children exist in relation to their parents, grandparents, siblings, and so on. Farmers exist in relation to merchants, soldiers, and government officials, and vice versa. Human life is a network of relationships. You can measure the quality of a life by the quality of those relationships. How should one live, then? Be the kind of person who contributes to good relationships.

As Confucians typically do, Mencius starts at home. Living virtuously begins with acting virtuously toward those closest to us. In other words, his sense of how we should act corresponds to his sense as a Confucian of our responsibilities: concentric circles that begin with our parents and extend outward from there. That brings us back to our second question from the start of the chapter: Whatever we think it means to act rightly, who should we have in mind as we do so? Going back to our Smokey Bear picture, we need to know: How big should our "forest" be?

How Big Is Your Forest?

Imagine you're walking to work one morning. Your route passes a pond, and as you get close to it, you see a small child struggling to stay above the water. The water isn't deep. You can easily wade in and rescue the child, at no real risk to your safety. What do you do?

You help, right? *Of course you help! It's a child!* It would be wrong not to help. That answer—that instinctive *of course*—means other people have a place in your forest. It's not just you. Your responsibility extends beyond yourself, at least a little. That's a not very intense implication for a rather intense thought experiment.

But Peter Singer, the Australian utilitarian who came up with it (independently of Mencius's example of the child falling into a well, it seems), thinks the thought experiment has a much sharper edge to it.

If we're obligated to save the imperiled child we come across, then we're just as obligated to do what we can to save those around the world dying from preventable diseases and hunger. Why should it make any difference if they're far away from us? Why should they count for any less than someone nearby? How could geographical proximity be morally relevant?

What Singer's getting at here is a core utilitarian belief: everyone's happiness counts the same. It doesn't matter whose happiness it is. Bentham's pupil, John Stuart Mill (1806–1873), thought this pure impartiality follows directly from the idea that pleasure is good and pain bad. Pleasure is pleasure, no matter whose pleasure it is, which means that one person's pleasure is just as valuable as another's. The only presupposition is that "the truths of arithmetic are applicable to the valuation of happiness, as of all other measurable quantities." In other words, if you can add and subtract amounts of happiness, then there's no excuse for privileging one person's happiness over another's.

Singer and Katarina de Lazari-Radek put the principle nicely: "Maximize goodness impartially." In other words, the whole world is your forest. If you can affect it, you're responsible for it. When discerning how to live your life, you should take the pleasure and pain of every sentient being in this universe, from now until the end of time, into account.

This is a powerful, demanding ideal. Many people today feel it. We recognize that how we live impacts the lives of others around the world, and not just humans. We see images of suffering in parts of the world we will never visit. We know the tug that follows, the sense that we can't ignore our impact on the world, that we ought to take it into account, that we can't privilege ourselves just because we happen to be us. After all, are you really ready to say that— objectively, in the grand scheme of things—you matter more than somebody else?

And yet . . .

It can be hard to shake the sense that you *do* have a special responsibility toward yourself. Now, not a lot of us are willing to go to bat for full-on, no-holds-barred egoism. We're not about to let the child drown.

But that kind of egoism isn't the only way to make yourself the center of your forest. There's also what the Canadian philosopher Charles Taylor calls "the ethic of authenticity." This is the view that each of us is irreducibly unique and ought to live in line with that uniqueness. The good life isn't one-size-fits-all. Each of us has our own way of being human. (One size never actually fits all, does it?) The ethic of authenticity lies behind slogans like "Be true to yourself" and "You do you." Even if some advocates of authenticity are easy to dismiss as shallow (and some most certainly are), the ideal itself can't be written off quite so easily. It demands that each of us wrestles with a moral responsibility to contribute to the world what only we can.

Lots of our students feel torn between these two answers to the forest question. Total altruism versus individual self-actualization. A limitless forest or one central tree. It's tempting to try to synthesize them. But how could you actually live up to both? How could you both actualize yourself in all your uniqueness and devote yourself impartially to the good of everyone? And yet to just take one of these answers can be hard to swallow. Universal concern can be a crushing weight. Authenticity alone can feel shallow and small.

As it turns out, this isn't a totally new predicament.

During Mencius's time, two philosophies enjoyed wide popularity in China. Yang Zhu (ca. 440–ca. 360 BCE) took the side of egoism. Mozi (ca. 470–ca. 391 BCE) advocated concern for the whole of society. Aligning himself with Confucius, Mencius sought a different way. Here's how he put it: "Yang Zhu is 'for oneself.' This is to not have a ruler. Mozi is 'impartial caring.' This is to not have a father. To not have a father and to not have a ruler is to be an animal."

If you're for yourself alone, you don't belong to a larger community that makes valid claims on you. That's what it means to say you don't have a ruler. If you care impartially, then nobody can make *special* claims on you. Everyone has equal standing. A stranger counts as much as your parent. Hence, "impartial caring" means not to have a father. Either option, Mencius says, is beastly. The stakes here aren't just that if you follow Mozi you might care for the wrong people. Rather, by trying to become someone who cares impartially—someone who tries to adopt the point of view of the universe—you might diminish your humanity.

But what would be a more human way?

The governor of a province once came to Confucius and boasted, "Among my people, there is one we call 'Upright Gong.' When his father stole a sheep, he reported him to the authorities." Perhaps bemused, Confucius replied, "Among my people, those we consider 'upright' are different from this: fathers cover up for their sons, and sons cover up for their fathers. 'Uprightness' is to be found in this."

For Confucius, people of integrity don't act with *impartiality*. That would be not to have a parent. Confucian integrity aims not at impartiality but rather at being *rightly partial*. Your scope of concern starts at home, with those who brought you into the world.

The forest doesn't *end* with your parents, though. The idea is that you can't be a good citizen without being a good child or parent or sibling or nephew or aunt. Your forest of responsibility radiates out from the cluster of close relations to reach the whole world. But you never skip over the family relations. And you never leave them behind. Mencius's forest is vast (maybe even universal), but it always and unapologetically has a center.

In the previous section, we considered three alternative views of what it means to lead life well: to maximize happiness, to cultivate our innate virtues, and to follow the God of Abraham. So far in this section, we've seen a utilitarian answer to the forest question and Mencius's Confucian answer. Turning to the Abrahamic view, we might hope that deciding to live by God's commands would have the benefit of answering the forest question for you. (Indeed, shouldn't it answer all questions for you?) But then the God of Abraham gives a command like "Love your neighbor." And you need to know: Well, who is my neighbor?

Thousands of miles and a couple of centuries away from Mencius's China, an expert in religious law posed exactly this question to Jesus.

Jesus answered with a story. (Jesus had a habit of answering with stories.) He told of a man who had been robbed and beaten up by bandits on a nearby road. As he lay dying, a priest came along—and ignored him. Then another devout religious professional did the same thing. Finally, a third person came. This one was different. He was moved by compassion and helped the injured man, at significant personal expense. He was also a member of a different ethnic and religious group, known as the Samaritans. In other circumstances, the injured man likely would have despised his rescuer.

Jesus closed the story with a question to the lawyer. "Which of these three, do you think, was a neighbor to the man who fell into the hands of the robbers?" he asked.

"The one who showed him mercy," the lawyer replied.

So Jesus said to him, "Go and do likewise."

This is a different approach to the forest question than we've seen from the utilitarians or Mencius or the ethic of authenticity. The Samaritan has no prior relationship to the injured man. Apparently, being a neighbor doesn't depend on a fixed social category. It's something you can do, and ought to do, for anyone who comes your way—or whose way you come, as the case may be. That might reduce the risk of focusing your forest too narrowly around your family and ignoring people who are different.

At the same time, the Samaritan's concern isn't exactly universal. He's responsible for caring for *this* person, not for figuring out the best possible use of his time for the world as a whole. That might help alleviate the crushing character of a universal forest.

And yet the Good Samaritan approach is not without its own questions. Singer might point out that with modern technology we're effectively just as able to help an undernourished child in Guatemala, where half of all children are stunted because of inadequate nutrition, as we are an injured person on the side of the road. Does the Good Samaritan approach turn out effectively the same as the utilitarian one? On the other hand, isn't it at least possible that our close relations need to take priority over strangers? Flashy stories about unusual, one-time heroics are all well and good, but what about everyday life?

There's no easy answer to the forest question. Bentham and Singer say everyone should be part of your forest. The ethic of authenticity says you are your most important responsibility. Mencius and Confucius say your forest starts with a particular set of someones and continues to others only after that. Jesus suggests (potentially) anyone could belong to your forest. None of these answers is without its costs. What do you say?

So How *Should* We Live?

You know by now that we're not going to give you a straight answer. Here, of all places, it's your job to discern the answer as best you can. (We're doing our best to answer the question for ourselves too.)

But what can you take with you from the voices you've heard in this chapter?

First, keep an eye on ends. Think seriously about what a well-lived life is after. Don't just assume it's after happiness. Don't assume it seeks *any* consequence in the world. Maybe a well-lived life is one that hews to God's law, come what may. Or maybe your character matters more than your accomplishments (even your accomplishments as a do-gooder).

Second, make sure to answer the forest question. How you answer it can dramatically change the implications of your answer to the ends question. Suppose you were convinced that good agency maximizes happiness. A self-centered forest would make you a pleasure-seeking narcissist, while a universal forest would make you a radical humanitarian. Or suppose Mencius convinced you that good agency cultivates virtues that then sustain good relationships. Well, whose virtue should you try to promote? Just your own? Yours and your family's? Everyone's? And which set of relationships should the virtues support?

Third, get comfortable with being unsure. Any of these options will leave you in a place where it's really difficult to be certain about how to live. Optimizing the consequences of your actions? Good luck forecasting the impact of anything you do in this crazy world. Trying to live in obedience to God's will? Get ready to do a lot of discernment; get comfortable with mystery. Aiming at cultivating virtue? Sorting out your moral sprouts from the weeds trying to choke them isn't always straightforward. Even trying to be true to ourselves means discerning some truest, "authentic" self hiding deep within. That's never a matter of precision.

Finally, you can't give a good answer to the question of how to live without answering the questions from the other chapters. If the Buddha is right, and wealth is an impediment, then you should live your life in a really different way than if material abundance is crucial to flourishing human life. If Wilde is right and sorrow is part of the good life, then seeking to eliminate any and all pain is wrongheaded. The questions wrap around each other and pull on each other like the cords of a strand of rope. In fact, the intertwining of these questions and their answers goes a long way toward making a real *vision* of true, flourishing life.

Your Turn

1. Reread your answers to the "life inventory" questions on pages xxxii–xxxiv.
   * What ends do they suggest you are seeking in exercising your agency?
   * What standards seem to guide your conduct?
   * What, practically speaking, do you treat as you forest?

2. How *should* we live?
   * What end(s) *should* we seek through our agency?
   * What standard(s) should we be held to?
   * Who and what are in your forest?

3. How do your answers to the questions in items 1 and 2 line up? Are you living in pursuit of the ends and by the standards you recognize as worthy of your humanity? If not, how would your life be different if you were? Again, be careful. As we said at the beginning, it would be a mistake to let this kind of question lead us into making New Year's–style resolutions. As we'll see in chapter 15, resolutions are doomed to fall short if we try to use them to live into our deepest insights about the Question. In answering this question, you're not making a to-do list. You're trying to get a glimpse of the kind of life you hope to be living.

Part 3

....

BEDROCK

SEVEN

The Recipe Test

For several chapters now, we've been taking the preposterously big question that is the Question and breaking it down into at least slightly more manageable sub-questions. The risk of this strategy is that it can start to seem like a list of one question after another with no connection between them.

But that can't be right. As huge as it is, the Question is a unified question. It has to do with the shape of our lives as a whole and our world as a totality.

Our responses to the various sub-questions go together. They're more like a recipe than a grocery list, and they can fit together like the ingredients of a good recipe into answers to the Question—or not. Sure, you could come up with a recipe that combines Italian sausage, mint chocolate-chip ice cream, asparagus, and pickled eggs. Maybe those are even your favorite individual foods. But would the combination be edible? Not even close.

So part of your task is not just to give the best responses you can to the questions from each chapter of this book, but to test out how those answers go together. It's to discern a coherent vision of flourishing life. Call it the "recipe test."

But we also know that when we work in the kitchen, our goal isn't simply to create something delicious. Nutrition matters too. So when we plan a meal, perhaps even before we think about what ingredients go together, we think in terms of food groups. Proteins. Fruits and vegetables. Grains and starches. Our desired balance between food groups is a product of our nutritional goals. If we're on a keto diet, grains and starches may not have a place on our plate. We'll need to look for a recipe that works without them. On an extreme version of the Atkins diet, maybe there's only protein.

When it comes to the good life, our "food groups" are the three aspects of life we've been thinking about in the last three chapters. Our responses to these three questions cover in broad strokes our positive vision for all of life. We said that "How should we live?" is a question about agency, about our active presence in the world. "What should we hope for?" covers the rest of the world, the circumstances of our lives. And "How does a good life feel?" gets at the felt experience of our lives, our affective responsiveness to the world around us as we perceive it.

These questions concern three modes of being in the world: active, passive, and, when it comes to emotions, both together. Disregard any of them, and your vision of life worth living will remain incomplete—or at least you'll have to explain why one or two can be left out. Call this the "nutrition test."

Agency, circumstance, and affect, then, are the three basic food groups of a good life. It's hard to find a feature of human life that doesn't belong in at least one of those buckets. Sure, there's plenty more to ask beyond these questions. But the center of gravity is here. So it makes a big difference not only how you answer these questions, but how you put them together.

That's true not only because some recipes just don't work (some answers to these questions just don't fit together), but also because lots of things that are really good candidates for components of a good life involve a synthesis of agency, circumstance, and affect.

Take friendship, for example. Thinkers ranging from Aristotle to Mary Wollstonecraft have considered it integral to a flourishing life. It's clear that having friends is a matter of circumstance, of life going well. Without someone else being your friend, you don't have a friendship. And yet friendship doesn't fall neatly into the circumstances bucket. Having a friendship also requires being a friend. Your agency is essential. If you don't reciprocate and act as a friend, then you might have an admirer or a lackey or a benefactor, but you won't have a friend. Feelings, too, matter for friendship. A friendship without any affection at all would still have something good about it. You might help each other out regularly, for example. But if it happened only through gritted teeth, the friendship would be missing something crucial. It's tempting to say that it wouldn't really be a friendship at all.

So this one good thing, friendship, bundles up agency, circumstance, and affect. It's got ingredients from all three of our good life "food groups." It requires them to be knit together. And that makes sense. After all, life doesn't come to us in tidy snippets of pure agency, pure circumstance, and pure feeling. It's a complex, interwoven amalgamation of them all. So much so that even as we distinguish the three, we shouldn't lose track of the ways that they intimately influence and condition one another. Though they are distinct, each of these three aspects of life already has the other two inside it, so to speak.

First, *agency is not just agency*. When we talk about agency, we're not talking about some absolute omnipotence. No matter what we were told by kind adults when we were children, we can't do anything we set our minds to. What we can do and who we can be are deeply shaped and constrained by both our circumstances and our affective lives. Circumstances meant that a sixteenth-century British monarch exercised a different sort of agency than an ancient Egyptian peasant, or a daughter in a contemporary, middle-class Canadian family. And affect influences agency too. An emotion like fear makes us more likely to act in some ways rather than in others, and even if we resist those tendencies, the very fact that we have to resist gives us some sense of how affect shapes our agency.

Second, *affect is not just affect*. Our feelings and emotions are influenced by both our circumstances and our agency. The first one is easy to see. Our feelings are largely responses to our circumstances as we experience them. We peer over the edge of a cliff and feel fear. Or we receive a thoughtful note of encouragement and feel gratitude and motivation. What's maybe a little more surprising is that our own agency also shapes our emotional lives. Within limits that researchers are only beginning to understand, it is possible to take actions that change not only the way we feel in one or another specific instance, but the ways we tend to feel in certain kinds of situations. For an example, let's begin by distinguishing two emotional responses to another person's suffering: empathic distress (you feel their pain with overwhelming intensity) and compassion (you are concerned by their suffering and motivated to help). Recent research suggests that the practice of Buddhist-inspired loving-kindness meditation can increase our disposition to feel compassion rather than empathic distress.

Finally, *circumstances are not just circumstances*. It might seem that circumstances are immune from being shaped by the other two aspects of life. Circumstances are the given. They are the obstinately actual, the unyielding reality of a world that confronts us as it is, with utter disregard for our preferences. But that's not entirely right. As both individuals and communities, we act in ways that influence our circumstances, sometimes even transform them. That influence isn't absolute. It's not even reliable or predictable. It is, however, real. Somewhat more subtly and indirectly, our emotions and feelings also bear on our circumstances. Our favorite park or place to unwind may so embody feelings of peace and serenity that we consider these feelings part of the place—the circumstance—itself. Our feelings actually change what that place means to us.

So as a matter of fact, circumstance, agency, and affect are bound up together in complicated ways. When we think about the kind of lives we aspire to, that fact underscores the importance of the recipe and nutrition tests. A hodgepodge vision will be less livable than one that hangs together. We need to get our recipes right.

The rest of this chapter is meant to help you get to know your way around the kitchen, so to speak.

We'll focus on emphasis. Some good life recipes elevate one food group head and shoulders above the rest. They look at life and say, "What we have here is a steak. Why mess around with a bunch of unnecessary ingredients? All we need is some salt and pepper and we're ready to grill." Nobody would mistake a well-seasoned steak for a meal of salt and pepper nicely complemented by a little beef. There's one ingredient from one food group that drives the whole recipe. Other recipes are less extreme. They still emphasize one ingredient, but the emphasis isn't as pronounced. In kung pao chicken, for example, the peanuts, chili peppers, and Szechuan peppercorns are essential to making the dish what it is, but it's still kung pao *chicken*. Still other approaches aim for a nearly perfect balance between a variety of ingredients. Think paella, gumbo, vegetable soup—that sort of thing.

All to say that different visions of the good life tend to emphasize different aspects of the good life. Some emphasize agency, some affect, some circumstances. And they also vary in terms of the degree of that emphasis. Some are rather extreme, others more subtle. In some cases, it's hard to tell which is emphasized at all. A vision can be balanced in such a way that any of the three aspects can be treated as a window into the whole.

Let's take a look at three examples of visions of a good life, each centering on a different aspect. We'll start with a rather stringent focus on agency (Stoicism), then consider a slightly more nuanced focus on affect (utilitarianism), and end with a quite subtle focus on circumstance (Confucianism).

Before we start, though, we want to remind you of our disclaimer from the introduction: in a few short pages, we can't give you definitive accounts of these visions. We have to leave out almost all their rich complexity and internal disagreements. The point here is to get a sense for the range of possibilities exemplified by these visions as we present them.

Virtue Is All You Need

The Greek philosopher Chrysippus (279–206 BCE) once wrote a multivolume book called *On the Means of Livelihood*. It was supposed to answer the question of how a wise man ought to make a living. As it turned out, though, Chrysippus thought there was a more important question: Why make a living at all?

This might strike you as an odd question. Surely we make a living so we can enjoy our lives. Chrysippus says no. Pleasure, he says, is "indifferent." It's a "take it or leave it" sort of thing. It's not a good reason to do anything. (Take that, Jeremy Bentham!)

Let's say we grant Chrysippus this point. Surely, we might think, we ought to make a living in order to survive. But Chrysippus says even survival is "take it or leave it." Just like pleasure, "living is a thing indifferent." It simply doesn't qualify as a reason to do anything.

Living is a thing indifferent. That sounds . . . bonkers. If anything counts as a good reason for us, it must be survival. Chrysippus thinks differently—and he's not alone.

Chrysippus was a Stoic. For the Stoics, agency (specifically, being virtuous) is all there is to the good life. In fact, it's more important than life itself. Stoics look around at the world, at all the external things people invest themselves in—money, fame, power, success, family—and they see that every one of these things is unstable. We can't guarantee that we'll get them. If we have them, we're always at risk of losing them. So if our flourishing depends on these things, it's fundamentally out of our hands. And, the Stoics think, that just can't be right. If anything at all should be in our hands, it ought to be the goodness of our lives. The only solution is to recognize that the good life is a life led well. Period. Being good and living the good life are the same thing. This has a dramatic effect on how the Stoics answer the question of what it means for life to go well.

Chrysippus's teacher, Cleanthes, once went to the theater in Athens, where he sat in the audience with all the local notables. A well-regarded poet got onstage to recite a poem and suddenly threw some unprovoked shade at Cleanthes in front of everyone. But Cleanthes sat entirely unfazed, with not a hint of anger on his face. That's how a Stoic is supposed to react to bad circumstances.

But that's nothing compared to the story the famous Roman orator Cicero (106–43 BCE) tells about the much earlier philosopher Anaxagoras (fifth century BCE). When someone brought Anaxagoras the news that his son had died, he simply said, "I was already aware that I had begotten a mortal."

Sure, health and wealth and the survival of your children are preferable to sickness and poverty and their deaths. But people can be virtuous and therefore flourish even if they don't get what they prefer and even if they lose all those things. No matter the circumstances, the Stoics thought, there is always the opportunity to act well. In a strict sense, therefore, circumstances have no place in a Stoic vision of what matters most. That's why Chrysippus thinks there's no good argument for making a living. You don't need to make a living to be virtuous. You don't need to be happy to be virtuous. You don't even need to survive. Sometimes the most virtuous thing to do is die well.

Yes, that's a radical approach to the Question. But there can be something really inspiring about it—especially if your circumstances are decidedly outside your control. One of the great Roman Stoics, Epictetus (ca. 50–ca. 135 CE), was born into slavery, for example. And when we taught Life Worth Living at the federal prison in Danbury, Stoicism was a hit. The students there recognized the power of focusing on what you can control. By focusing on the core of agency that no one can take from you—that ability to direct your own internal posture—students felt the possibility of dignity under any circumstances.

The Stoics take a more nuanced stance toward emotions than toward external goods like health and wealth. Now, as ancients, they don't use the category *emotion*. That's a modern idea. But they do talk about a good chunk of what we mean by emotions under the rubric of the passions. And the Stoics consider the passions not just irrelevant, but bad.

Things like fear and anger reflect and reinforce inappropriate investment in things outside our control. They subject us to domination by the capricious whims of the world. They lead us away from virtue and, therefore, from the good life. Fair enough, you might say. Who makes fear and anger important parts of the good life, after all? Well, the Stoics don't stop with fear and anger. They place what we would consider positive emotions, like hope and elation, in exactly the same category. Hope and fear, they say, are very much alike. Both are evidence of unwise investment in the future. Both place your happiness outside your control. No place for them in the good life. "You will cease to fear, if you cease to hope," advises Seneca the Younger (ca. 4 BCE–65 CE). That's quite the exchange: no more hope for no more fear. It'll keep your "good life" secure, but if you place any value on feelings themselves, it will sap much of the color out of life.

That said, not everything we think of as emotion falls into the Stoics' "passions" bucket. They insist that certain "good passions" will be by-products of a virtuous life. Most important, there's what they call "joy." They mean it in a very specific sense: quiet, stable satisfaction in one's own good agency. Seneca advised a younger friend, "Look to the true good and take joy *only* in that which comes from what is your own. What do I mean by 'from what is your own'? I mean you yourself and your own best part." What he means is, be satisfied with your virtue.

So for the Stoics, there's nothing more to the good life than leading life well. It's not just that virtue is the "hero" ingredient to their recipe for the good life. It's pretty much the only ingredient that matters, because agency is the only "food group" necessary.

And for a Stoic, that strict focus is a good thing. Focusing exclusively on virtue draws your attention away from potential distractions— like the passions and life's circumstances—that will only wreck your life.

For Pleasure's Sake

The utilitarian philosophers Jeremy Bentham, John Stuart Mill, and Peter Singer put a different ingredient at the center of their good life dish. All of them undeniably prioritize the affective aspect. Recall what Bentham said: "Good is pleasure or exemption from pain. . . . Evil is pain or loss of pleasure." For these utilitarians a good life is simply one that is full of good feelings and free from pain.

Unlike the Stoics, they don't claim that nothing else matters. All sorts of things other than feelings matter. But for the utilitarian thinkers above, these things matter only because they promote or diminish happiness. For example, certain circumstances are more likely to produce pleasure and reduce pain than others. Utilitarians worry a lot about life's basics: sufficient food, education, health care, and money to buy various goods and services. These things are valuable because they tend to lead to more pleasure and less pain. Circumstances, however, have no independent value of their own. They matter *only* to the extent that they increase pleasure or reduce pain.

And as we've seen, utilitarians' focus on happiness actually ends up animating a really demanding account of how we should exercise our agency. Everyone's happiness matters the same. There's nothing special about your own or your kids' or your friends' happiness. If you're really committed to a utilitarian view of pleasure and equality, then you ought to help others until it would hurt you more to give than it would help anyone else to receive. A life led well is one that ruthlessly seeks the greatest overall happiness, at whatever expense to oneself that entails.

The striking thing is, for a utilitarian, even this life of radical care for others isn't valuable for its own sake, strictly speaking. If it were possible to have a world of unending bliss where no one had to care for anyone else at their own expense, that would be preferable. As it happens, we don't live in such a world—at least not yet.

But what if we could build such a world? The idea is less and less far-fetched. More than fifty years ago, philosopher Robert Nozick (1938–2002) proposed a thought experiment. Suppose you could plug into an "experience machine" that would give you any experience you could want. While plugged in, you wouldn't know you were there. You'd think all your experiences were real. (Cue Morpheus from *The Matrix*: "What is real?") Suppose everyone else could plug in as well, so you needn't stay out of the machine to take care of others. Nozick wants to know, "Would you plug in? *What else can matter to us, other than how our lives feel from the inside?*"

Nozick expects that we will not want to plug in. His argument depends on it. We want to actually do things. We want to actually be certain ways. We value contact with reality, not just the experience of its verisimilitude. Nozick concludes, "We learn that something matters to us in addition to experience by imagining an experience machine and then realizing that we would not use it."

Nozick's expectation, however, may be falling out of step with the zeitgeist. Each year, we ask our Yale undergraduates whether they'd plug in, and each year, more and more of them say they would. And it's not necessarily because they're budding techno-utopians (though some may be!). It may be that plenty of them simply agree with Bentham, Mill, and Singer that the experience of pleasure and freedom from pain are the only things worth wanting for themselves.

For now, the metaverse seems unappealing enough to relegate the experience machine to the realm of fiction. But it may not always be so. And even if plugging in isn't on the table, valuing how life feels above all else may not be something you're ready to do. Maybe care, even costly care, is something valuable in its own right. Perhaps acting and being acted upon by reality need their own place in life's recipe.

A Recipe for Harmony

There is, Confucius thought, a pattern for how the world ought to be. Life isn't static, so the pattern works less like a drawing and more like an animation. It's less like a pose, more like a dance. Not a destination, but a way—*the* Way. It's the shape of life and the world that coheres and resonates with the deepest truth of things. Maybe it *is* that deepest truth.

Nowhere that's been written down, at least, did Confucius ever come out and say what the Way is. He didn't give a definition. He didn't offer a detailed, comprehensive description. Nevertheless, we can get a sense of what it's about from the book that collects Confucius's sayings and stories about him, the *Analects*.

For one thing, the Way is a pattern for whole societies, but it also reaches down to the details of social rituals, family relationships, and individual speech and action. Everything is tightly knit together. We can see this integration in a characteristically enigmatic story about Confucius. Someone, it is said, once asked him to explain one of the traditional ritual sacrifices. The Master said, "I don't know. Someone who knew its meaning would understand all the affairs of the world as if they were displayed right here—and he pointed to his palm." The whole order of how things ought to be is so cohesive that if you were to really, deeply understand this one ritual, you would unlock the whole.

A second important feature is that the Way has fundamentally to do with relationships—with how people and groups relate to one another and to the material world. The right kinds of metaphors for it are things like order, structure, or (maybe best of all) harmony.

Taken together, these two features mean that there's a decided accent on circumstances in Confucius's vision. A certain arrangement of things is essential to full flourishing. It's a little like a lock. Inside are a set of pins called tumblers. When even one tumbler is out of alignment, the lock is shut. But when all of them come into alignment—click!—the lock opens. Suddenly, there is freedom of movement. The whole system functions differently.

What the wise person wants most of all is to live in a society that lives according to the Way and therefore prospers and has peace. They are no Stoic sages, who can live the whole good life even in the worst society. Confucius advises his students, "Do not enter a state that is endangered, and do not reside in a state that is disordered. . . . Hide when the world loses the Way." As the Stoics predict, if you allow circumstances a foothold in your vision, having a good life is no longer entirely up to you. Your flourishing is dependent on circumstances outside your control. It's tied up in the flourishing of the world around you. Confucius and the Stoics would presumably agree on this point. What they disagree about is whether Confucian interdependence is a bug (so the Stoics would say) or a feature (so Confucians).

But the circumstance of a society that lives according to the Way isn't quite as all-consuming in Confucius's vision as virtue is for the Stoics or pleasure is for the utilitarians. Affect and good agency have much more significant places in his "recipe." And yet, as in a good recipe, their roles don't clash with the circumstantial side of the Way. They complement it and contribute to a cohesive whole.

Let's take affect first. Confucius uses various terms when alluding to how a good life feels. One is particularly illuminating: *joy*. Confucian joy is neither the utilitarians' pleasure nor Stoic (self-) satisfaction—nor, for that matter, Subha's contentment. Confucius thinks a wise person is joyful because they are in tune with the Way. They resonate with the world as it most fundamentally is and ought to be: the Chinese character we translate as "joy" serves as the basis for the character for "music." The relationship to good circumstances is baked right into Confucius's account of affective flourishing.

For Confucius, life feeling as it should (affect) also has an inner connection to leading life well (agency). "A man without humanity cannot long bear adversity and cannot long know joy." *Humanity* is Confucius's term for the heart of good character. So he's saying that leading life well is essential to finding long-term joy.

Let's turn now to the relation of agency to circumstance. One important point comes out best by way of contrast. In some utilitarian visions, a perfectly flourishing world with no human agency at all is imaginable. Hooking everyone up to the experience machine would be good enough. Great, even. Is it going to happen? Probably not. But would Bentham have any reason not to *want* it to happen? No.

Confucius's view is different. The picture of a cohesive and harmonious set of circumstances may be an illuminating point of view from which to consider the Way. But remember, if the Way is a set of circumstances, it's a set of circumstances in motion—a set of dynamics, including innumerable human actions. Rulers act with virtue, wisdom, and propriety. They delegate to capable ministers. Those ministers serve uprightly and for the good of the society. Children exhibit proper deference and respect for parents, and younger siblings for older. Everyone participates in the prescribed rituals respectfully and joyfully. And so on. All these things help to create the web of interlocking social relations that define good circumstances. So like affect, agency has its own standing in Confucius's vision. The Way is always something that is put into practice. Remember those four sprouts Mencius wants you to cultivate in your life? The idea is that those virtues will help you live in the Way.

All this is to say that, at least in one plausible interpretation, Confucius's vision of the good life is a fairly balanced recipe. No one food group took up all the space on the plate, so to speak. The Way can be understood in a certain light as a set of ideal circumstances—a whole world in harmonious motion. But precisely as such, Confucius's account of the Way includes flourishing emotions like joy and flourishing agency.

What Are You Going to Do About It?

Hopefully these three examples give us a sense of what visions of life start to look like if we put an ingredient from one or another food group (aspect of the good life) at the center of our recipe. And hopefully they also help us see what difference it makes whether that central ingredient is basically the whole meal or if, instead, it shares the spotlight. Stoics strictly emphasize agency to the effective exclusion of circumstance and affect. Utilitarians focus on affect but give space for circumstance and agency insofar as they impact how people feel. Confucius envisions a harmonious set of circumstances, of which people's agency and emotional resonance are important facets.

There's a catch, though. When push comes to shove, in a certain sense, agency *always* holds first place. As long as we're able to face the Question, an inescapable practical priority goes to the question of how to lead life well. All the other sub-questions verge on idle musings unless they have implications for how we live. When we come to the Question, we're not just looking for a topographical map laying out the terrain of what's worth wanting. We're looking for a destination and a compass.

There aren't many things the great religious traditions and philosophers mostly agree about. It turns out, though, that this is one of them: when push comes to shove, the decisive facet of the Question is, How should we live?

This practical emphasis on agency shows up even in visions that prioritize affect or circumstances. For example, as much as Bentham and his ilk are happy to reduce the good life to pleasure and the avoidance of pain, a lot of what they *say* has to do with what you should *do* if you agree that happiness is what matters. Namely, you should act so as to maximize the amount of happiness and minimize the amount of suffering in the world. They argue passionately that each one of us should count equally when we assess the next right thing to do. Everyone's pleasure and pain all count the same, they insist. Nobody gets a special deal. In a utilitarian calculus, there is no multiplier for being rich or powerful or super nice or really charming, or even for being *you*. That's not the way we normally think. As a result, the utilitarian line of thinking can end up advocating that we ought to act in ways that strike us as at once profoundly reasonable and deeply counterintuitive. Pages and pages of their books are devoted to helping us stop imagining ourselves as the center of the universe and inviting us to act accordingly.

Similarly, Confucius spends more of his energy encouraging his listeners to lead their lives well than he does describing a society that fully realizes the Way. Since the actual society of his day (and ours) fails to follow the Way, the key question for anybody looking to live in light of Confucius's vision is how to follow the Way in a society gone astray. If the world isn't following the Way, rewards go to precisely the wrong people. Cheaters prosper. The shameless get famous, instead of infamous. In a world gone awry, Confucius looks at any of us who have found wealth or made a name for ourselves and asks, This world is working for you? *This* one? If the world is out of joint and you find yourself living large, it's probably because you, too, are out of joint. If the society you live in has lost the Way, you can choose only one of these options: leading your life well or trying to make it go well. And if you have to choose, Confucius insists that you go in for good agency, come what may. He's even willing to put agency above the most basic of circumstances: being alive. "The humane person," he says, "never tries to go on living if it is harmful to humaneness. There are times when he sacrifices his life to preserve humaneness." For Confucius, living righteously aims to conform to and contribute to the ideal circumstances of a world that follows the Way. He gives circumstances a real priority. But we have a responsibility to live according to the Way even when those ideal circumstances don't obtain. Circumstances have *ultimate* priority, but agency gets *practical* priority.

As we emphasized in the introduction, human agency is fundamentally constrained. None of us is omnipotent. None of us is an absolute sovereign, even if some of us like to think we are. Many know the intense work required to claim agency within social systems that marginalize whole groups of people and deny them agency. And all of us are prone to the reshaping, restriction, or, in the extreme, complete loss of our agency through illness or injury. All agency, like all ability, is temporary.

In the big picture, there are more consequential things than how any one of us uses whatever capacities for agency we've received. None of us is at the center of everything. Every one of us, though, holds a privileged position in our own life. It's *ours*. Now, that doesn't mean that the weight is all on you. "Only you" responsibility doesn't mean that you're on your own. It may well be that an essential part of using your (limited) agency well is to seek out help, to find others to share life with, to admit that you alone are not enough.

Granting all these important qualifications, it's still the case that how we lead our lives is going to have a special urgency no matter how important we think it is that life feels good or goes well. Even if our recipe aims for near-perfect balance between the three aspects, we'll find that we really get cooking when we have a clear sense of what we ought to do. So as we put together our recipes, we'll need to keep in mind this special status for how we ought to live.

So How *Should* We Put It All Together?

The message of this chapter is simple. Pay attention to how your vision hangs together. If you're going to embrace a one-ingredient vision, it's important to know what you're getting into. One ingredient can only ever be from one food group. You better be a true believer in the dietary theory driving your meal planning. Otherwise, your vision may fail the nutrition test. And whatever overall balance we land on, there's value in trying to make sure the various facets of our answers to the Question complement each other. It's no good for our values and ideals to be pushing us in contradictory directions. We need to pass the recipe test as well.

Is it possible, though, that we're putting a little too much emphasis on the whole consistency thing? What's so wrong with a little self-contradiction anyway?

At the end of each Life Worth Living class at Yale, students write a short paper sketching their vision of a life worth living. It's a daunting task and undeniably above their pay grade.

It's also above our pay grade to authoritatively judge the truth or falsehood of the visions our students articulate. Each of us has to be free to do the difficult work of discerning the shape of flourishing life and articulating answers for ourselves. But we're still the teachers, and it's our job to assess our students' papers somehow, so we've come up with criteria for grading the papers that we hope still grant students the autonomy their "only you" responsibility deserves. We tell them they'll be graded, in part, on how coherent their vision is as a whole. We encourage them to apply the recipe test to their visions as part of the drafting process. Does it all hang together?

One year, a student came to Matt and, with admirable courage, objected to this criterion. The search for consistency, they said, is a mistake. For one thing, you're never going to find it. For another thing, it wouldn't be so great if you did. Life, they insisted, is unruly. A systematic, self-consistent vision of life would sell that unruliness short. It would do more harm than good.

We can learn two things from this bold student.

First, the student is almost certainly right that complete coherence is an unreachable ideal. We're never going to get it all in perfect order. The Question is too big and too complex for any of us to answer with strict and comprehensive consistency.

Given that there will be inconsistencies in our visions, the important question is what we'll do when we find them. Rather than fearing them or trying to ignore them, perhaps we'll see that these inconsistencies present opportunities. They give us an occasion to dive into discernment again, to weigh the various facets of our de facto responses to the Question, and to try to bring them into a richer synthesis. Granted, we'll never get all the way there. Even so, bringing our visions into greater coherence is an important goal, unless we believe something like the student's conviction that life is inherently unruly.

That *unless* points to the next lesson.

Our student was surprisingly *consistent* in their reasons for championing inconsistency. They appealed to things they took to be true about the world and reasoned from those things to the conclusion that visions of a life worth living ought not to aim for tight coherence. The student's approach points to an important feature of wrestling with the Question: all our answers take shape in dialogue with our sense of the really big picture of, to borrow a phrase from Douglas Adams (author of *The Hitchhiker's Guide to the Galaxy*), "life, the universe, and everything." That's where we'll turn in the next chapter.

Your Turn

1. Go back over your answers to the exercises from the last three chapters.
   * How do they fit together?
   * Where are there tensions or contradictions? If you had to resolve them, which question(s) would you change your answers to?
   * Does one of the three aspects (agency, circumstance, affect) take priority in your vision, or do you try to balance them? If you tend to give one priority, what reasons can you give to justify that priority?

EIGHT

The Really Big Picture

Every time we teach Life Worth Living at Yale, there's a seminar session where we discuss Yale's vision of the good life. The idea is to think together about the various answers to the Question that permeate our shared social space at the university. Each year's conversation is different, but one theme comes up without fail: *meritocracy*, the idea "that advantage should be earned through ability and effort rather than inherited." Our students are right to identify it as an influential ideal at Yale.

They disagree with each other about how consistently the university implements its meritocratic ideal, how widespread that ideal is in society, and whether or not the ideal is a good one. What they almost invariably do agree on is that meritocracy isn't nonsense. They accept the premise that merit is real.

One year, however, a student turned that assumption on its head.

These aren't the student's precise words, but they said something like, "Well, neuroscience shows that humans don't have free will. Everything we do is completely determined, which means we're not responsible for our achievements. So the whole idea of merit makes no sense." Same, they went on to say, with blame. In other words: We're not free. But responsibility presupposes freedom. Therefore, we are not in fact responsible for our acts, achievements, or anything.

Reward and punishment, in turn, are supposed to go to responsible agents. But there's no such thing as responsible agents. Therefore, it doesn't make sense to practice reward and punishment. To do so is to act as though something (responsibility) is the case, when in fact it is not. Hence, the student concluded, we shouldn't reward and punish. There should be no meritocracy. (And no prisons to boot.)

This was a line-in-the-sand moment. If this student's claim and the argument they built on it were true, it would scramble the whole conversation. And not just this one. Suddenly, all our discussions about flourishing, the shape of a good life, and the like were thrown into question.

The Picture and the Question

This classroom episode shows that our ideas about the really big picture of things—the fundamental nature of physical reality, the metaphysics of human agency, and the like—matter for our attempts to address the Question. They rule out certain answers. (To use an example from chapter 3: we can't very well be responsible to God if God isn't real.) And they tilt us in the direction of others.

So whether we like it or not, learning to think about the really big picture is an important part of learning to address the Question.

There is, admittedly, reason not to like it. It's understandably tempting to try to ignore the really big picture. It is really big, after all, which makes it daunting. When it comes to the really big picture, we're back in the same predicament as when we first tried to get our heads around the Question. If figuring out the shape of flourishing is above our pay grade, surely things that philosophers call by intimidating names like metaphysics, ontology, and episte-mology are too.

It might be helpful to use the same strategy here that we've used throughout the book: break down a truly overwhelming question into only moderately overwhelming parts. But it would take a whole other book (or two or three) to parse out even a rough over-view of the sub-facets of the really big picture.

To keep our momentum going, we'll focus for now on two questions (inspired by the Christian theologian Norman Wirzba) that sum up some of the most important features of the really big picture: *Where are we?* and *Who are we?* These two questions en-capsulate the really big picture's function of orienting us to our surroundings (in the broadest sense) and giving us an idea of just what kind of thing a human life is. In briefer, more technical terms, they help us articulate a *cosmology* and an *anthropology*, an account of the world and one of human beings.

These questions will help us get our heads around some broad-strokes descriptions of a few different understandings of the really big picture. They'll also help us see how apparently abstract issues connect with the real stuff of life.

We'll start by posing Wirzba's questions to Christianity, his tradition (and ours), before moving on to consider other traditions and perspectives.

A Story of Everything

At the age of thirty, a woman we know only as Julian (1343–ca. 1416) lay on the verge of death in her one-room chamber attached to the Church of St. Julian in Norwich, England. A priest at her side, she fixed her eyes on an image of Jesus dying on the cross, and she prayed. And then, Julian tells us, she received a series of visions. Shortly thereafter, she recovered and composed a short narrative of her experience.

As part of the first vision, she says, God "showed a little thing, the size of a hazel-nut in the palm of my hand, and it was as round as a ball. I looked at it with my mind's eye and thought, 'What can this be?' And the answer came to me, 'It is all that is made.' I wondered how it could last, for it was so small I thought it might suddenly have disappeared. And the answer in my mind was, 'It lasts and will last for ever because God loves it; and everything exists in the same way by the love of God.' In this little thing I saw three properties: the first is that God made it, the second is that God loves it, the third is that God cares for it."

For Julian, from beginning to end, the story of our hazelnut-sized world is the story of God's love. Having spent more than fifteen years mulling over and wrestling with the meaning of the visions she had seen, Julian came to this sudden insight: "I saw quite certainly in this and in everything that God loved us before he made us; and his love has never diminished and never shall. And all his works were done in this love, and in this love he has made everything for our profit, and in this love our life is everlasting."

Humans have a special status within this creation of love. Quoting the Bible, Julian says that we were made in God's "image" and "likeness." We have, however, marred that image by failing to live well, by breaking the relationship of love that God intends for us. Julian is painfully aware of how far short of the mark we fall.

But crucially, God's love covers even this. God loves without fail, despite our failures. "He who made man for love, by that same love would restore man." As broken as things may seem, God will make them right and bring them into the fullness of love. Julian hears God's voice say in one of her visions, "I may make all things well and I will make all things well and I shall make all things well; and you shall see for yourself that all manner of things shall be well."

What responses does Julian's experience suggest to our guiding questions? *Where are we?* In the fragile, vulnerable world that God created out of love and for love. *Who are we?* Beloved but failure-prone creatures made in the image of God and loved without fail by the God who promises that "all manner of things shall be well."

What might a really big picture that focuses on God's unfailing love for creatures imply for life? How might it impact our responses to the Question? It's hard for us to answer briefly. In our day jobs as Christian theologians, we've written whole books addressing it. But we'll try to have some self-discipline and note only two connections here.

First, there's nothing to prove. We don't have to demonstrate our value by being perfect or pure or super impressive. Our value doesn't come from what we do or who we are but from the One who loves us. And that love is thoroughly, unconquerably, unfailingly dependable. Nothing "will be able to separate us from the love of God in Christ Jesus our Lord," to use the apostle Paul's language. Not even any failure of ours. And that means we don't need to live under the weight of guilt or shame or striving to prove ourselves. We can live in freedom.

Second, because we are loved, we ought to love. And this isn't just a reciprocal thing, us loving God because God loves us. God loves the world, and in loving God, we ought to love what God loves. So we ought to love the world. A passage from the Bible lays out the fundamental inference: "Beloved, if God so loved us, we also ought to love one another." This love should be a finite echo of the infinite love of God. It should, therefore, be unconditional. Because God loves us despite our failures, we should love others (*all* others) despite theirs.

That's a daunting standard. Christians have not met it. We have not come close to universally demonstrating the love of God to the world. At times it has seemed this was due in part to the way we thought about the really big picture.

Late Arrivals on Turtle Island

Even after decades of cleanup work and remediation, the water of Onondaga Lake is contaminated with mercury. Eat too much fish from the lake, and your hair, teeth, and fingernails might fall out. The lake bed is full of toxic heavy metals like lead and cobalt, as well as harmful hard-to-pronounce chemicals: polycyclic aromatic hydrocarbons, polychlorinated biphenyls, chlorobenzene, and more. Some stretches of the shore feature sixty-foot-deep beds of industrial waste where the soil should be.

Robin Wall Kimmerer, an environmental biologist in the lakeside city of Syracuse, has reasons to be suspicious of Christian accounts of the really big picture. Kimmerer is a member of the Potawatomi Nation, an Indigenous people whose traditional homeland is present-day eastern Michigan. Over several centuries, European settlers who proclaimed Christianity pushed the Potawatomi south and west, from Lake Huron to Lake Michigan, and eventually forced their removal from the Great Lakes region to reservations and private land plots on the Great Plains in Kansas.

The society those settlers built is the one that devastated Onondaga Lake.

Kimmerer is nuanced. She neither flat-out rejects modern industry and technology nor simply blames Christianity for colonial expropriation of land or environmental wreckage. She does, however, implicitly critique certain features of a Christian really big picture in her influential book *Braiding Sweetgrass*.

For one thing, a Christian really big picture seems inclined to treat the entire planet as an effectively undifferentiated whole. Where are we? God's creation. Everywhere is equally that. So it would seem that every place is, in the really big picture, effectively the same.

For another, Christianity's orientation toward the future can tend to construe us humans as mere exiles on Earth, "just passing through an alien world on a rough road to [our] real home in heaven," as Kimmerer puts it.

And finally, Kimmerer suggests, Christianity sets humans too far apart from other creatures by giving us a privileged place. The idea that we were created in the image of God authorizes human power in ways that separate us from other creatures. Facts like the incredible rate of extinction of other species on this planet (over one thousand times the expected natural rate) suggest that we haven't used that power well.

Kimmerer draws on North American Indigenous traditions to paint a different really big picture. She works mostly with sources from Algonquin-speaking peoples related to her Potawatomi Nation and from the Haudenosaunee (or Iroquois) Nations, on whose traditional lands in upstate New York she now lives.

In Haudenosaunee legend, there was no land here below until a woman fell from the sky. But for the geese who rose from the water to break her fall, she would have perished. But for the turtle who offered its back, she would have drowned. But for the muskrat who gave his life in a dive to the ocean floor to bring back mud to spread on the turtle's back, so that plants could grow and the floating island become a home for her, she may well have starved. Thanks to these and other helpers, Skywoman did not die. In gratitude, she sowed the bundle of seeds from the Tree of Life that she had grasped as she fell from the world above. The land blossomed and brought forth fruit.

What does the story of Skywoman have to say about where we are? To begin: we, at least those of us who live in North America, are on Turtle Island. But what exactly does that mean?

Note first that the community of animals supports Skywoman in her need and fragility. She can live here only because "here"—in the form of living creatures with their own gifts and ways of life—has received her and nurtured her. Put generally, we live in hospitable environments made up of a multitude of other-than-human creatures, and these environments are essential to our survival and thriving.

But the story of Skywoman isn't primarily meant to put things generally. Rather, it is a way of articulating the specific relationship between the Haudenosaunee peoples and their homeland. Whatever it says about humans and our world generally, this is first and foremost a narrative description of a particular "here." Kimmerer emphasizes that each of us is in a specific place with its own peculiar other-than-human inhabitants and temporal rhythms. The Central Asian steppe is a very different life-world than the Amazon Basin. Much closer together, Puget Sound (where Seattle sits) has a markedly different ecology than San Francisco Bay.

Braiding Sweetgrass threads together a plethora of different implications of this sense of ecological situatedness. We'll mention two especially central ones. First, Kimmerer concludes that we ought to "become indigenous to place," to "learn to live *here* as if we were staying." Very few of us, even if we live in the very house where we were born, are indigenous in Kimmerer's strong sense of the word. Very few of us, that is, live according to patterns of reciprocity that recognize and support the particular network of other-than-human species that constitutes the place where we live.

Second, the Skywoman story represents relationships between species as fundamentally cooperative. Reciprocity, not exploitation, is the basic truth of things. "All flourishing is mutual," as Kimmerer pithily puts it. To seek our own gain at the expense of those around us (human and otherwise) is to live at cross grain with the deepest way of the world.

The story of Skywoman also illustrates some of Kimmerer's responses to the question of who we are. Skywoman enters a world already populated by wise, intelligent beings. She is a newcomer who must learn from and work with the existing inhabitants to make a home in the world. In line with this, Kimmerer says, various Indigenous traditions think of us humans as younger siblings of other-than-human creatures. The Anishinaabe (a larger cultural group that includes the Potawatomi) tell of Nanabozho, the mythical First Man, walking the land and learning from it and its inhabitants how to live and thrive. The human stance that corresponds appropriately to this little-sibling status is one of humility and learning.

At the same time, each creature has a particular gift—something peculiar and proper that it alone can offer to others—and, therefore, a particular responsibility. We are called to recognize our gifts, acknowledge that they are gifts, give thanks, and then give to others out of our giftedness. "Whatever our gift, we are called to give it and to dance for the renewal of the world. In return for the privilege of breath." The picture of humans as gifted creatures in a community of other gifted creatures leads to a response to the Question that emphasizes gratitude and reciprocal giving.

Recall that Kimmerer is a biologist. Gratitude and gift are not the usual categories of empirical biology. Kimmerer has dedicated much of her life to synthesizing the wisdom she sees in the really big picture of North American Indigenous peoples with the data offered by scientific research. But Kimmerer is far from the only one who faces the question of how modern empirical science relates to our accounts of the really big picture. Anyone who acknowledges the value of findings ranging from radio waves to penicillin has to wrestle with it. The issue is all the more pressing because a number of influential scientists have argued that empirical science actually provides the really big picture itself and so sets the terms for all plausible responses to the Question.

Paradise on a Pale Blue Dot

From down here, Earth looks and feels enormous. In 1990, though, earthlings got to see things from a decidedly different perspective—from 3.7 billion miles away, to be (relatively) precise. The spacecraft *Voyager 1* snapped photos of the solar system from its outer reaches and sent them back to Earth. From out *there*, Earth looks tiny and insignificant. A "pale blue dot," as the astronomer Carl Sagan (1934–1996) famously put it. In the really big picture, it would seem, our planet is rather small potatoes.

If the planet that seems so enormous to us is a mere dot, what does that make us? Sagan writes, "On the scale of worlds—to say nothing of stars or galaxies—humans are inconsequential, a thin film of life on an obscure and solitary lump of rock and metal."

So where are we? Empirical cosmologists and astrophysicists currently give a rough estimate of something like ten billion trillion stars in the observable universe, mostly clustered into something like two hundred billion galaxies. We're on a "lump of rock and metal" that orbits a rather unremarkable one of those myriad stars in a fairly run-of-the-mill galaxy.

As Sagan sees it, this situation has serious implications for the Question. It radically undercuts human pretensions to greatness and relativizes both our differences and our conflicts with each other:

> Think of the rivers of blood spilled by all those generals and emperors so that, in glory and triumph, they could become the momentary masters of a fraction of a dot. Think of the endless cruelties visited by the inhabitants of one corner of this pixel on the scarcely distinguishable inhabitants of some other corner. . . . There is perhaps no better demonstration of the folly of human conceits than this distant image of our tiny world. To me, it underscores our responsibility to deal more kindly with one another, and to preserve and cherish the pale blue dot, the only home we've ever known.

We're small and fragile and marginal, Sagan says. And that means we should be humble and gentle and kind.

When we zoom in on Sagan's "lump of rock and metal" to take a look at its "thin film of life," astrophysics and cosmology give way to biology as the most relevant empirical scientific discipline. Contemporary biology not only paints a picture of how living organisms today function and interact with one another; it also investigates how current species came to exist through processes of evolutionary selection under conditions of competition.

This adds a more granular layer to the astrophysical perspective on where we are. We are on a planet that hosts complex, interlocking ecological systems filled with millions of species of living beings, all of which are in the midst of ongoing processes of evolutionary change that have been going on for somewhere around 3.5 or 4 billion years.

It also suggests at least some features of an answer to the second question: Who are we? At the broadest level, humans are one of those millions of species. We are particularly intelligent, but like all other species, we are inheritors of a certain set of genetic characteristics that produce behavioral tendencies we call instincts. Our instincts aren't as inflexible and specific as, say, those of ants, but they are still real and influential. Increasingly, contemporary biologists argue that our instincts are products of two different types of evolutionary selection: individual selection and group selection.

Individual selection arises from competition for resources and reproduction between *members* of a species. It's the phenomena that lends a bit of credence to the old picture of evolution as a cutthroat, everyone-for-themselves, all-against-all fight for survival. And in human evolution it tends to favor those genetic variations that prescribe strength, cunning, freeloading, cheating, selfishness—whatever gives the individual a leg up within the group.

Group selection, as you might suppose, arises from competition between different *groups* within a species. Just like a football team that works together will outperform one where every player is out for their individual glory, so cooperative groups have an evolutionary advantage over ones that don't work together well. That means that group selection tends to favor genetic variations that prescribe generosity, honesty, mutual support, and altruism—within the group at least.

As the evolutionary biologist E. O. Wilson (1929–2021) summarizes, "Within groups selfish individuals beat altruistic individuals, but groups of altruists beat groups of selfish individuals." Individual and group selection worked simultaneously in human evolution. Consequently, we have tendencies produced by both, which pull us in divergent directions. In Wilson's pithy phrase, "Risking oversimplification, individual selection promoted sin, while group selection promoted virtue."

One important caveat is that competition between groups promotes traits that Wilson calls "tribalism": the tendency to think of our own group as superior and to treat in-group members better than outsiders.

So who are we, in Wilson's view? We are "at once saints and sinners, champions of truth and hypocrites," pulled between total commitment to community and an opposite instinct to seek our own good at the community's expense, and possessing a stubborn tendency to privilege our own groups over others. At the same time, because we are highly intelligent, we are the Earth become conscious and curious. We are the galaxy come to know itself.

Wilson thinks that evolutionary biology has plentiful implications for the Question. For one thing, there's no getting out of our conflicted nature. The competing pulls of "sin" (selfishness) and "virtue" (altruism) are essential to who we are. The best we can do is learn to tamp down the worst effects of selfishness and enjoy the creativity that our conflicted nature produces. The one thing we can and should seek to overcome completely, he says, is tribalism. There's no rational reason to believe our group is better or more important than others, and the consequences of that belief are deadly. We should, therefore, use the rationality evolution gave us to pursue a united humanity. If we do, Wilson says, we can hope "to turn Earth into a paradise both for ourselves and for the biosphere that gave us birth" in little more than a hundred years.

Stepping back, what are we to make of Sagan's and Wilson's attempts to paint the really big picture using the color palette of modern empirical science?

One important thing to note is that Wilson and Sagan face an acute version of a common problem: How does *is* relate to *ought?* In other words, how do descriptions of the way things are relate to prescriptions about how they should be? This question poses a dilemma. On the one hand, just because something is a certain way doesn't mean it ought to be. ("I stole your wallet. Therefore, I ought to have stolen your wallet." Nope. The more serious an example you choose, the more abominable the idea appears.) The gap between *is* and *ought* is the only thing that gives *ought* any teeth.

On the other hand, what *reasons* could we possibly give for an *ought* without appealing to one or another *is?* For example, utilitarians like Bentham and Mill claim that we *ought* to seek the greatest overall happiness. Why? Because happiness *is* desirable. A sharp distinction between *is* and *ought* risks turning every *ought* into the expression of a mere preference. It risks a version of what philosophers call "emotivism": the view that *ought* statements aren't truth claims but just roundabout ways of saying, "That's how I happen to want it to be."

One common way of responding to this problem is to make a distinction within *is*. To claim that there's a *realer* real, a deeper truth, something more fundamental than the ordinary, everyday way things are, and to identify that realer, deeper, more fundamental *is* as the criterion for *ought*. For example, Jews and Christians and Muslims might point to God's truth or God's will as the definitive reality and claim that we humans ought to live in accordance with it. In Kimmerer's case, she seems to distinguish between the deep truth of interdependence and reciprocity, on the one hand, and the actual ways that so many of us live (as if we were independent and owed nothing to other-than-human creatures), on the other. Her message is to live in line with what we most deeply are.

Whether this kind of move works is a thorny philosophical question. (Our sense is that it can work if done well.) But regardless, at least it opens up some room for *ought* while trying to ward off unmitigated emotivism.

Sagan and Wilson don't have grounds for making this two-realities move. They are emphatic that there is only one level to reality: the empirical, material one governed by laws of physics and biology. (Not all empirical scientists share their view on this point.) So they seem to be stuck with just *is*. How can a telescope tell us what matters? In what sense is it better to respond to the vastness of the universe with humility and intergroup harmony than with despair over our cosmic insignificance or a tooth-and-nail fight to hold on to the miniscule bit of life and resources that we have? What reason do we have to call selfishness "sin" and altruism "virtue," as Wilson does? They're both baked into who we are. And why shouldn't we go on denigrating and competing with outsiders? That's the way it's always been. Who's to say it should be otherwise?

Beyond (Being) Meat

Maybe the better question is, "Who's to say it will stay the same?" Maybe the really big picture of where we are and who we are isn't nearly as fixed as Wilson claims. Maybe there's serious change in store. And maybe that change is just around the corner.

The inventor Ray Kurzweil tells a six-stage story of everything. First was the origin of chemistry as we know it (atoms and molecules and the like), with more complex structures emerging in the millions of years after the big bang. Eventually, some agglomerations of molecules became self-replicating, and life was born, bringing on the second stage of the story and kicking off the evolutionary process as modern biology understands it. After millions of years, the third stage began: organisms with brains and nervous systems evolved. One such organism, humans, gained the capacity to envision future possibilities (like the consequences of taking a burning ember from a lightning strike and touching it to a pile of dry grass and sticks) and act to bring them about. That capacity sparked the transition to the fourth stage: human technology, which has developed at an exponentially increasing rate to bring us today to the cusp of the fifth stage. Soon, Kurzweil says, humans will merge "the vast knowledge embedded in our brains with the vastly greater capacity, speed, and knowledge-sharing ability of our technology." That will ignite an astonishing explosion of intelligence, as nonbiological intelligence reorganizes matter for its computational purposes and comes to saturate the universe.

In short:

Physics and chemistry

Biology and DNA

Brains

Technology

The merger of human technology with human
intelligence

The universe wakes up

Where are we, according to Kurzweil? Right at the crucial
transition point from stage four to stage five. We still inhabit our
biological bodies and depend in large part on our biological intelligence, but we are beginning to be able to enhance those bodies
and push beyond the limits of brain-based thinking. "What we are
doing is transcending biology. . . . We are upending biological evolution altogether." Kurzweil calls this decisive moment of change
"the Singularity." It spells the end of all distinction between human and machine, physical reality and virtual.

If a shiver of dread goes down your (biological) spine when you
think about it (with your biological brain), you're not alone. Kurzweil is used to it, and he has an account of who we are that he
thinks should put you at ease.

First, note that the actual stuff that makes up our bodies
changes constantly. Indeed, we get an almost completely new set of
particles every month or so, even in our brains. What makes us us,
Kurzweil says, is the pattern (of body and brain-dependent mind)

that persists over time. But even this pattern changes over time. We grow, we learn, we age, and so on. The pattern just changes rather slowly and continuously. We are, Kurzweil says, simply constantly evolving patterns. So there's nothing for each of us to fear from evolutions of our particular pattern that take it beyond biology.

Second, as a species, our definitive trait is the drive to overcome whatever our current limitations are. "Being human means being part of a civilization that seeks to extend its boundaries." So to push beyond the human-as-we-know-it is the most human thing we could do.

There is no end point for Kurzweil's transhumanist story of everything. Physicists currently hold that our universe will at some point end, although they disagree on just how the curtain will fall on our cosmos. But however it happened, the demise of the universe would be a less-than-happy end to Kurzweil's version of the big story. Kurzweil is optimistic, though. We should expect that intelligence trillions of times more powerful than all our feeble meat-brains combined will find a way to avert the death of the universe, or else make a new one if this one can't be sustained indefinitely.

Kurzweil envisions—and hopes for—this unending world of ever-increasing intelligence getting what it wants with (to us) mind-boggling speed, efficiency, and imagination.

Cycles of Ill

"This . . . is the noble truth of ill."

In the deer sanctuary outside Benares (modern Varanasi), not

far from the Ganges River, the Buddha spoke to his first followers. He laid out the fourfold basic insight from his enlightenment,
a set known throughout Buddhism as the Four Noble Truths.
They provide the four cornerstones to his account of the really big
picture.

As the traditional stories tell it, the Buddha lived in a cultural
world that wouldn't bat an eye about the prospect of universes succeeding universes in an endless string of worlds. Time, it was
thought, proceeds in massive cyclical epochs spanning millions,
billions, or even trillions of years. Cosmic systems grow, decline,
and perish, only for a new system to arise and restart the cycle.

On the micro level, individual beings mirror this pattern of
birth, death, and rebirth in the process often (somewhat mislead-
ingly) called "reincarnation." Driving that process, according to
this version of the really big picture, are two principles. On the one
hand, there's karma: every (im)moral action has consequences for
the agent who performs it, and these consequences can echo
through multiple lifetimes. On the other hand, there's what the
Buddha calls "craving": desire seeks its own satisfaction, and when
it finds this satisfaction, a new desire arises in its place.

The overall picture is one of a churning, perpetual, cyclical process of cause and effect, birth, death, and rebirth—at both the micro and macro levels. The technical term for it is *samsara*, which is
a pretty good candidate for a one-word Buddhist answer to the
question of where we are.

Buddhism developed out of and alongside a variety of other
South Asian religious and philosophical traditions. Some of those
traditions hold that there is an enduring, stable "self" (*ātman*) that
persists through the iterations of *samsara*. The Buddha, in contrast,
taught the doctrine of "non-self" (*anātman*). We are shifting con-

glomerations of "aggregates." We persist across time but without an unchanging essence.

It might seem like there's a rather straightforward vision of the good life to be had here. We don't have to worry about death, this vision would say, because it's not the end of us. And because of karma, the argument would continue, we have an opportunity to work our way up to better and better lives. Do well by doing good, as they say.

Not so fast, says the Buddha. The whole samsaric cycle, as he sees it, isn't just the neutral background for our lives. It's a problem. *The* problem. The first two of the Buddha's Four Noble Truths lay it out. First is the "noble truth of ill [*duhkha*]": "Birth is ill, old age is ill, disease is ill, death is ill, association with what is not dear is ill, separation from what is dear is ill, failure to get what one wants and seeks is ill, body is ill, feeling is ill, . . . consciousness is ill, in a word the five *skandhas* [aggregates] of grasping at material things are ill." The Buddha got an inkling of this truth when, as Prince Siddhartha, he saw the old man, the sick man, and the corpse and resolved to renounce his royal life. The basic idea is that everything tends to dissolution. Nothing is truly stable.

But that's just the fact of the matter. In the second noble truth, the Buddha says that it's craving that takes this fact and makes it ill. Craving is passionate attachment. It's the kind of desire that invests us in things being this way and not that. It's desire that doesn't want to let go of its object. But since no object is stable, craving binds us to things that are passing away. And so there is an "illness" knit into the fabric of our lives in the cycle of *samsara*—a dis-ease and restlessness.

The solution, offered in the third and fourth noble truths, is to cease craving entirely by following the path laid out by the Buddha. The answer isn't to do good so that good things come to you, or to crave only what you can get, or to expand your ability so you can get whatever you want. All of those approaches would leave us trapped within the logic of craving. They would invest us in the ceaseless, fruitless struggle to ward off the fundamental tendency of things to pass away. And that means that for the Buddha, Kurzweil's Singularity doesn't escape the true problem, but rather leaps into it with gleeful abandon. Given the Buddha's really big picture, massive superintelligence shaping the universe into its own image on an indefinite timescale isn't a matter for hope. It's the apotheosis of samsaric ill.

Imagine the Buddha returning to meet a being with trillions of times the computing power of a human brain. What might he say? Perhaps he would cross his legs, breath calmly, and begin, "This . . . is the noble truth of ill."

Taking It All In

We've covered a lot of ground in this chapter. From God to grateful reciprocity, and from the Singularity to *samsara*. If one thing is certain, it's that you haven't come out of this whirlwind tour with a fully formed, metaphysically robust really big picture to inform your response to the Question. So what are we to make of all this?

At the risk of oversimplifying, here are four takeaways:

1. *Think about it (but not too much).* Like we said at the beginning of this chapter, there's no escaping the really big picture, so we may as well consider what we take to be true about it. At the same time, we're never going to get all the way to the bottom of it. Obsession with filling out the really big picture

isn't just exhausting. It tends to pull us away from trying to actually *live out* responses to the Question. At some point, each of us just has to take some things for granted. It's inescapable.

2. *Acknowledge disagreement.* We've been on a whirlwind survey of five accounts of the really big picture. It should be clear by now that they're not all just different versions of some essentially universal human understanding of the world. Science isn't going to ride in and save the day. Kimmerer, Sagan, Wilson, and Kurzweil are all thoroughly committed to accepting the findings of empirical research. So are many Christians and Buddhists. And yet their takes on the really big picture are not mutually compatible. They disagree not just on some details but on central issues. It can be uncomfortable to recognize how deep these disagreements are, but papering over them is only going to lead us astray.

3. *Face up to the is/ought conundrum.* This is especially important for those of us who are skeptical about any sort of "transcendent" reality, any realer real or truer truth that might prescribe how things ought to be. Are we willing and able to give up on *ought* altogether? Or to reduce *ought* to *I prefer*? If not, what alternative can you find?

4. *Don't sweat it (too much).* When it comes to the really big picture, just like with the Question, there's always risk involved. No matter how hard we try, we might get things—important things—wrong. (Given the widespread disagreement between people, odds are that *most* of us will get *a lot* of things

wrong.) That doesn't mean we should just throw in the towel. It does, however, suggest that we need to learn to live with the risk. We need to take it seriously without letting it paralyze us. Another way of putting it is that something like *trust* is an essential feature of pursuing the Question.

Your Turn

1. What traditions have shaped your sense of the really big picture?

2. What is your sense of *where we are*? The following questions might help you start to formulate an answer:
   * What stories shape your sense of the world and your place in it?
   * What is the world to you? A vast universe? God's creation? A network of mutual interdependence? Something else?
   * How do you *feel* when you think about the world and your place in it? Do you feel small? Loved? Fragile? Responsible? Grateful? (All of the above?)
   * What do you feel compelled to *do* when you think about the world in the context of the really big picture as you see it? What actions seem to fall under your responsibility?

3. What is your sense of *who we are*? The following questions might help you formulate an answer:
   * What stories shape your sense of what it is to be a human being?
   * What are human beings to you? Evolutionary accidents? The universe becoming aware of itself? Beloved creatures? Younger siblings to nonhuman species?

* How do you *feel* when you think about human beings in the way you just described?
* How do you understand our relationship as human beings with nonhuman life?
* What do you feel compelled to *do* when you think about human beings in the context of the really big picture as you see it? What actions seem to fall under your responsibility?

Part 4

························

FACING THE LIMITS

....

NINE

When We (Inevitably) Botch It

A s Oscar Wilde sat in prison, he looked back over the fateful relationship with Alfred Douglas that had landed him there. What he saw dismayed him. This was not, however, a case of a penitent criminal feeling remorse for his crimes. Wilde knew the laws and system that had convicted him were unjust. He didn't regret that he had broken the law and defied the system. Laws—especially unjust ones—were for the small-minded who worried about what others thought. What dismayed him was who he had become in the context of the relationship. The true crime was against himself.

It had been pleasant enough—perhaps too pleasant. Lazy mornings and leisurely luncheons, seeing and being seen. Wilde was that rare bird: a genius recognized in his own age. (Don't believe us? Read Wilde. He'll tell you as much!) Surely his decadent desserts were well deserved. But the life he lived with Douglas had a terrible impact on his productivity. "I am not speaking in phrases of rhetorical exaggeration but in terms of absolute truth to actual fact when I remind you that during the whole time we were together I never wrote one single line," the brilliant playwright wrote from his cell. And yet, he insisted, his censure fell not mostly on Douglas, but on himself: "In allowing you [Douglas] to stand persistently between Art and myself I give *to myself* shame and blame in the fullest degree."

Maybe Wilde's dismay strikes you as an overreaction. Every artist goes through dry spells, right? But from within Wilde's vision of life, his hand-wringing makes sense.

Wilde, you see, was an individualist. He believed there are countless beautiful and wonderful and fascinating ways to be human. The best way for a person to live is to find their own particular expression of humanity and develop it to the full. Wilde knew in his bones that his way, his gift and genius, was for art. To squander his artistic vocation was, for Wilde, a devastating failure. It amounted to a squandered life.

There is something deep and significant about Wilde's self-diagnosed failure, all the self-protective arrogance and vitriol notwithstanding. It was not that he had failed to get what he wanted. He had gotten *precisely* what he wanted—a life of luxury and leisure in the arms of a young lover—and he had gotten it in spades. The problem was that in getting what he wanted, he had betrayed his own highest ideals. He had failed to live in correspondence with his own best understanding of what kind of human being it was truly worth being.

Let's call the kind of failure Wilde saw in his past "personal failure" because it has to do with who we are as people, not just what we achieve in our projects. It has to do with whether we are living the lives we believe to be worthy of our humanity, whether we are succeeding or failing as human beings.

The first thing to know is that we are going to fail like this—each and every one of us. Our failures might not be catastrophic. They might be entirely unspectacular. Little lies here. Tiny broken promises there. A bit of cold indifference where there ought to be compassion. A string of small compromises—each one completely understandable—that tug you bit by bit away from the vocation you hold dear. And in all this, you drift from one vision of life to a different one that offers a bit more instant gratification or that fits better with what everyone else is chasing after. In short, multiple small personal failures can add up to something much harder to stomach: Personal Failure-with-a-capital-*F*.

And when you realize that you've botched it—assuming you're lucky enough to have that realization—it will hurt. You will be disappointed with yourself. And you'll need to know what to do about it.

How It Feels to Be Wrong

In her 2011 TED Talk, journalist Kathryn Schulz asked the audience, "How does it feel to be wrong?" People answered predictably enough: it feels dreadful and embarrassing. Schulz thanked the audience for their responses. But she insisted they were all answering the wrong question. They were answering the question, How does it feel to *realize* you're wrong?

Being wrong without realizing it feels exactly the same as being right. That's the trouble. Same with doing wrong. If we don't realize it, doing the wrong thing feels the same as doing anything else. We're just doing what we do, living as we live.

There's a serious danger here. We can have good values—maybe even the right values—and be mindlessly living out of step with or even in direct opposition to what we take to be worthy of our humanity. And once we get going in that direction, the incentives to stay ignorant start to pile up. After all, we don't feel like we're missing the mark. We feel like we're doing what's right. Without even knowing it, we're deceiving ourselves, and cycles of self-deception are easy to get going but incredibly difficult to disrupt.

Something has to upend us to clue us in. It could be a crisis like the one Wilde found himself in. When the regular flow of life and relationships is disrupted, it can present the opportunity to see our habits and our choices in a new light.

More often, perhaps, what snaps us out of it is a person. If we're lucky, it's a friend or mentor kindly letting us know that we're not living up to our own standards. Maybe like the mentor who once pointed out to Matt that the way he was treating one of his friends was "unbecoming" of him. It still stings. But people who care for us often call us out in order to call us forward. They want to see us grow and live in sync with our values.

More often than we'd prefer, it's someone we've harmed who sounds the alarm. They name the harm and our role in it. Maybe they come to us. Maybe they tell it to someone else. Either way, we're found out. The jig is up.

As painful as it may be, something important has happened in these moments. We're being confronted with the truth of our behavior. And telling the truth is a precondition of whatever we might hope comes next.

If it takes being upended to see when we've failed, maybe a key to leading our lives well is to be upendable. Never waste a good crisis, a friendly callout, or an uncomfortable truth. But that may mean fighting your strongest instincts for what to do next.

Deny, Deny, Deny

Your first instinct when you're called out might be to deny it. To yourself. To your friends. To anyone who asks. You'll feel the pull to refuse to admit that you've done wrong or missed the mark.

Denial can take at least three forms. You can deny the facts of the matter. (*Wasn't me!*) You can deny that you're responsible for the failure. (*I had no choice!*) Or you can move the goalposts: admit the facts but deny that they amount to personal failure. (*So what if I did? Nothing wrong with that!*)

Either way the message is the same: *Nothing wrong here! Everything's just fine! Move along!* The goal is to sweep personal failures under the rug and just move on.

The denial instinct is completely understandable. Admitting a personal failure puts you in the position of having to admit that you were in the wrong and then having to do something about it. And pretty often, we don't know *how* to deal with it. In twelve-step programs, the first step is admitting you have a problem. But if you don't know what steps two through twelve are, then admitting the problem might just be a horrible-feeling dead end. Conflating what we do with who we are, and bereft of any hope for the future, we throw our hands up: *OK, I'm awful. Now what?*

And even if we do have a sense of how to respond to our own personal failure, denial can still seem like the wise move. We suspect that others will always define us by our worst. That we'll never be able to shake the burden. That there's a scarlet letter and a flood of mean tweets waiting for us. There are even people who would be happy to use our weakness to harm us and advance their own interests.

We know this from experience. Plenty of us have been the people who define others by their worst, who turn the screws, who paint the scarlet letters and score points off others' mistakes. We know how merciless we can be when others fail. Why would we expect anything else from them? And who wants to slog through that gauntlet? So the urge to sweep things under the rug makes plenty of sense. That doesn't mean it's good.

For one thing, denial is still deception, both of others and of ourselves. When we deny our personal failure, we get ourselves invested in proving the lie of our innocence and excellence. For another, denying a personal failure makes it more likely that you'll fail that way again. It's like a leaky roof. There's no good reason to hope it will get better if you just leave it alone. It might be a few days before it rains again, but when it does . . . And of course, things have a habit of coming to light even if you deny them. Then you have to deal with not just the failure itself but the denial too.

It's not often that the friends we've brought to our conversation about the Question all agree. But there is striking consensus on this point: we can't respond well to personal failure if we deny it. Only someone as idiosyncratic and iconoclastic as Nietzsche will disagree. "Don't be cowardly about your actions!" he wrote in the twilight of his sanity—how much to himself and how much to others we cannot know. "Don't abandon them afterwards!—The pang of conscience is obscene." To admit personal failure, in other words, is a failure of nerve.

It's a tempting idea. It promises unassailable pride and self-assurance. But unless you're willing to go all the way with Nietzsche—and that is a long, hard, likely unlivable way—an essential step in responding to personal failure is always going to be owning up to it. Indeed, perhaps that's what true courage requires.

So let's say you overcome the instinct to deny. You admit that in some act or omission or habit you have failed to live up to your own standards. What next?

The Daniel Tiger Approach

There's an episode of the fantastic kids' show *Daniel Tiger's Neighborhood* where the titular tiger is playing ball with some friends. All the other kids catch the ball on the first try, but Daniel drops it. He gets upset and wants to quit, but his friends convince him to keep trying. "Just keep trying; you'll get better!" they sing every time he drops the ball. And then, of course, he catches it. And all is well.

"Just keep trying" is one of our culture's favorite answers to the problem of personal failure. You did something wrong? You didn't live up to your standards? Well, get back on the horse. Give it another go. You'll do better next time. The solution is willpower and practice.

"Just keep trying" can be inspiring. It lays down a challenge and then tells us we have what it takes. Who doesn't love a grit-and-elbow-grease success story?

But what if just trying isn't enough? "I'm going to put down my phone and focus on my kids" is a fine resolution until your mind wanders and your fingers start to creep toward your pocket. Sometimes personal failure looks less like onetime slipups and more like deeply ingrained habits (see chapters 13 to 15).

And when the failure is big and deep, it can rob us of our confidence in our very ability to try again. We thought we were one kind of person, and it turns out otherwise. How do we put the pieces back together? "Just keep trying" won't cut it. *I was trying, and look how that turned out.*

What's more, trying again doesn't address the actual past failure, even if it's successful. Some of our failures create wounds that ache to be healed, wrongs that demand to be righted. Even if you could try your way to never betraying another friend, what about the friend you already did betray?

In the rest of this chapter, we'll consider some views about how to respond to personal failure that aim to solve one or both of these problems with "just keep trying": (1) when trying harder doesn't cut it, and (2) what to do about past harm.

Start Small

The news reports from East Bengal (now Bangladesh) in 1971 were appalling. The already-impoverished population was devastated by a government mass-killing campaign, the resulting civil war, and a cyclone. Millions were displaced, and even more were hungry or sick.

As all this happened, the young Australian philosopher Peter Singer looked around and found, distressingly, that the world didn't seem to care very much. Hungry people were starving. The sick were dying. And the world wasn't doing enough about it. *He* wasn't doing enough about it.

Now, "doing enough" is not a low bar for Singer. He's a utilitarian. His forest is every sentient being, and every tree in the forest counts the same. That means no privileging yourself. It means the right thing to do when faced with a disaster like the famine in Bengal or the fact that today more than 350 million children worldwide live on less than $1.90 per day is to give until the point where giving anything else would hurt you more than it would help others. To do anything less would be to shirk your moral duty.

Singer admits that he has never met this standard. And he

knows that almost none of the rest of us will ever meet it. We're all failing all the time.

Some people have said this is an argument against utilitarianism: it's just too hard for actual humans. Singer doesn't buy it. Why, he says, should our failure to be moral change what it means to be moral? But if that's right, what should you do—practically, as the person you are, not as some utilitarian moral hero?

In short, Singer has argued, the answer is to start small. Don't try to meet the standard all at once. In his book *The Life You Can Save*, Singer lays out a proposed starting point for everyone, challenging people to give a certain percentage of their income (starting at just 1 percent) toward reducing the suffering of the world's extremely poor.

The basic idea is to use whatever inspiration you can get from the utilitarian ideal to make a little change in your behavior. Maybe (probably) you'll find that it's not so bad. And then you'll feel confident taking another step. You'll likely never reach the standard. You'll always be falling short to some extent. But you'll be getting closer, and the world will be a better place because of it. That, at least, is Singer's hope.

Singer has a fairly clear answer to the first problem we found in the Daniel Tiger approach (sometimes trying again is just setting yourself up for failure). When you start small, you set yourself up for success. You don't try to bite off more than you can chew. You give yourself a chance to book a win and build—maybe slowly, but at least somewhat surely—toward a life that's more fully in line with your vision of flourishing.

It's less clear how Singer would recommend we approach the guilt incurred by our past personal failures. On that question, the ancient Jewish rabbis have quite a bit to say.

Repent!

In an eighth- or ninth-century text by unknown rabbis, we find a retelling of the story of creation. Before the creation itself, God first thought to create the world. And so, like "a king who wishes to build a palace for himself," God began to sketch out the architectural plans for literally everything. God found, however, that the envisioned structure was unstable. If God built it, it would collapse. Something was missing, something foundational. It wasn't until God thought to first create repentance that the world could remain standing and the creation could proceed.

How is it that repentance could be so literally fundamental? How could the very existence of the world depend on it?

First of all, the rabbis are convinced that human beings are inevitably going to fail. Personal failure is like the thick, oozy mud in the children's book *We're Going on a Bear Hunt*: we can't go over it, we can't go under it . . . we've gotta go through it. Which is to say, we have to have some way of handling it.

But that's not all. Both the rabbis and the Hebrew Bible have a pronounced sense that personal failure is more than just personal. Our failures don't affect just us. They rupture relationships. Since this is a vision where we're accountable to God for following the commands of God, personal failure inevitably ruptures our relationship with God. And let's admit it: a ton of our personal failures harm other people as well.

All this gives personal failures serious gravity. They don't just knock us down a peg from the realm of awesomeness into the realm of somewhat-less-awesomeness. To use the weighty language of these early Jewish writings, they're a matter of sin.

So to answer our question: if (a) personal failure is as big a deal as that, and (b) we can't simply avoid it, then it starts to make sense why human life would need repentance to stay on its feet.

To get a sense of what the rabbis mean by *repentance*, we can start from the Hebrew word they use: *teshuva*. The root word is a verb that means "to turn around." Repentance is about a 180-degree change of direction that restores relationships. The twelfth-century Jewish scholar Moses ben Maimon (or Maimonides; 1138–1204) says that "repentance brings near the far apart." It takes the relational fabric torn apart by personal failure and stitches the pieces back together.

Repentance of this sort has two sides. One looks back toward the failure itself. It involves confession, restitution, and receiving forgiveness. Its point is to make things and relationships right. The other turns around and looks forward. It involves commitment to change, and its point is to do the right thing from here on out.

Let's start with that look backward. The first thing to do is confess. The idea here is that there's always someone other than us who suffers for our personal failures, and so it's not enough to just recognize our personal failure internally, for ourselves. To begin to repent—to start to turn around—it's important to name the failure and acknowledge it in the context of the relevant relationships. As Maimonides and the rabbis see it, every sin ruptures our relationship with God. That means confession to God is a part of all repentance. But many of our personal failures also rupture relationships with other people. In that case, interpersonal confession is essential. Indeed, Maimonides says that when your sin has harmed another person, you ought to confess publicly, not just to the one you harmed but to a wider community. Doing so gets things out in the open. It also puts you on the hook with your community for changing your ways.

Confessing, though, isn't always enough. It's all well and good for us to say we're sorry, but that doesn't change what happened. So the backward-looking side of repentance often also requires making restitution: doing our best to compensate for whatever harm we've done. Maimonides says that God won't absolve someone for a sin against another person until the offender makes monetary restitution and begs the offended for forgiveness.

Confession and restitution look backward in order to make things right. Repentance, though, is also about turning around. It's about a new direction, a fundamental course correction. So looking forward and resolving to change our ways is an essential feature of this understanding of repentance. Rabbi Adda bar Ahavah (third or fourth century CE) insists that "confession alone is futile, but one who also abandons his transgressions will receive mercy." It's not enough to say you're sorry. It's not even enough to make amends. Responding well to our sin requires that we amend our ways.

The two-sided model of repentance—make things right, do what's right—takes seriously the real impacts of our personal failures on others and on our relationships. But is it realistic enough about our ability to actually do what's right after we've failed? Does the "do what's right" side of it amount to just another version of "just keep trying"? Unless there's hope of becoming righteous, how can we expect to consistently do what's right?

The rabbis recognize that we're prone not just to fail, but to fail again and again. Close to the human heart, they say, there is an "evil impulse" or inclination. It's in our power to struggle against it. That's the hard work of repentance. To really overcome it, though, is beyond us. We need help. We need God, both to forgive the wrongs we've done and to help us do what's right. Rabbi Shimon ben La-kish (ca. 200–ca. 275 CE) puts it this way: "A person's evil inclina-tion overcomes him each day and seeks to kill him. . . . And if not for the Holy One, Blessed be He, Who assists him with the good inclination, he would not overcome it." God is there, providing a countervailing force to the evil impulse that pushes us back toward sin. And without that divine help, our efforts would be fruitless.

So we might deal with personal failure by naming it as sin, pur-suing repentance, and receiving forgiveness. The Jewish rabbis are not alone in this perspective. Christian and Muslim thinkers take up and develop similar ideas. But what if all this talk of "sin" is actually the problem?

Take Note

As the contemporary American Buddhist teacher Pema Chödrön sees it, the problem is not sins that we need to repent of but the whole category of sin itself and the destructive patterns it produces. "The elemental struggle," she says, "is with our feeling of being wrong, with our guilt and shame at what we are." The only solution is to "befriend" that feeling, which will allow us to begin to find our way through to a more compassionate way of living with ourselves and with others.

The Buddha, Chödrön says, teaches that there are "four fac-tors," the possession of which will overcome past misdeeds. Basi-cally, it's his answer to personal failure. The whole process, she says, is one of confession, but in a dramatically different sense than what Jewish, Christian, and Muslim thinkers mean by it. "You don't confess to anybody," and "no one forgives you." It is personal and internal. Chödrön takes up and interprets the four factors as follows.

First, there's regret. That might sound like wallowing in guilt, but Chödrön insists that it's liberating. It's a matter of clearly seeing what you have done and giving up all your self-protective attempts to deny it. It's a matter of "getting tired" of the neurotic patterns that lead you into destructive ways of thinking, speaking, and acting. There's no self-flagellation here, because regret benefits you. It clips the threads of denial and shame that tie you to your past actions and propel you to throw good money after bad, trying again and again to justify yourself and investing more and more in destructive patterns.

Second, having recognized your personal failures for what they are, you refrain. That can sound harsh, like the stern voice of your conscience shouting "Thou shalt not!" at you again and again. But again, Chödrön offers a correction. The heart of the Buddhist path, as she interprets it, is compassion. So a harsh, punitive stance toward ourselves is counterproductive. "When we buy into disapproval, we are practicing disapproval. When we buy into harshness, we are practicing harshness. The more we do it, the stronger these qualities become." In other words: "In order to feel compassion for other people, we have to feel compassion for ourselves."

Refraining isn't a Herculean effort of will. It's the natural fruit of seeing the harmful consequences of your misdeeds. "You refrain because you already know the chain reaction of misery" that cascades from "the initial bite, or the initial drink, or the initial harsh word." The internal voice of refraining doesn't yell. It gently encourages us with the reminder, "One day at a time."

Third, you undertake remedial action. This is not specific restitution for a specific harm done, as the rabbis and Maimonides envision it. Instead, it's taking up a practice like loving-kindness meditation to nurture in yourself the ability to think and act differently from the ways that brought about your personal failure in the first place. It's building the infrastructure of compassionate living.

Fourth, you resolve not to repeat your errors again. Yet again, there's an analogy between Chödrön's step and Jewish ideas about repentance, as Chödrön's fourth step seems to correspond to the resolution to change our ways discussed by the Jewish rabbis. But yet again, it would be a mistake to draw the analogy too tightly. The accent in Chödrön's teaching is on the need to avoid self-judgment even here. Resolution isn't a matter of commanding ourselves not to fail the same way again, but of reminding ourselves that we don't have to fail the same way again and that, deep down, we don't want to.

For Chödrön, we turn to the past not because it needs to be set right but because it shows us how things go wrong. Taking note of the patterns that produce suffering allows us to gently break them. Condemnation is worthless. Compassion—for ourselves and for others—is what matters. Compassionately seeing our personal failures for what they are will naturally produce the fruit of restraint, remedial action, and resolution to change.

So How *Should* We Respond to Personal Failure?

Start small. Repent. Take note. It's tempting to want to turn these into a list of tips you could put into practice one after another or just tools you can use when the task seems to require them. But hopefully by now we're getting a sense that these are actually really different approaches to the question of what to do when we fail. Singer's "start small" takes our impulse to "try harder" and upgrades it to "try smarter." The basic impulse is the same—don't worry about the past; just focus on positive change in the future—but the strategy is a bit savvier: start with something doable and build from there. Chödrön and the rabbis are concerned with the past. But remember: Chödrön explicitly contrasts her approach with the rabbis'. For the rabbis, the world itself turns on repentance, while for Chödrön the language of repentance gets us stuck in a moralistic morass. There's no pretending these folks are offering us the same answer—or even compatible ones—to our question.

Unfortunately, time spent thinking about how to respond to personal failure is no mere academic exercise. Personal failure isn't something "out there." It's a reality right here in each of our lives. Seeing that is difficult. Owning up to it hurts.

To see our personal failures—and how they can add up to Personal Failure—requires cultivating a posture of receptivity. We need to be upend-able, ready to capitalize on a crisis or callout that might come our way. We need to find a way out of denial.

Once we move past the need for acknowledgment, the consensus among our conversation partners quickly dissolves. What one sees as the solution, another sees as the heart of the problem. As you discern for yourself how we ought to respond to personal failure, two lines of questioning are especially important.

First, how are you going to make the changes stick? What can you rely on to keep you from falling into the same kind of failure in the future and to help you respond well when, in all likelihood, you fail again? (For more on this, see chapters 13 to 15.)

Second, how much does repairing the harm of the past matter?

Do we need to make amends and seek forgiveness from and reconciliation with whomever we've wronged or harmed? (And if so, what steps are we going to take? Will we take time to listen and understand the impact of our actions? If not, we might not come to agree with those we've wronged about what actually happened. And that might well make genuine forgiveness and reconciliation impossible.) Alternatively, might it be sufficient to fix the source of our failure and avoid future wrongdoing and harm?

These last questions draw our attention to harm. Our personal failures often give rise to suffering—our own, but also others'. And the suffering in our lives and our world deserves careful attention in its own right, whether or not it's our fault.

Your Turn

1. Think of a time when someone else's personal failure affected you.
   * How did you respond?
   * How did you want *them* to respond?

2. Think back to a time when you failed to live up to your own standards for yourself.
   * How did you come to realize you had missed the mark? Was it through a moment of crisis? A friend who called you out? Someone you hurt who told the truth about the consequences of what you did?
   * Did you pause to learn the truth about the impact of your actions on others, or did you rush to seek (or even demand) forgiveness?
   * How much did you focus on repairing damaged relationships and making things right?
   * How much did you focus on doing better next time?

3. How *should* we respond to our personal failures?
   * How much does repairing the harm of the past matter? Ought we to make amends and seek reconciliation with whomever we've wronged or harmed? (If you're inclined in this direction, consider the *language* that you use. When someone

apologizes to you, for example, do you say "Don't worry about it" or do you say "I forgive you"?)

* Do we already have the resources we need to refrain from falling into the same personal failure again, or do we need to seek help from beyond ourselves?

....

TEN

When Life Hurts . . .

The air is piercingly cold outside. Your joints ache, and your toes are numb. You can feel the snot freezing in your nostrils as you breathe in. Inside, an enticing glow beckons from the fireplace. Relieved, you open the door, shake the snow off your boots, and step inside. You peel the gloves off your hands and inch forward, leaning deeper and deeper into the soothing warmth. The sensation draws you in.

As you move closer, you stumble on the upturned corner of a rug. Reaching out to catch yourself, your hand lands in the fireplace. It's scorching hot. You flinch from the pain and draw your hand away at once.

Pleasure attracts. Pain repels. We seek the one and avoid the other.

Bentham thought this was the driving principle of our motivation: "Nature has placed mankind under the governance of two sovereign masters: *pain* and *pleasure*. . . . They govern us in all we do, in all we say, in all we think: every effort we can make to throw off our subjection, will serve but to demonstrate and confirm it."

Philosophers call this doctrine "psychological hedonism," and they vigorously debate its merits. But even as they've debated it, the basic idea has taken tight hold across large swaths of the contemporary world. There is serious cultural weight behind the idea that we invariably seek to avoid pain. And not just in the reactive, pull-your-hand-back-from-a-searing-fireplace way, but as a guiding maxim for our behavior and, indeed, for our life plans. It's not that we all hold a principled belief in psychological hedonism. It's more like a pervasive feeling, an unreflective general sense that pain—and suffering more broadly—is an unmitigated evil and should be eliminated to the greatest extent possible.

The present moment is especially open and fervent in its aversion to suffering, but perhaps we can glimpse traces of this feeling in the images of a pain-free paradise, either at the beginning of the world or at its end, found in many cultures. Perhaps it is one of the deep dreams of humanity.

There's good reason to believe, however, that things aren't so simple. As the psychologist Paul Bloom points out, we often choose suffering of one sort or another. For one thing, people sometimes find pleasure in pain. Some runners relish the burning sensation in muscles pushed to their limits, for example. And connoisseurs of spicy food delight in the fire on their tongues. Pleasure and pain, it turns out, are not always mutually exclusive. In other cases, even when the pain isn't pleasurable, we sacrifice pleasure for the sake of meaning. Think of the pain of bearing a child and the plentiful sorrows of raising one. More grimly, countless people have willingly suffered the hell of war, whether in order to gain glory or for the less self-focused motive of doing their part to defend the homeland.

The popular fixation on psychological hedonism may be a red herring. There's more going on with pleasure and pain than simple attraction and aversion. Indeed, living lives of pleasure and meaning—not to mention lives worthy of our humanity—may require that we embrace certain kinds of suffering: for our beliefs, for our loved ones, for a truly noble cause.

The fact of the matter, though, is that most suffering—and there is no shortage of suffering in the world—is not chosen. Malice and negligence have unleashed tears enough to fill an ocean. (Most who suffer war's horrors did not choose them, after all.) Much of our suffering, however, comes from just being the fragile creatures we are, living in the physical world as it is. These two forms of unchosen suffering present two related challenges. First, how do we work against suffering to eliminate or mitigate it? And second, how do we live with the suffering that inescapably remains? We will take up these two questions in this chapter and the next.

Help Until It Hurts

When Julia Wise was young, her parents helped her see that the world is unfair and that her family was privileged, lucky to have as much as they did when so many people had so much need. She drew a simple but uncomfortable inference: If we have more than we need, shouldn't we give a lot of what we have away?

Julia threw herself into a mission: live modestly; give the rest away. When she met her future husband in college, he suggested they should keep separate budgets if they ever got married. She won him over in the long run, though. Eventually, they started meeting other like-minded people in the growing "effective altruism" movement, a network of people committed to (1) giving a lot and (2) figuring out where their giving will make the most difference. Julia is now the community liaison for the Centre for

Effective Altruism. She's also a regular visitor to our Life Worth Living class at Yale.

Every year since they got married, Julia and her husband have donated 30 to 50 percent of their total income to organizations whose work reduces suffering and poverty. The average American household gives 2 to 5 percent. (And only a fraction of that goes to the kinds of anti-suffering, anti-poverty causes Julia and Jeff give to.)

The thing is, Julia will flat-out acknowledge that at some level, she probably ought to be doing more. Like many effective altruists, Julia has been influenced by utilitarian philosophers. Peter Singer, whom we met in chapters 6, 7, and 9, is a major figure in the movement. And as Singer sees it, what morality actually demands is that we give "until we reach the level of marginal utility." In other words, your duty is to give to others until it would hurt you more than it would help them. And who are you obligated to help? Any and all people. So, basically, as long as (1) there's someone out there poorer than you and (2) there's a way for you to give them some of what you have, you are morally obligated to do it. That may be a standard none of us actually lives up to, but from Singer's perspective, that doesn't make the standard any less *true*.

Every year when Julia tells her story to our Life Worth Living class at Yale, it blows our students away. Here's this otherwise regular person who has made extraordinary generosity an ordinary part of her life. Many of them are drawn to it. Some of them become effective altruists themselves. Inevitably, though, one of them asks some version of this question during the Q&A session: What about the systems? You're giving an amazing amount of money and dedicating an amazing amount of energy to, in effect, putting out fires. Don't we need to figure out why they're being started in the first place? Or, to use the hackneyed example, you're pulling drowning people out of the river. Shouldn't we go upstream and make it so they don't fall in? Your giving is radical, but is the change it makes radical enough to really address the depths of the world's problems?

"Till Society Be Differently Constituted"

Mary Wollstonecraft (1759–1797) was born into a downwardly mobile family. Her father belonged to the lowest ranks of the English gentry, and he was horrible with money. As he squandered the family's livelihood, the diminishing resources went increasingly to Mary's brother, while she and her sisters were left to fend for themselves.

Wollstonecraft, despite the odds, managed to stay on her feet. She educated herself and started a girls' school outside London. When the school failed, she became a governess. When that didn't work out, she became a freelance writer, honing her thinking and rhetorical skills by churning out book reviews for a small-time monthly magazine called *Analytical Review*. Eventually, she made a name for herself with works like her classic *A Vindication of the Rights of Woman*, and she is known today as one of the great early feminist thinkers.

Like the Stoics, Wollstonecraft thought that leading life well is far and away what matters most. Virtue, she says, is the heart of human flourishing. The purpose of life is to develop one's reason and act virtuously, which is to say the way that reason dictates. Unlike the Stoics, however, she thought that circumstances could seriously affect our chances of being virtuous.

Two things, in particular, are essential: education and equality.

Education is how we learn to develop our capacity for reason. And equality is the seedbed of virtue. "Virtue," she said, "can only flourish among equals." Inequality makes superiors into "voluptuous tyrants" who always get what they want and never have to exercise virtue. (Like the Buddha thinking about Rāhula's inheritance, Wollstonecraft thinks wealth and power are generally *bad* for you.) On the flip side, inequality makes inferiors into "cunning envious dependents" who just want to get whatever advantage they can.

Wollstonecraft also gave more weight to life going well and life feeling good than the Stoics did. While she envisioned this world as a "hard school of moral discipline," inescapably filled with challenges, she thought a society of virtuous people would enjoy genuine goods like friendship and a true, reliable sense of happiness.

But to Wollstonecraft's dismay, she looked around and saw a society set up to produce exactly the opposite of flourishing. It fostered not virtue but vice. And consequently, it yielded not happiness but an empty, unstable simulacrum of it for some and sheer misery for others.

On the one hand, education was a mess. Only rich boys got it, and what they got was more focused on giving them gentlemen's manners than wise men's virtues.

On the other hand, equality was nowhere to be found. Wollstonecraft's social world was shot through with "preposterous distinctions of rank." Kings were elevated above everyone, nobles above commoners, rich above poor, and so on. Most pervasive of all, she thought, was the unequal relation between men and women. Throughout society, Wollstonecraft wrote, women suffered under "the galling yoke of sovereign man." Patriarchy meant that even relatively unimportant men like her father were morally warped by their power over a household of women. And even relatively well-off women like her and her sisters suffered degradation that stunted their moral growth.

Wollstonecraft wanted to see all of this change. Because the root problems were social problems, the solution had to be social change. "It is justice, not charity, that is wanting in the world!" Wollstonecraft insisted. "Till society be differently constituted," there would be little hope for widespread improvement at the personal level.

Her program had three central pillars: (1) political representation for women through the right to vote, (2) economic self-sufficiency through access to previously male-dominated trades, and (3) equal education for all through coed day schools. Put these into place, she argued, and people—both women and men—would "quickly become wise and virtuous." A differently constituted society would open the path to flourishing for all.

Many of the reforms Wollstonecraft called for have been implemented, even if imperfectly. It's hard to imagine, though, that she would be happy with the world today. It's not exactly teeming with supremely rational paragons of virtue. Nor is unnecessary suffering missing.

This raises questions. Have societies simply not gone far enough down the road to political representation, economic participation, and equal education? Did Wollstonecraft pick the wrong reforms? Is an even more comprehensive reordering of society needed to set things right?

Rectify the Names

Somewhere in the misty region between history and legend sits the great Emperor Yao, facing south, in the proper ritual position.

Tradition relates that a terrible flood submerged the land. The people were displaced. Many died of starvation or illness. The whole society was upended. Worse still, the flooding didn't relent. For years, the land was drenched and uninhabitable. Yao wisely appointed the virtuous Shun co-emperor and heir and tasked him with saving the land. Shun performed rituals, toured the empire, and instituted administrative reforms. In turn, Shun's deputy and heir, Yu, dredged the rivers and dug channels. The flooding subsided. At last, the people could live in peace and prosperity. Wise leaders of a united society had brought disaster to an end. By Confucius's time, Yao, Shun, and Yu were revered as almost godlike heroes, exemplars of the Way in action.

As we saw in chapter 7, the Way takes pride of place in Confucius's vision of flourishing. When a society follows the Way, everything fits together. With the exception of things like illness and natural disasters, such a society would be relatively free of unchosen suffering. And Confucius sees the flood story as an illustration that even when suffering can't be avoided, a society that follows the Way can reduce the effects of disaster.

On the flip side, if things have gone awry, that's a telltale sign that a society has lost the Way. Most likely, the problem started at the top. A fish rots from the head down, as the old proverb goes. When those in power cease to follow the Way, the consequences metastasize throughout the society. The chief minister in Confucius's home state of Lu once asked Confucius for advice. It seems that theft was distressingly common in the country. What should he do? Confucius replied, perhaps surprisingly, "If you could just get rid of your own excessive desires, the people would not steal even if you rewarded them for it." Greed in the halls of power makes for a society built on the same logic as robbery. It's not a big step to actual robbery.

The later Confucian Mencius criticizes rulers who think about statecraft in terms of advantage or profit. It's a surefire way to send the whole society spiraling into ruin. If leaders think and act on this basis, then everyone else eventually will. And "it has never happened that people embrace profit in their contact with one another yet fail to be destroyed." Everyone out for their own advantage is most definitely not the Way.

So avoidable suffering can be traced back to a society losing the Way, most likely because its leaders lost the Way first. What's the solution?

Well, in the broadest terms, it's just the Way. "When the world is drowning, one pulls it out with the Way," Mencius says. To begin with, it's a matter of getting the leaders back on track. Just as waywardness at the top percolates down through all of society and leads to all sorts of hardship and distress, so virtue among leaders attracts others and pulls them toward the Way.

How do you make virtuous leaders out of wayward ones? Education. Powerful people must be taught the rituals and relearn the traditions. Asked what he would do if invited to intervene in a state gone wrong, Confucius replied with just one task: "I would rectify names." That is, learn to call things (and treat things as) what they truly are. "Let the ruler be a ruler; the subject, a subject; the father, a father; the son, a son." Once words again mean what they ought to, once everyone has relearned their roles—starting with the ruler on top—flourishing life comes naturally.

Confucius sometimes talks as though getting the leadership issue sorted out is all that's needed: "If a true king were to arise [meaning one who ruled via the Way] . . . we could certainly see a return to Goodness after a single generation." It's as though the leader's example is enough: "To 'govern' means to be 'correct.' If you set an example by being correct yourself, who will dare to be in-correct?"

Given how comprehensive the Way is, though, it might take incredibly wide-ranging social changes for a society to actually get out of its wayward state. Mencius, at least, thought just that. Like Wollstonecraft, he has some favorite proposals. Things like dis-tributing land fairly among households, appointing officials based on their virtue, manageable taxation, sustainable use of resources, and providing schools where people (men, Wollstonecraft would point out) can learn the virtues proper to their social roles.

Only leaders who follow the Way themselves would implement a program like this. Most leaders, though, aren't nearly so virtuous as Yao and Shun were said to be. That raises a serious question for the rest of us. Are we simply at the mercy of the virtue or vice of the people in power?

Confucius and Mencius insist that anyone is capable of follow-ing the Way and that everyone is called to do so, even when their society has lost the Way and things are falling apart. But are those of us who don't hold influential positions effectively unable to work against the real causes of suffering and social dislocation in our societies? Confucius is definitely willing, even eager, both to cut us some slack by acknowledging there's only so much we can do and to throw us a bone by pointing out a way we can contribute. Some-one once critiqued him for not "participating in government." He quoted some lines from an ancient book and then said, "In being a filial son and good brother one is already taking part in govern-ment." In other words, each of us can do our part by following the Way in our particular social roles. It's worth wondering, though: *Is that enough?*

There's potentially an even bigger issue with the elite focus of

Confucius's and Mencius's recommendations. The problem has two sides. First, might meaningful change take more than replacing a few broken stones at the top of the social pyramid? Is it possible that the problems are more structural than that? Second, Confucius and Mencius don't give much opportunity for those who bear the brunt of social breakdown to speak. What would the view of suffering look like from somewhere less close to the top? Perhaps a reliable diagnosis would need to come from someone closer to the ground.

Together—Helplessly and Forever

James Baldwin was no optimist. He had seen—had felt in his flesh—the cruelty humans all too often visit upon each other. He knew firsthand how injustice warps lives and relationships. Baldwin grew up Black in mid-twentieth-century Harlem. More than one officer of the law had beaten him for goodness knows what supposed offense. As an adult, he traveled the South and witnessed key moments of the civil rights movement, as well as White citizens' and officials' caustic, often violent opposition to it.

What drove this hostility? What could account for the injustice inflicted on his people, the racialized inhumanity that marred the history of his country at every turn?

When Baldwin followed the roots down, he found them tangled thick in the soil of the human condition. "Evil," he remarked, "comes into the world by means of some vast, inexplicable and probably ineradicable human fault." If we reckon with life and people as they actually are, then "it goes without saying that injustice is a commonplace."

The deep roots of evil and the commonplaceness of injustice do not, however, mean that we simply leave them alone. The answer isn't to throw up our hands in resignation. It is to struggle. "One must never, in one's own life, accept these injustices as commonplace but must fight them with all one's strength."

To fight injustice requires that one see it as it is and understand where it comes from. Not every injustice is the same. Context matters. So Baldwin spent his life seeing America and diagnosing its deep ills.

Much of the trouble, he came to believe, arose from suppressed fear and aversion to pain. In a country where White people have power that Black people do not, Baldwin observes, White people use their power to secure themselves against pain. In a bitter irony, their broken responses to suffering produce much of the country's most severe suffering and injustice. These broken responses come in many forms: shame at one's own weakness, unspoken horror over violence one or one's kin had perpetrated, embarrassment or violently conflicted responses to interracial sexual attraction, and so on. Baldwin noted and examined them all.

Baldwin, like Oscar Wilde (see chapter 4), is convinced that a current of suffering runs through all of life. We are fragile, often lonely beings, prone to being hurt, unable to secure ourselves. But exactly because this *is* who we are, this vulnerable place is where our flourishing is to be found. Baldwin thinks our tender fragility is precisely where we can find the meaning, dignity, and beauty of life: "Life is tragic, and, *therefore*, unutterably beautiful."

This potent, painful combination of beauty and tragedy ought to draw us together, so that we might hold one another in the midst of it. But this is, as Baldwin sees it, a hard truth. Some of us fear that the *therefore* is too weak to hold our weight; that if life is tragic, then it is not beautiful but ugly. And worse than ugly. Damnable. Others of us are simply afraid that when the tragedy of life comes for us, it will break us. Light reflecting off broken glass strewn across the ground may be beautiful, but what good is that to the shattered window?

These are the fears that Baldwin saw poisoning American society. They are the seeds of much of America's malaise and malevolence, including White supremacy. When White Americans have tried (in vain) to secure themselves in the face of life's fragility, they have done so in large part by defining themselves in terms of superiority to Black people. The fruit of this dynamic is a dreadful two-fold harvest. First of all, it harms Black Americans, both materially and spiritually, including through the corrosive power of bitterness and rage. But second, it is morally poisonous to the White Americans under its sway. "Whoever debases others is debasing himself." (Baldwin echoes Wollstonecraft's idea that inequality is bad for all parties involved.)

In a situation like the one Baldwin describes, what is to be done?

Baldwin did advocate for political and social reform. He saw it as essential. But he also believed "the political institutions of any nation are always menaced and are ultimately controlled by the spiritual state of that nation." So the only truly adequate response to egregious, gratuitous suffering and injustice is something akin to *conversion*. The work of social change and the work of personal transformation, both our own and our neighbors', belong inseparably together. Just as *we* belong together.

The first step is to be honest and unflinching. To accept the reality of who we are and where we've come from. To face the pain and disappointments we find there. "Not everything that is faced can be changed; but nothing can be changed until it is faced." The work of acceptance and change is arduous. ("It has always seemed much easier to murder than to change," Baldwin laments.) But if White Americans would commit to it, there would be the prospect for a new social reality, grounded in the recognition that "each of us, helplessly and forever, contains the other."

The tragic character of life would remain. But by accepting it, we might give one another shelter from its fiercest storms. Baldwin says, "The sea rises, the light fails, lovers cling to each other, and children cling to us. The moment we cease to hold each other, the moment we break faith with one another, the sea engulfs us and the light goes out."

In diagnosing America, Baldwin diagnoses the human. So while the details of his analysis might not apply always and every-where, he offers a stance that others might take up for themselves, should they find it compelling. He both (a) protests against injus-tice and egregious suffering, and (b) holds that some form of suf-fering is an unavoidable feature of life. And he seeks both social change and personal transformation. He knits the two tightly to-gether. One essential part of working against suffering in the world is to work with our own suffering, so that we might become the sort of people who don't inflict our pain on others.

This aspect of Baldwin's vision brings us to the second of the two questions we identified at the start of this chapter: How do we live with the suffering that inescapably remains? We'll take up this question in the next chapter.

Your Turn

1. What is your instinctive response to your own pain? To the pain of others? How, if at all, are these two responses different?

2. What kinds of responses to the world's suffering do you have the most hope for? (Personal transformation? Practical, material interventions? Systemic—political, economic— change?)

3. What do you think you ought to do to alleviate the suffering of others? Think of a concrete step you might take (e.g., donate to a worthy cause, take a step to mend a broken relationship, join a phone bank for a cause you believe in, commit to working through some of your own pain so you can be compassionate to others).

ELEVEN

. . . And There's No Fixing It

J ames Baldwin left us with a question: If some forms of suffering are inescapable, how should we live with them? His ideas about facing painful truths and the truth of pain point to something important about our responses to this question. These responses won't focus on changing conditions. That's the main way we reduce suffering, and it's essential for repairing injustice. But when it comes to bearing suffering well, the focus will fall on changing ourselves and our stances toward suffering. In this chapter, we'll consider various approaches to doing just that, starting with one so radical that it purports to entirely solve the problem of suffering for a person without having to change a single one of their circumstances.

A Burning House

Siddhartha Gautama's early life was markedly free of suffering—at least as we usually understand the word. As we said right at the beginning of this book, he had a life of luxury, power, and comfort. And yet he left it behind. Why he did so reveals a lot about how the Buddha viewed suffering and its place in flourishing life.

As the poet Aśvaghoṣa (ca. 80–ca. 150) relates it, compassion was central to the "great renunciation." Siddhartha saw earth being plowed near his palace and noted with horror the dead insects and worms turned up by the plow, the weary toil of the oxen, and the sunburnt, leathery skin of the poor workers. "He grieved greatly, as if a kinsman had been killed," and compassion overwhelmed him.

Beyond just making him feel sorry for bugs and cattle and less privileged people, this compassion sparked a dreadful realization: even though he lived in a palace, he was in exactly the same boat as the plowed-up worms. Disease, old age, and death are inexorable laws. Their long arms reach out for everyone eventually. Even princes. Siddhartha's father, the king, tried to convince him to stay and take over the kingdom. There was a well-established custom of older men retiring from political life to focus on spiritual pursuits. There would be time for the Question when Siddhartha was older and had done his duty as a ruler.

So Siddhartha offered a deal. He wouldn't immediately seek enlightenment, so long as his father could promise him four things: "[1] My life shall never be subject to death, [2] disease shall not steal this good health of mine, [3] old age shall never overtake my youth, [4] no mishap shall rob this fortune of mine."

The king was understandably offended by the obviously impossible terms. He insisted that his son offer a better deal. But the prince replied to his father, "If that's not possible, don't hold me back; for it is not right to obstruct a man who's trying to escape from a burning house." And so he left.

After his quest for enlightenment, the Buddha gathered those who would listen to his message and taught them. What did he teach? In the words recorded as part of his first sermon: "Both in the past and now, I set forth only this: suffering and the end of suffering." The problem of suffering and its solution was his central and all-encompassing theme. The whole arc of the Four Noble Truths, which summarize the Buddha's teachings, is about just that. The Four Noble Truths lay out:

1. The reality and pervasiveness of suffering

2. The source or cause of suffering

3. The means to ending suffering

4. The path to achieving this freedom from suffering

The key to the whole is the Buddha's diagnosis of the immediate cause of suffering, because diagnosis leads naturally to the prescription of a treatment. All suffering, the Buddha says, arises from "craving," which means something like ego-centered attachment. It's the kind of desire that grasps or clings to things, whether they be pleasant feelings, wealth, power, political ideals, or your own identity. But craving also manifests as aversion, the kind of rejection that shows an underlying attachment, like the horrible thought of losing a spouse, a lover, or a child.

This dual character of craving means that two common routes to dealing with suffering are closed. We can't overcome suffering by getting everything we crave, because indulging our cravings just reinforces them. The more we get what we want, the more attached we become to getting what we want. But extreme deprivation won't do either. It rejects things so passionately as to remain inextricably attached to them. During his years of seeking enlightenment, the Buddha had learned this the hard way. He had nearly starved himself, going so far as to try to live on one grain of rice a day, and it had led nowhere. He still suffered.

The only solution is what the Buddha called the "middle way." Neither indulgence nor deprivation. Because the *things* we crave aren't the problem. *We* are. Craving depends on the sense that the craver is a stable, coherent entity, a self-standing "I" such that things could be "mine." But that, the Buddha says, is an illusion. With the recognition that one is a "non-self"—a contingent, changing, flowing collection of phenomena—the fires of ego-attachment die out like a lamp deprived of oil.

This is a radical approach. It does not seek to eliminate suffering in the world through careful planning and clever arrangement of circumstances. It seeks to cut suffering off at the root by letting go of the kind of self that can suffer. After his enlightenment, the Buddha still felt pain and illness, but the claim is that he no longer suffered from these things because he had extinguished the flame of craving. Pain is inescapable, but suffering can be solved because it is entirely a matter of one's relation to things, both painful and pleasant.

The Buddha held that suffering has a cause, but he denied that it has a reason. Suffering is no bushel of lemons waiting to be made into lemonade. There's no making sense of it, no rationalizing it, and consequently no redeeming the suffering we have undergone. This view pushes against a common, deep-seated impulse.

Everything Happens for a Reason

In 2014, the hip-hop artist Drake got a new tattoo on his forearm: "Everything happens for a reason, sweet thing." They were far from the most original words of his career. It's such a common thought, so clichéd, that it's been said by or attributed to a bevy of famous people, from Oprah to Marilyn Monroe to Shaquille O'Neal.

And celebrities aren't alone in holding that everything happens for a reason. Psychologists Paul Bloom and Konika Banerjee found that 69 percent of study participants expressed some degree of belief in the idea that significant life events happen for a reason and "an underlying order" determines how things turn out. Perhaps unsurprisingly, they also found that people who said they believe in God were more likely to view events in their lives as happening for a reason. Why wouldn't things happen for a reason if a benevolent, omnipotent God is in charge of the universe? Indeed, what would keep you from making the yet bolder claim that this world, with all its suffering and pain, is the best of all possible worlds?

Among Westerners, this "best of all possible worlds" idea is associated with the philosopher and mathematician Gottfried Wilhelm Leibniz (1646–1716), but he was hardly the first to come up with it. Six centuries earlier, it had been expressed by the eminent Muslim thinker Abu Hamid al-Ghazali (1058–1111).

The fundamental Muslim conviction is that God is one. And since God is the creator and source of the world, to say that God is one is to say that there is only one creator and source of all that is. That means God faces no constraints in creating. There's no material God has to work with, like a sculptor working clay or a musician manipulating sound waves. There's no "way things work" that God has to account for. Everything—absolutely everything—flows from God's creative activity.

Al-Ghazali takes this to mean that "there is no agent but God the Most High." Whatever has been done, God (in some ultimate sense) did it. "Sustenance given or withheld, life or death, riches or poverty, and everything else that can be named"—God and God alone "initiated and originated it."

So far, this might seem like small consolation. Or worse. All our suffering flows from the decree of a singular, all-powerful God? That might just as well inspire despair and resentment as hope and trust.

Al-Ghazali, however, insists otherwise. God is not merely all-powerful, but supremely wise and unsurpassably benevolent. Among the ninety-nine "names of God" that Muslims find in the Quran are The Infinitely Good, The Merciful, The Just, The Benevolent, The Wise, and The Doer of Good. That means that we can trust that God has ordained things for the good. Indeed, for the best. As al-Ghazali puts it:

> Everything which God Most High distributes among His servants: care and an appointed time, happiness and sadness, weakness and power, faith and unbelief, obedience and apostasy—all of it is unqualifiedly just with no injustice in it, true with no wrong infecting it. Indeed, all this happens according to a necessary and true order, according to what is appropriate as it is appropriate in the measure that is proper to it; nor is anything more fitting, more perfect, and more attractive within the realm of possibility.

In the grand scope of things, everything works for the best possible overall good. Any deficiencies in the world here and now will bring about enhancements in the world to come. And any deficiency someone suffers in the next world will bring about benefit for others: "If there were no hell, the inhabitants of paradise would not know the extent of their blessing."

Supposing that were true (not a small supposition), how ought we to relate to our own suffering? For one thing, it calls for and motivates an attitude of patience. God's purposes and wisdom far surpass any powers of ours to ferret out the meaning of things. The appropriate thing to do is to bear suffering patiently while we wait to see what good it brings.

But the ability to bear suffering in patience depends on trust that God is indeed wise and has good purposes. There's no good reason to wait if we don't think we can depend on God to come through in the end.

Finally, because everything comes to us from the all-wise, infinitely good God, the appropriate stance is thankfulness "under all circumstances . . . both in prosperity and in hardship." We may not yet see how our suffering redounds to the good, but trusting in God, we can give thanks not merely *in* our suffering, but in an important sense *for* it—and for the entire reality of the world, past, present, and future.

For the Buddha, serenity in the face of suffering rested on non-attachment. Al-Ghazali doesn't think you need that. Trusting in the good God's reason for everything will get you there.

Patience, trust, and gratitude. The paradigmatic figure of this stance is the prophet Job as he appears in Muslim tradition. A man of great wealth and fortune, he was nevertheless humble, thanking God for his many blessings. He then lost all he had and suffered grievous physical afflictions, but through it all he remained patient and trusted in God.

Al-Ghazali's fundamental conviction is that there is a reason to it all, a divine reason. He says to the faithful, "Everything, small and large, is recorded and carried out by Him according to the divine decree . . . and if you were not afflicted you would not make progress, and were you not making progress you would not be afflicted." Reflecting on the goodness and wisdom and power of God thus makes it possible to "trust in divine providence" and praise and bless the God who gives both everything and its reason.

But what if you simply cannot believe in the almighty and benevolent God who has a reason for everything?

What Doesn't Kill Us

Friedrich Nietzsche did not know that those crisp autumn days in the northern Italian city of Turin would be the last days of his sanity. Possessed by a thrilling sense of vitality and insight, he wrote incessantly. Among the thousands of words to flow in a frenzy from the genius's pen were likely his most famous ones: "What doesn't kill me makes me stronger." They're printed on motivational posters, painted on gym walls, quoted by Tupac and *The Simpsons*, and tattooed on goodness knows how many chests around the world. Rarely quoted are the words that immediately precede these. The full quote is, "From life's school of war—What doesn't kill me makes me stronger."

Nietzsche considered himself a graduate of that school of war. He had literally been to war, serving as a medical orderly in the Franco-Prussian War (1870–71) and contracting diphtheria and dysentery while in the army. Such physical suffering had not, however, been a passing experience. For most of his adult life Nietzsche weathered literally blinding headaches and relentless nausea. He was incapacitated by pain for weeks at a time. Psychologically, he had endured rejection, betrayal, and the breaking of most of the meaningful relationships in his life.

So it was not entirely without reason that Nietzsche thought of himself as someone who could speak from experience on suffering and how to live with and through it. He saw his life as a largely triumphant struggle of self-overcoming: the transmutation of pain, trials, and misfortune into depth, nobility, and strength.

Nietzsche's view is just about the strongest pushback you can imagine against seeing pain as the supreme evil and pleasure as the supreme good. He thinks that kind of hedonism is the mindset of the pathetic "last men" who blithely claim "We invented happiness" and who self-medicate to dull whatever pain creeps into their trifling little lives. Whether or not they believe in God, they practice "the religion of compassion," which views suffering not as part and parcel of existence or an opportunity for self-overcoming but "as evil, hateful, deserving of annihilation, as a defect of existence."

This religion, Nietzsche says, gets the nature of happiness wrong. Happiness and unhappiness, pleasure and pain, joy and sorrow: in reality, these all go together. "Happiness and unhappiness are sisters, even twins that grow together." So all we get when we try to minimize unhappiness is the minimization of happiness as well. Both remain stunted. For one to grow, we must let the other thrive too.

Behind this view is a simple but provocative thought: if you suppress suffering, you suppress life. Life, for Nietzsche, is fundamentally a process of growth. And it grows by overcoming obstacles, setbacks, and suffering: "The discipline of suffering, of great suffering . . . has been the sole cause of every enhancement in humanity so far." Nietzsche saw this in his own biography. It was by managing to translate his own sickness and weakness into health and strength that he became who he was. The only route to greatness, nobility, and genius is through the wretchedness of pain, sorrow, and sickness. And, he says, that's true not only of the individual but of humanity in general.

So Nietzsche takes his stand as a defender of suffering against its milquetoast modern haters. He calls for the embrace of suffering for the sake of the enhanced humanity it helps produce. Never mind that it leaves the path to greater forms of being human littered with the suffering of innumerable actual human beings.

In Nietzsche's view, the religion of comfortableness promotes pity. It says that we ought to relieve others' pain and suffering—and do so as quickly as possible. But that is, paradoxically, to deny them the only route to true happiness. Moreover, pity belittles the sufferer. It treats them as helpless and—well, pitiful. Consequently, "not wanting to help can be more noble than the virtue that leaps to help."

Suffering is baked into life. The decisive thing is not to get rid of it or to avoid it, but to learn to take it in and grow from it. To look upon the tragic character of one's own life with the austere yet cheerful eye of a triumphant sovereign. But Nietzsche pushes beyond even this, because it is not only one's own suffering that demands to be taken in and affirmed; it is the suffering of the whole world, "this monstrous sum of all kinds of grief." Why this astonishing leap?

Nietzsche holds that everything is connected. Each of our lives sits atop the heap of all history that went before it, and each life would not have come about without every ounce of that history. So to say yes to one's life—even just to a moment of it—is to say yes to *all* that. "Have you ever said Yes to one joy? Oh my friends, then you have said Yes to *all* pain. All things are enchained, entwined, enamored." So if you've ever wanted to relive an experience—the sunshine on your skin at the beach, your child's smile, a personal triumph, a first kiss—"then you wanted *everything* back!"

Nietzsche aspires to these heights (and depths) of affirmation of suffering. He expresses the extremity of his view in what he called his "abysmal thought": eternal recurrence, the idea that everything that can happen has already happened and will do so again and again in an endless cycle. Eternal recurrence puts our ability to affirm the world despite suffering to the ultimate test. What kind of person could say yes to it all in every detail, not once but over and over again? What would it take for you to become the kind of person who could look at yourself and your life and speak a yes so profound as to make the holy profane, give sense to the senseless, redeem the past—all of the past—and give birth to a radically new future?

Here we find a secular echo of al-Ghazali. No God, no reason, no perfection. Just the brute reality of the world—and yet an analogous love for absolutely all of it. That's Nietzsche's victory over suffering.

For the Buddha, suffering is a problem with a cause and therefore a solution (admittedly, a radical one). For al-Ghazali, suffering has a reason and is to be borne with patience, trust, and thanksgiving. For Nietzsche, no reason for suffering is forthcoming from on high. The challenge is to take it in, grow from it, and thereby *give* suffering a reason. In itself, suffering is senseless. The challenge is to live so thoroughly, profoundly, and irrepressibly as to *make* sense of it all.

Perhaps, however, all this is a bit too simple—rather too tidy and submissive (the Buddha and al-Ghazali?) or decidedly too heroic (Nietzsche?).

Job's Protest

We mentioned Job earlier. As with many of the prophets recognized by Islam, he shows up first in the Hebrew Bible. The story we get there is rather different from the one in the Muslim tradition. This Job does not simply trust in the wisdom of God and accept his affliction as a test. This Job protests. At one and the same time, he both accepts his lot and complains fiercely that it's undeserved and unjust. To keep faith with God is to do both.

The Book of Job, where this story shows up, is among the most enigmatic, challenging pieces of literature from the whole ancient world. It's been interpreted a thousand ways, and there's no consensus in sight. We're not about to change that in the next few pages. Even so, we can encounter a unique and challenging stance toward suffering in the book's story.

The rough outline is this: Job is a good guy with a nice life. He's successful and happy ("wealthier than anyone in the East"), and the really great thing is that he seems to *deserve* it. The text calls him "blameless and upright." One day, a shadowy figure called the Adversary shows up in God's heavenly court. God takes the opportunity to brag on Job: He's the best! Blameless and upright and everything! The Adversary replies, essentially, "But that's pretty easy for Job, isn't it? After all, he's got it easy. His setup is flat-out cushy, don't you think? I bet if you sent some trouble his way, he'd curse your name." To which God says, in effect, "Challenge accepted." (Nobody asks Job what he thinks about this deal.)

The Adversary proceeds to wreak havoc on Job's life. Bandits steal Job's livestock and kill his servants, and his children die in a freak accident. When none of this provokes Job to blaspheme, the

Adversary comes after Job's own body, afflicting him with painful sores from head to toe.

Three of Job's friends hear about these disasters and come to try to comfort him. Things are so bad that they just sit with him in silence for a whole week straight. Then, in reaction to Job's complaint, they get to talking. The bulk of the book is a series of poetic speeches made by Job and the friends, all responding to the egregious, out-of-the-blue suffering that has come his way.

Job maintains that he is innocent and the suffering is undeserved. By all appearances, God has wronged him, and he wants an explanation from God. The friends, who believe you always get what you deserve, suggest that Job must have done something wrong. He ought to figure out what it is, repent, and seek God's mercy and forgiveness. In effect, they blame Job for his suffering. (Few things are as bitter as pity laced with blame.) Eventually, God shows up in person and brings the conversation to a screeching halt with a fearful, awe-inspiring speech delivered from the midst of a whirlwind. In the face of it, Job falls silent and gives up his demand for vindication.

Let's think for a moment about the character of Job's complaint. Note, first, that it is directed against excessive, gratuitous affliction. It's nothing he could have avoided, but also not the sort of suffering that is knit into the fabric of the human condition. It's not the death of loved ones as such, for example, but the sudden, violent, premature deaths of his children. His complaint assumes the goodness of fragile, transient human existence. But within that fragility and transience, Job affirms the goodness of prosperity, fertility, health, good reputation, and the like.

Job insists that when extreme affliction befalls a person of integrity, something is amiss. It's a problem. It's worthy of vociferous complaint. It's wrong. This isn't how things ought to be. Job protests against the injustice that has befallen him. He protests against God, but not because he thinks that God is unjust. He protests because he believes that God is just and he knows that God's goodness was the source of the goods he lost. Job rejects the explanations of his fate because the only explanations on offer rationalize or trivialize or justify the suffering. They pretend it's not actually as bad as it really, truly is (especially given its gratuitousness).

After God's speech from the whirlwind, Job drops his suit, so to speak. He abandons his insistence that God either explain his suffering as just punishment or recognize it as unjust oppression. In effect, he throws up his hands in the face of the mystery of it. But then God does two surprising things. First, turning to one of the friends, God says, "I am incensed at you and your two friends, for you have not spoken the truth about Me as did My servant Job." Second, God "restored Job's fortunes and . . . gave Job twice what he had before."

The friends, God is saying, ought not to have blamed Job for his affliction. But there's even more to it than that. Job, it seems, had been right to ask God to give an account for everything that had gone wrong. Job was right to protest, even though God never offers Job an explanation for his suffering. We are left with an unsettling picture. God remains upsettingly beyond human comprehension.

What lesson are we to learn about suffering and how to respond to it? A (perhaps frustratingly) complex one, but one that honors the limits of human knowing and many people's deep moral convictions. On the one hand, the Book of Job suggests the importance of recognizing that we don't understand the moral fabric of the world. We can't make all the pieces of the puzzle fit. We can't really be sure that they do fit. On the other hand, Job's peace with God did not mean the end of Job's quarrel with the world. God affirmed Job's conviction that egregious suffering is simply not how God's world is supposed to be. We should not acquiesce to it, whether by cultivating nonattachment to the world, by insisting that there are good reasons for suffering, or by heroically celebrating the blind force of the world.

Even in the midst of egregious suffering, we ought to protest and struggle against it—in the name of precisely those goods that Job lost and the God who had given them to Job. This, you might notice, brings us back to the subject of the previous chapter: how we work against suffering to eliminate or mitigate it. Nietzsche might scoff at struggling against the suffering in the world. But to one extent or another, everyone else we've heard from in this chapter has room in their vision for that struggle. The work would take different shapes in the context of different visions of life. Buddhist compassion is different from utilitarian giving, which is different from the Muslim practices of charity that al-Ghazali followed, which is different from . . . you get the idea. But the full circle of these chapters does show that the questions of how to work against suffering and how to live with it are very likely two sides of the same coin.

So How *Should* We Work against and Live with Suffering?

First, we'll need to discern what we think is the right balance between the more "objective" work of reducing what suffering we can and the more "subjective" work of learning how to live well with suffering. How much should we focus on one versus the other? Even if we're convinced, like Baldwin, that the two belong inseparably together, there are trade-offs of time and energy. The life of a dedicated effective altruism advocate is going to look pretty different from that of a Buddhist monk.

Second, it's probably wise to be cautious about giving advice to people who are suffering. Another's suffering is always at least somewhat beyond our grasp. However convinced we are that we have a theory to account for it or the right way to live with it, empathy may be what's most needed. There can be wisdom in reticence, even if a time for processing and sense-making will come.

For three years, our friend Angela Williams Gorrell worked with us at Yale and taught Life Worth Living. Angela is a truly amazing teacher, and the class wouldn't be what it is without everything she brought to it. So it was a sad moment when she stood up to speak to the gathered students and teachers on the last day of class of her last semester before heading to a new job.

Angela had come to Yale to work on a research project on the theology of joy. Just before and during her first semester teaching Life Worth Living, she had suffered three tragic losses in quick succession. The bitter juxtaposition put the challenge of living with and through suffering front and center.

On that last day of the semester, she told the heartrending story of one of those losses, the loss of a family member to suicide. Here's how she recounts it in her book *The Gravity of Joy*:

> I opened the passenger door and grabbed my cell
> phone from the floorboard of the car.

I was stunned to discover that I had missed seven calls from Mom and a text from her.

The text read, "Dustin killed himself." . . .

Tears streamed down my face like water rushing over a tub filled to the brim. Before thinking, I called Mom back.

I remember screaming "No!" over and over again, crying and demanding she tell me it wasn't true. . . .

I was wandering through the parking lot as I listened to her tell me that it was true. She was still crying when she answered the phone, though she had known for a few hours.

Suddenly, I dropped the phone on the pavement of the church parking lot and wailed.

Angela looked out at our students when she had finished. There was reverent silence. She took a breath and said to them, "I hope you have a vision of life that will sustain you in the moments on the pavement. There will likely be a day when the world stops and your heart breaks and you will need a vision of a life worth living that can survive the storm. Surely, your vision will be deepened, transformed, sharpened by the days on the pavement, but I hope your vision already has a compass that can orient you or, better yet, an anchor that will hold you."

Everyone in the room that day left with a sense of the way life's "pavement moments" test and refine our visions of flourishing life. There's much more to surviving the storm than having a sturdy vision of life worth living, but like Angela said, it's better to have an anchor already on board if you can.

We are reason-seeking animals, and we are (all too often) people in pain. We need responses to suffering that both help us cope and help us fit the pain and disjointedness we find in our lives and our world into a larger picture. Just because a way of thinking about suffering makes us feel better doesn't make it true. Just because a practice for weathering suffering helps get us through doesn't make it good. But that said, what good are responses to the question of suffering if they don't actually help us respond to its reality? The Question, after all, is the question of our lives.

Your Turn

Note: We mean what we said above about being cautious when advising others about their own suffering. So we want to preface the exercises for this chapter by acknowledging that we don't know what you may be going through right now. If you have things you need to process with someone—a counselor or a trusted friend—rather than with a book, please do so. If now is simply not the time to dig deeper and process, surely you know that better than we do. Sometimes what we need most is time and distance from our pain.

1. How did you feel as you read about the Buddha's proposal that suffering ceases when we recognize the emptiness of the self and so cease craving?
   * What do you think lies behind your feelings?

2. Is it comforting to think that perhaps there's a grand plan for the world's suffering? Is it troubling to think that God might cause or permit suffering? Why?
   * Do you think the truth about suffering is more likely to be comforting or troubling? What reasons can you give for your answer?

3. Does thinking about suffering as an occasion for growth (Nietzsche) belittle the pain? Alternatively, does it offer a path to meaning and value?

4. Have you ever found yourself in Job's position—protesting
   suffering you can neither overcome nor understand?
   * How did it feel?
   * How did others respond?
   * What have you done when you've been in the
     position of Job's friends?

5. How much do you think it matters to understand suffering?

TWELVE

When It Ends

A massive, two-dimensional, disembodied head and shoulders hovered over the lecture hall. It was a little fitting that Zoltan Istvan, who was speaking to our students about the philosophical movement known as transhumanism, wasn't there in the flesh. Technology had a lot to do with his vision of flourishing, so a technologically mediated lecture felt about right.

Unlike most of the traditions with which we have engaged in Life Worth Living over the years, this one had a political party. And Istvan had been its candidate for president of the United States. His campaign consisted of a simple, one-plank platform: make Americans immortal. You see, Zoltan shares Ray Kurzweil's common transhumanist belief that with enough effort, we could discover the technological means to radical life extension within a few decades. Istvan wanted to spread the word, so he had traveled the country campaigning in a coffin-shaped bus.

His remarks to the class laid out his reasoning. Your biggest problem, he argued, is that you are going to die. It blows every other problem out of the water. What could possibly matter more to you than *life*! And yet your government is doing nothing at all to solve this overriding problem. Seems like a catastrophic case of misplaced priorities not to at least *try*.

You could make something of the same argument about this book so far. With a few exceptions here and there, death hasn't played much of a role in our consideration of the Question. But Istvan is not wrong about at least one thing: you *are* going to die. What's more, you don't know when. The prospect of death shadows every moment of life, whether we notice it or not.

No vision of flourishing life worth its salt will ignore the fact that these lives of ours—no matter how well we live them, how well they go, or how they feel—will end in death. What a vision has to say about death will tell you a lot about its stance toward life.

The Cure-All

On an otherwise uneventful day in 399 BCE, an Athenian jury delivered its verdict in the trial of a noteworthy citizen on the charges of "impiety" and "corrupting the youth." Guilty. The convict was condemned to die by poisoning.

In the time between the sentence and its execution, the man conversed with a small group of friends on the subjects of justice, the soul, and death. Some of his supporters came up with a plan to ferry him out of the prison, down to the sea, and away into exile. He declined.

When the time came, his friends wept, but he did not. He calmly drank the hemlock-laced cup presented by the executioner. As his life drained away, Socrates (b. 470 BCE), the giant of Greek philosophy, made one final request. His most famous student, Plato (ca. 427–348/7 BCE), portrays the teacher turning to his old friend Crito and saying, "Crito, we owe a cock to Asclepius; make this offering to him and do not forget."

Asclepius was the god of medicine. To owe him a rooster would mean that the god had answered one's prayers for healing. So Socrates is saying, with characteristic flair, that death is quite like a form of healing. But if death is a cure, then it would seem that "life is a disease," to quote Nietzsche's interpretation of the scene.

Now, Socrates wasn't a dour guy. Penchant for putting people on the spot with tough questions aside, he seems to have been fairly easygoing. By all accounts, he was pretty happy most of the time. He wasn't a self-denying ascetic. He didn't starve himself or forgo wine or sex or parties. So what gives?

As Plato presents it, the heart of the matter is the soul. Your soul is the best part of you. In fact, when push comes to shove, it's the real you. What matters in life is the good of your soul. That it be wise and just and the like. Above all, that it grasp the eternal truth of things. The best life, then, is one that cares for the good of the soul.

The body, Socrates argues, doesn't add anything to this kind of goodness. In fact, it tends to distract us from caring for our souls. For one thing, our bodies are super needy. They're also pretty bossy. They throw fits when they don't get what they want. And they break down both inevitably (as when we age) and unexpectedly (as in the case of disease or injury). Perhaps worst of all (to Socrates), the body's notoriously unreliable senses inhibit pure reasoning. It's hard to think straight in a world of optical illusions, phantom sounds, and all sorts of deceptive appearances.

It's not clear, though, how any of this would make death a blessing. It's the end of life, after all, and only someone who's alive could be wise or virtuous.

Socrates is pretty cagey about what he thinks happens when you die. But in Plato's *Phaedo*, he goes to great lengths to convince his friends that the soul is immortal. At death, your soul departs from your body. The two things then have very different fates. Your soulless body becomes an inanimate corpse and decays. But your bodiless soul stays intact. Death doesn't harm the soul directly. Nor does it harm the soul by separating it from the body. If anything, this separation is a boon. It allows the soul to "escape the contamination of the body's folly." And we have good reason to hope that if we have lived well, we will "live in complete happiness, beyond the reach of evils."

The philosophical life, for Socrates, is "training for death." By examining and reflecting on the eternal truth of things, it gets the soul ready to be separated from the body. It anticipates the soul's "escape" here and now. To live well is to invest your time and energy, as much as you can, in the soul that will last, rather than in the body that will perish. It's to live such that death will be a blessing for you.

But what if death is neither the single biggest problem of our lives nor a potential blessing? What if death is actually nothing at all? There's a serious perspective out there that says just that.

No Birth, No Death

Vietnamese monk and champion of "engaged Buddhism" Thich Nhat Hanh (1926–2022) thinks we can see the truth about death by looking at a cloud.

Some water evaporates from the ocean and rises as vapor into the atmosphere. When conditions are right, it condenses into liquid or solid particles, and these particles cluster together in a cloud. Many clouds simply dissipate as the particles evaporate once again.

When the conditions are right, however, the tiny particles begin to coalesce into larger, heavier ones, which then begin to fall as rain. The rainwater seeps into the ground, where plant roots absorb it, or it gathers into rivulets, brooks, and streams, flowing downhill into larger rivers and eventually into the ocean.

OK. But what does an elementary-school earth science lesson have to do with death?

"The cloud," Nhat Hanh says, "does not come from nothing. There has only been a change in form." Similarly, the cloud does not become nothing. "If you look deeply into the rain, you can see the cloud."

The coming and going of the cloud is a continuous process of change. Nothing comes to be or ceases to be. There is only a series of shifting "manifestations." It's like the waves on an ocean. Different waves ceaselessly come and go, but it's always all just water in motion. The upshot is this: "There is no real death because there is always a continuation. A cloud continues the ocean, the river and the heat of the sun, and the rain continues the cloud."

The same is true, Nhat Hanh says, of us. The phenomenon that is each of us is a manifestation. It has no underlying, stable basis. Nothing new comes into being when we are born, and nothing ceases when we die. "Our true nature is the nature of no birth and no death." You might recognize this as the teaching of non-self, which we discussed in chapters 8 and 11. Nhat Hanh pairs it with an emphasis on the closely related idea of impermanence, which holds that "nothing remains the same for even two consecutive moments." *Everything* is always shifting, changing, giving rise to whatever is next.

Death is just an idea, a category we use. It doesn't name anything substantial. To see this is to change everything, Nhat Hanh says. It is "the cream of enlightened wisdom. . . . When we have this insight we will have no more fear." Since so much of the fear in our lives is connected to fear of death, to be freed from fear of death is very nearly to be freed from *all* fear. Hence the title of his book: *No Death, No Fear.* If we can truly touch our own impermanence and non-self, we will be able to "ride on the waves of birth and death, smiling serenely." Nothing life—or death—can throw at us will faze us. "We can enjoy life and appreciate it in a new way."

This might seem like a bum deal. It sure feels like the only reason Nhat Hanh can say that "things do not really die" is because they do not really live either. Doesn't his perspective amount to disarming death by embracing annihilation?

Nhat Hanh thinks otherwise. We shouldn't think of things like impermanence and non-self as doctrines that state a truth opposed to the falsehoods of permanence and self. They are, instead, tools to help us get free of our deceptive ideas of permanence and selfhood. But the aim is actually that we get free of *all* ideas, including impermanence and non-self, because "reality is free from all concepts and ideas." So just as "there is no permanent self" (bummer?), "there is no annihilation" (yay?).

Shakespeare's Hamlet famously declared that "to be or not to be" is "the question." Nhat Hanh imagines the Buddha turning Hamlet on his head: "'To be or not to be is *not* the question.' To be and not to be are just two ideas opposing each another. But they are not reality, and they do not describe reality." Reality is the constant interdependent transformation of phenomena "in a constant process of manifesting."

When we take this view of reality, then "instead of birth and death, there is only continuing transformation." It's not that "things" come into being and then cease. The ocean, the cloud, the rain, the river—they are all simply manifestations, transforming one into the other. Same with us. Think about the difference between "you" now and "you" as a newborn infant. The long way from then to now is a continuous series of transformations. And Nhat Hanh insists that there's no metaphysical difference between how we continue from moment to moment in our lives and how we continue after our deaths. In neither case are "we" something stable, some solid existent "self."

What follows from this view is a cheerful unconcern for death. It takes practice to cultivate this stance, but Nhat Hanh believes it's possible. "If your practice is strong, at the moment of dying you will sing a song of happy continuation."

This is a *very* different sort of continuation than the one Socrates looked forward to as he drank the hemlock. It's not the continued conscious existence of a rational soul, but a continuous fluid process of manifestations arising and then yielding to other manifestations.

It also implies a strikingly unconventional stance toward time. Nhat Hanh criticizes the tendency to think of happiness as something that we'll achieve in the future. That tendency is silly because the future never comes. There is only ever *now*. So now is the only time we could be happy. What's more: there's nothing but ourselves stopping us from being happy now. No matter what's going on, "the conditions for happiness are already here." But can we really isolate happiness from all past and all future?

Writing about the ancient Greek Epicurean school of philosophy, philosopher Martha Nussbaum notes that a human life "projects beyond its present states toward the future." Our actions take time. Our relationships grow and change. So we are, apparently inevitably, tied to the future. Indeed, part of what it means for projects and relationships to be what they are and to matter to us is for them to be oriented toward the future. Marriage is a good example of this. It is *intrinsically* a relationship intended to have a future.

Sure, we only ever inhabit the present. But the futures of things like relationships, projects, or a game of chess dwell in the present with us. Those futures partly *make up* our present. It's often not that we're waiting to be happy in the future, but that the future is part of what makes happiness and meaning possible *now*. And death, Nussbaum says, disrupts this. It "intrudes upon the value and beauty of temporally evolving activities and relations."

Shortly after the death of his wife, the poet Joy Davidman (1915–1960), C. S. Lewis wrote, "It is hard to have patience with people who say, 'There is no death' or 'Death doesn't matter.' . . . You might as well say birth doesn't matter."

Maybe Nhat Hanh is right that "no birth, no death" lets us enjoy life in serenity. But Nussbaum and Lewis raise a pressing question. Such a life might be enjoyable. But could it *matter*?

This (One and Only) Life

Our Yale colleague Martin Hägglund does not want to die. But he doesn't want eternal life either. As he puts it, "an eternal life is not only unattainable but also undesirable." Seems like those are the only two options, though: die for good or live forever. Now, Hägglund doesn't think that he or any of us gets to choose which of the two is our fate. But if the choice were his, Hägglund would cast his lot with mortality. Finite, mortal life is better than eternal life.

How so? If life is good, it would seem that endless life would be better.

To the contrary, says Hägglund. "Any life worth living must be finite." The key to understanding his view lies in the word *living*. Living is something we *do*. Agency is its essential core. And Hägglund thinks that for our agency to be ours and to make any sense, our lives must end in death.

To be an agent is to have purposes. It is to act for the sake of something, which implies that we care about something. But caring only makes sense, Hägglund argues, if what we care for is vulnerable—if we can make a difference to it. "Caring about someone or something requires that we believe in its value, but it also requires that we believe that what is valued can cease to be," he says. And eternal life of the kind we saw Socrates hoping for doesn't meet this standard. Nothing eternal, Hägglund claims, can need anything from us—or from itself. It's already eternal. It's completely secure. If our lives are eternal, then, we can't care for them, which means that we can't be concerned with our own agency. "Eternal activity does not depend on being sustained by anyone." So in an imagined eternal life, there's no reason to do anything. Indeed, properly speaking, there's no *doing* at all.

Similarly, what we do with our lives—whether we do this or that, now or later—can matter to us only if our time is limited. "If I believed that my life would last forever, I could never take my life to be at stake and I would never be seized by the need to do anything with my time. I would not even be able to understand what it means to do something sooner rather than later in my life, since I would have no sense of a finite lifetime that gives urgency to any project or activity."

Hägglund's conclusion is this: "What I do and what I love can matter to me only because I understand myself as mortal." No death, no agency. No agency, no meaning.

It might seem that Hägglund is talking to Socrates but ignoring Nhat Hanh, who offers what appears to be an alternative to the dichotomy between mortality and immortality. But from Hägglund's perspective, it's no real alternative at all. As he sees it, Socrates devalues life by making us immortal, while Nhat Hanh devalues life by denying that there's any real "us" to live and die. The telltale sign is that both counsel us not to fear death or be disturbed by the loss of loved ones. "Being invulnerable to the fear of death," Hägglund writes, "would amount to being completely indifferent." Which is to say, nothing would matter.

And that's precisely what Hägglund thinks a Buddhist position like Nhat Hanh's does. It cuts our ties to our lives and the earth, Hägglund says, by seeing everything we might care about as ephemeral and illusion-like. Its purpose is to get beyond all purposes. But without purposes, nothing can matter. So its goal is for nothing to matter. "Such an ideal," Hägglund judges, "is empty and not worth striving for."

If Hägglund's claim is true, it has serious implications for the whole project of this book. If our lives must be mortal for things to matter, then the question of how to spend our lives makes sense only if death is a real and final end. The Question of the shape of flourishing life would only really be a question for people who deny enlightenment, eternal life, and anything of the sort.

It would mean that the billions of people who do believe in such things would betray their own highest ideals any time they let something in life matter except as a means to ultimate fulfillment. The only "meaning" allowable in their lives would be the project of getting to some state where life, if it can be described as life at all, is meaningless.

Putting on Imperishability

Popular imagination paints Christianity in Socratic brushstrokes. This life is a "vale of tears" that we pass through in order to reach eternal life in heaven. Death, therefore, is a blessing to be embraced. Surely, many Christians have thought of life and death this way. The early Christian leader Ignatius of Antioch (first and second centuries CE), for example, described this life as a "state of death." Having been sentenced to death, he asked influential Christians in Rome not to get his sentence reduced. "Do not keep me from living," he begged. By "living" he meant dying.

But this is not the only way Christians have thought about death. Let's return to the apostle Paul, whom we met in chapter 5, for a different perspective.

Paul writes of death as an "enemy" and portrays it as a domineering tyrant. It's no blessing. Rather, it's the paradigmatic curse. God had created humans finite and fragile and mortal. (Everything other than God is by definition finite.) But God's intention had been to give the gift of everlasting life.

Life as we know it, though, is marred because humans broke faith with God. In Paul's terms, we "sinned." So things are not as they ought to have been. There is an illness, but it is not life. It is the sin that severs humans' relation to the source of life.

In the context of this broken situation, our lives now have two essential stages. The first begins with our birth and ends with death. Even though things are messed up, this first stage is good. And that goodness cannot be taken away. God created it, after all, and God is supremely good. That this life ends in death is bad. It's a tragedy, and if it were all there is to the story, the whole story would be a tragedy.

The message Paul preached all over the eastern Mediterranean was that there was indeed more to the story. Death is an enemy, but when God raised Jesus into new life after he had been executed, the power of death was broken. We can look forward in hope, therefore, to a second stage of life, which begins with what Paul calls "resurrection," the raising into new life of those who have died. Resurrection isn't, though, the release of an already-immortal soul from its mortal body. It's resurrection of the *body*. Paul uses the metaphor of changing clothes. Our lives "put on imperishability." The same life that we live here and now is transformed and healed and sustained. The relation between these two stages of life is not, then, one of illness to cure, but of good to (a lot) better.

We can see the distinction in how Paul counsels Christians to respond to the death of loved ones. They should not try to muster the cheerfulness that Socrates (unsuccessfully) asked of his friends. But neither should they suffer "utter bereavement." They should mourn, Paul writes, but mourn in hope, neither seeing death as definitive destruction nor treating it with emotionless indifference, as if it weren't bad at all.

The foundation of Paul's view of death is affirmation of life. God has, from the very beginning, been the God who makes alive. God created humans (and other creatures) as living beings. And life is still the hallmark of God's work. Jesus Christ is "life-giving." Bringing life to others is just what he does. What's more, God's life-giving work takes place here in this world because the life-giving God is *God of this world*. This world and this life are no mere way stations as we pass on to the hereafter.

For Hägglund, the threat of death is, in a sense, primary. The negativity of death is necessary for agency and for life's meaning. Resistance to death is the foundation of commitment to life. But, Paul might insist, doesn't that get it backward? It's not that we care for others because we know they will die. It's that we work to preserve them (not to mention ourselves) from dying because we love them. The goodness of living is prior to the negativity of death. And the life truly worth living is above all a celebration of that goodness through love. It drives out fear and makes hope the primary mode of relating to life and death.

From Paul's perspective, without the prospect of resurrection into indefinitely extended life, a perennial mist of sadness would envelop our lives. We would likely experience life as meaningless precisely because not only our lives but the lives of those we love (and eventually the life of our planet and the entire universe) would end in death. From Paul's perspective, it is precisely eternal life (as he understands it) that is desirable. Whether it is plausible is a different question altogether. Even in the unlikely event that Paul convinced Hägglund that eternal life would be desirable, they would still have to hash out whether there are compelling reasons to believe in it.

What Is Worth Dying For?

We said at the beginning of the chapter that what a vision of flourishing says about death will tell you a lot about its stance toward life. That's especially true when we pose the question, What is worth dying for?

It's a challenging question, especially if you don't believe that there's any form of life after death. It summons you to ask whether there is something more valuable to you than—you. Even if you do believe in postmortem life, the question still prods you to ask whether you would bet your life on it. What is so valuable that it would be worth pushing all your chips to the center of the table?

Along with its challenge, this question brings a promise: if you know what's worth dying for, then you'll know what kind of life is truly worth living. Put the other way around: if you can't answer the question of what's worth dying for, then you might not really have a vision of life worth living. Your highest good would simply be to live.

A long discussion at this point would be redundant. At some level, everything we've discussed in the book so far has been pointing to various answers to this question. But it'll be helpful to highlight two broad categories of common responses.

First, many have held that we ought to be willing to die so that others might flourish. One passage in the Hebrew Bible says that Moses offered his own life in solidarity with his people. And we have already seen in chapter 5 that Paul did something similar. In a different vein, utilitarians believe that we ought to sacrifice our own happiness for the sake of others'. Giving one's own life so that others might thrive would be the costliest realization of this ideal. Some Buddhist traditions believe in *bodhisattvas*, people who are enlightened but who nevertheless remain in the cycle of birth and death so that they can lead others to enlightenment. They are willing not just to die but to keep on dying over and over for others.

Second, there's devotion to true life. Many (maybe even most) of our conversation partners from this book would say that staying true to one's vision of the good life is more important than life itself. It's both a matter of integrity and one of testifying against a world that opposes flourishing life. Some, like Socrates, have indeed died rather than do what they thought would be wrong. Given the chance to escape, Socrates declined, not only because he hoped for immortality, but because he thought breaking the laws of his home city would be wrong. It was more important to him to do the right thing than to keep living.

But you don't have to be the founder of a philosophical school or religious movement to die for your vision of life worth living. An ancient Christian text, for example, tells the story of two young women, Perpetua and Felicity, who were arrested and imprisoned along with some companions for not being willing to offer sacrifices to the Roman gods to honor the emperor. Perpetua was a nursing mother. The text reports in her own words that she worried grievously for her son, eventually entrusting him to her mother and brother. Felicity was pregnant and gave birth in the prison. She gave her child to be raised by other community members. Both were offered freedom if only they would give in and perform the sacrifice. Both refused and were killed in the town amphitheater during gladiatorial games for the emperor's birthday. This story is just one of countless instances of ordinary people putting greater value on devotion to true life than on extending their own lives.

From the Question of Death to the Matter of Living

Once we've come to see the Question as the question of our lives, there's no escaping the further question posed by death. At least to begin with, death puts meaning, value, and goodness into doubt. Over the course of this chapter, we've seen various competing ways of responding to this challenge. Socrates urged us to live so that death might be a blessing to our souls. Nhat Hanh tried to show us that both death and birth are mere ideas that don't reflect the true nature of things. Hägglund proposed that, bitter though it may be, death is actually what *gives* meaning to life. And Paul named death an enemy but proclaimed the enemy defeated by God on our behalf.

Even if we're willing to sign on to one of these perspectives on death and its corresponding vision of flourishing life, we haven't arrived yet. We're not even halfway there. Serious challenges remain. Perhaps most pressing of all is this: How can we come to actually *live* a life we recognize as worthy—a way of life that would be worth dying for? How could we make a life like that so thoroughly our own that we *actually would be willing* to die for it? The next three chapters will help us start to respond to this challenge.

Your Turn

1. Which future-oriented projects and relationships are meaningful to you?
   * Do these projects and relationships become more or less meaningful when you consider that they are destined to come to an end in death?

2. If it were true—if it *is* true—that death is nothing because life is nothing (as Nhat Hanh says), how would your life have to change?

3. Regardless of whether you believe in it, do you think eternal life would be desirable? Why or why not?
   * If you knew that you and those you cared about would live forever, what (if anything) would still give this life meaning?

4. What would be worth dying for?
   * Are there people you hope you would be willing to die for? Why might it be worth it?
   * Are there ideals you hope you would be willing to die for? Again, why might it be worth it?
   * What do your answers to the last two questions say about what's worth living for?

Part 5

··

BACK TO THE SURFACE

THIRTEEN

It Turns Out We Have Some Work to Do

We hold these truths to be self-evident, that all men are created equal . . ." These words document a genuine insight into the kind of life that is worthy of our humanity.

It is bitterly ironic that over the course of his life, the man who penned them held some six hundred human beings in slavery. It did not have to be that way. Thomas Jefferson's original draft of the Declaration of Independence included a veritable screed against the slave trade. He called it a "cruel war against human nature itself." That first draft would have been a Declaration of Independence and an Emancipation Proclamation in one. But politics—and, it must be said, Jefferson himself—could not bear to put the insight into practice, and so we got the bare ideal: "all men are created equal."

That's not to say that no one in power at the time understood the far-ranging implications of these words. Many did. In 1780, a mere four years after the Declaration, Massachusetts used Jefferson's language in its state constitution. Within three years, the state supreme court had abolished slavery. Slaveholders in the South, too, saw the power of the phrase, changing "all men" to "all freemen" in six southern constitutions.

In time, Jefferson's personal emancipatory ideals would dissipate. In 1792, he wrote in his ledger that he had calculated that his plantation was yielding a 4 percent annual return through the birth of enslaved Black children. It struck him as a sound investment strategy. He even recommended it to George Washington and others. It seems Jefferson found dollars and cents a stronger motive than self-evident truths. Journalist Henry Wiencek notes the suspicious timing: "Jefferson began to back away from antislavery just around the time he computed the silent profit of the 'peculiar institution.'"

In 1776, Jefferson had an insight. By his death in 1826, that insight had led him to free precisely *two* of the more than six hundred enslaved persons he had claimed to own.

In 1777, Robert Carter III also had an insight.

It may have started with a fever dream. In June 1777, when God's presence suddenly overwhelmed him, Carter had just been inoculated against smallpox, a risky business in colonial Virginia, even for a wealthy plantation owner like him. But Carter took it to be more than a dream: it was a divine encounter, the sort of sudden conversion that American Christians love to celebrate. In his diary, he would call it a "most gracious Illumination." A month later, he would declare that while he had once doubted the divinity of Christ, he did no longer.

Another vision in December led him further along his spiritual quest—and as he reflected, it began to reveal to him something he had previously missed. Two enslaved people, Sarah Stanhope and Harry-Ditcher, had been with him for this second vision. They had seen the same great, strange light shining in the sky. Carter began spending more and more time among the people he held in slavery and his servants. Eventually, he was baptized in the mixed-race congregation of a Separate Baptist church. In the words of his biographer, Andrew Levy, "in the course of three short years, he had turned away from the religion of Thomas Jefferson, and embraced the religion of Thomas Jefferson's slaves."

Thus began the long and winding road to Carter's understated, bureaucratic, but legally airtight emancipation of all enslaved persons on his properties.

Like Jefferson, Carter believed deeply in freedom. Like Jefferson, Carter "owned" hundreds of enslaved people. Like Jefferson in the late 1770s, Carter recognized the incompatibility of those two facts. Unlike Jefferson, Carter did something about it. In 1791, he registered a detailed plan for the gradual release of all 420 enslaved persons whom he had the legal right to set free. As Levy describes Carter, he was the "anti-Jefferson," a "man who did not lack the will to free his own slaves but who did lack the vision and clarity to make his love of freedom eloquent."

Carter did not wax eloquent about freedom. (The closest we get is a meandering "whereas" clause in his court filing.) Jefferson, undoubtedly, would get the better grade on his final Life Worth Living paper at Yale. But whatever critiques we might offer of Carter (and surely we might want more from our heroes than that they quit enslaving fellow human beings), it is not hard to judge which life more deeply honored our shared humanity.

Insights are one thing. Actions are another.

Suffice it to say: if, thirteen chapters into this book, we've come to significant insights of our own about the Question, we still have a fair bit of work to do.

It's about Living

We've spent a lot of time in this book thinking about what distinguishes one vision of flourishing life from another. And that is well and good. The differences are real, and they're important. It can be tempting to paper over them and claim that all traditions basically, deep down, endorse the same vision of life. But hopefully by now it's clear: that's just not true. And we do ourselves no favors trying to pretend otherwise.

One benefit of being honest about the many divergences is that when there actually are substantial agreements, they really stand out. Here's one: just about everyone agrees that no matter how valuable it is to know what the good life is like, the real point is to live good lives. The point of considering the shape of flourishing life is to find our way to it and open the way to others.

The consensus here is far-reaching. There are, of course, the obvious cases. It's hard to imagine a purely abstract utilitarian, someone interested only in what, hypothetically speaking, would do the most good for the most people. The point is to act. If we can help but don't, we're not just missing the opportunity to do something good. We're doing something wrong. As Peter Singer says about his argument for radical giving to others: "In this instance, taking our conclusion seriously means acting upon it."

Similarly, Robin Wall Kimmerer sees herself as sharing wisdom that demands *actions*. The insight is this: "We are all bound by a covenant of reciprocity: plant breath for animal breath, winter and summer, predator and prey, grass and fire, night and day, living and dying. Water knows this, clouds know this. Soil and rocks know they are dancing in a continuous giveaway of making, unmaking, and making again the earth." Kimmerer has invested much of her career so that her fellow humans, the "younger siblings" of the earth, might know this as well. But this knowledge brings with it an urgency to act. "The moral covenant of reciprocity calls us to honor our responsibilities for all we have been given, for all that we have taken. It's our turn now, long overdue."

Perhaps of all people, we might expect the ancient philosophers to be in favor of knowledge for its own sake. And that might be true for some sorts of knowledge. (Like geometry. They were really into math for math's sake.) But not when it comes to the kind we've been after in this book. Aristotle says near the beginning of his book on ethics, "We are inquiring not in order to know what excellence is, but in order to become good, since otherwise our inquiry would have been of no use."

The Jewish rabbis agree. Despite devoting his life to learning, Rabbi Shimon ben Gamliel (ca. 10 BCE–70 CE), son of the venerable Rabbi Gamaliel, remarks, "All my life I grew up among sages and I found that nothing is better for a person than silence. Not learning but doing is the main thing; and one who talks too much causes sin." *Not learning but doing.* So says the son of a great rabbi after a childhood spent learning at the feet of sages.

We shouldn't drive too sharp a wedge between knowledge and action. The goal for the rabbis is to have both. But they have no doubt which you should emphasize. Rabbi Hanina ben Dosa (first century CE) says, "For one whose good deeds exceed his wisdom, wisdom endures. For one whose wisdom exceeds his good deeds, wisdom does not endure." If you don't put wisdom into practice, it tends to wither and die. In contrast, even good practices that we *haven't* thought very hard about may yet blossom into wisdom.

Rabbi Elazar ben Azarya (first century CE) offers a perhaps surprising botanical metaphor:

> To what may one whose wisdom exceeds his deeds be compared? To a tree with many branches but few roots. When a wind comes, it uproots and overturns it. . . . To what may one whose deeds exceed his wisdom be compared? To a tree with few branches but many roots. Even if all the winds of the world come and blow against it, they cannot dislodge it from its place.

Did you catch that? *Deeds* are the roots, *wisdom* the branches. Wisdom grows out of the goodness of life. The two mutually nourish each other like the roots and branches of a tree. But it's our practices, not our good ideas, that keep us rooted.

Jesus says something similar in the Gospel of Luke. What sounds at first like a complaint about disobedient disciples turns into a parable about the sorts of resilience that intellect alone cannot provide:

> Why do you call me "Lord, Lord," and do not do what I tell you? I will show you what someone is like who comes to me, hears my words, and acts on them. That one is like a man building a house, who dug deeply and laid the foundation on rock; when a flood arose, the river burst against that house but could not shake it, because it had been well built. But the one who hears and does not act is like a man who built a house on the ground without a foundation. When the river burst against it, immediately it fell, and great was the ruin of that house.

Hear the words, sure. But the firm foundation isn't the hearing. It's the doing. It's our practices, not just our abstract insights, that we can count on and build on.

For Confucius, too, deeds distinguish the student who really gets it. In a humorous passage, Confucius describes how his favorite student could be misjudged by those who don't know what to look for. "I can talk all day to Yan Hui—he never raises any objection, he looks stupid. Yet, observe him when he is on his own: his actions fully reflect what he learned. Oh no, Hui is not stupid!" The top student at the seminar table isn't the one who takes up the most "airtime." It's the one who does the work to change their life.

There's an important dynamic at play in Kimmerer's call to reciprocity in the face of the looming ecological crisis, in Rabbi Elazar's tree and its roots, in Jesus's parable of the house built on the rock, in Confucius's praise for Yan Hui—really, in just about every tradition we've encountered. (Not to mention quite pointedly in the stories of Jefferson and Carter.) The time when we find ourselves with an insight but haven't yet put it into action is a moment of peril. James Baldwin renders it with characteristic clarity: "People are always in great danger when they know what they should do, and refuse to act on that knowledge." So to the extent that reading this book has sparked any insights for you, you're in risky territory. If you don't do anything about what you've learned, you may be in serious danger.

Now We're Cookin'

Chances are, reading this book hasn't led you to a total revolution in your response to the Question. It probably hasn't given you a new comprehensive vision of flourishing life. All-at-once conversions or enlightenments are fairly rare. Not everyone is the Buddha sitting under the fig tree or Simon dropping his nets to follow Jesus. More often, change starts smaller. Usually, reflection like the kind we've been doing in this book leads us to one or two or maybe a small handful of insights.

These insights come in all shapes and sizes, in varying degrees of power and significance and confidence. Maybe you picked up the nagging hunch that something matters more than you thought it did: developing a virtuous character, responding to personal failure, or living with suffering we can't eliminate, for instance. Maybe you've found some point more attractive and convincing than you would have guessed: Wilde on sorrow, Julian on God's love, or Baldwin on suffering, for example. Maybe you're thoroughly persuaded about a value or principle that had never occurred to you before: the utilitarians' insistence that everyone's happiness counts the same, the idea of an eternal responsibility before God, or the Buddha's suspicion of wealth and power. Or maybe insight has taken a different form altogether.

Whatever shape new insights take, living them out will require (a) integrating them into a more expansive response to the Question and (b) knitting them into the broader fabric of our lives.

An insight about how we ought to live, what we should hope for, the significance of death, what to do when we fail, or anything of the sort is a fragment of a vision of flourishing. It's a thread in a tapestry. It's a line of verse that belongs in a poem. It's an ingredient that goes with a recipe. It's the sort of thing you can't change without affecting everything else.

Each of us is always operating with a de facto response to the Question. We have an implicit vision of flourishing that influences how we approach life and the world. We've always got something on the stove, so to speak, whether we realize we're cooking or not.

When we come to a new insight or revise an old one, it's like we've realized some ingredient is missing or the proportions are out of whack. The problem could be nutritional: all fat, no protein, or something of the sort. Or it could be a matter of fit: you can hardly taste the carrots given how much garlic there is, or the like. Or maybe it's not really a matter of proportions at all. Maybe we suddenly find ourselves with a new ingredient that we're *sure* deserves a place in this meal and we have to figure out how to change the rest to accommodate it.

The point is this: a new insight is almost never like the last piece of a jigsaw puzzle falling into place and making the picture complete. Instead, it's a change in our response to the Question, and being true to the insight means being open to how it revises the whole. There's really no telling how far it will go.

Maybe it's just a tweak: stir in the new insight, add some salt to bring out its flavor, and voilà. Or we might instead realize that this new ingredient calls for a bunch of other new ones to complement it. Maybe there's already an ingredient in the pot that just won't do now that the new insight has priority. It might be time to take out the strainer. In some cases, seriously following the trail of a new insight might lead us to chuck out everything that's in the pot and start over. At the extreme, we might need to scrub the pot clean and really start from scratch. We can't predict in advance. It's all a matter of testing, refining, and seeing where the insights we've found lead.

Our recipes (our visions of life) need to fit together, because, in the end, our dishes (our lives) need to fit together. Ingredients that don't fit make for bad recipes. And bad recipes make for bad dishes.

Part of what makes a dish good is the fit and balance and interaction of its ingredients. So, too, in life. Part of the goodness of the good life is its dynamic integration. That's why we need visions of what matters most that fit together and have internal balance. Integrated visions help us live integrated lives.

Now, the choices we make in our real kitchens are largely matters of taste. Some of us really like spicy foods or cauliflower or dark chocolate, and others don't. No big deal. The situation with our responses to the Question is importantly different. They have to do with the truth of what matters, of how we ought to live, of what it means to flourish or languish, to succeed or fail as human beings. That means the stakes of following where new insights lead are high.

The really scary thing—and at the same time, the truly promising thing—is that it's not just our theoretical, idea-level responses to the Question that are at stake. If visions are for living, then an insight—even a rather unassuming one—has the potential to upend our way of life. Transformations for the better tend to do just that. An insight's implications can reach into every corner of what we think about things and even how we seek to live.

Think about Carter. He started with a conviction about the reality and presence of God. But as Carter followed the thread of that insight, he wound up making changes with significant social and economic consequences, not only for himself but for hundreds of others. Which raises another important point. We're not isolated individuals. We're not the only ones cooking in the kitchen, nor are we the only ones eating the meal. One person living out an insight (or failing to live it out) has ramifications beyond their individual life. So as we reflect on what we've learned, we would do well to ask ourselves: How should I involve others in testing, refining, and ultimately living out these insights?

Finally, a word of caution. Some of us are perfectionists. We want to get our ducks in a row—a tidy, evenly spaced, aesthetically pleasing row—before we set to waddling anywhere. It can be tempting to think that because insights are to visions as ingredients are to recipes, we need to have the whole vision put together and perfectly arranged before we get down to living.

Sorry to say, that simply can't be done. Life is too expansive and messy to build a perfect, all-encompassing, impeccably coherent vision that we can then just put into practice, like building a Lego set from the instructions. It's no good waiting until we have everything figured out before we get down to living because all that time spent waiting and figuring things out is already time spent living. We're living all the time. There's no pause button on life just because we have some thinking to do. It's no use getting the perfect kitchen equipment ready and fussing about every detail of a cooking process that we've never tried. The proof of the pudding, as they say, is in the eating. The proof of the insight, and of the vision, is in the living.

That said, we shouldn't expect a vision of life to provide a set of step-by-step instructions. Even if we had a fully integrated vision of life, it's not like we would have a point-by-point plan we simply needed to execute: do A, then B, then C, then B again, and *presto*— the good life! Visions of flourishing describe ways of life, not scripts. They're frameworks within which we improvise our lives and that render our improvisations meaningful. Ways of life are composed of practices, not steps. And these practices are not simply applications of wisdom we arrived at through pure reflection. Rather, they help make us wise. (Remember Rabbi Elazar's tree: wisdom is often the outgrowth of practices rather than the other way around.)

Don't Forget

We need to act. Fair enough. Even while we're reflecting, we're living. Even we three die-hard intellectuals will happily admit that. But if you're inclined to revel in reflection like we are, maybe this is just the warning you need to hear.

If you're naturally inclined toward action, on the other hand, maybe it's taken quite a bit of patience to get through all the reflection we've been inviting you to do. (Kudos for sticking with it!) Maybe you're itching to get back to "real life." We can't blame you.

But there is a danger when we turn from reflection to the rest of life: that we'll forget what we've worked so hard to discern about the shape of flourishing life. To recall the diving image from chapter 1, the risk is that we'll leave our insights behind in the depths and arrive back at the surface empty-handed. Remember, the surface is the autopilot mode of life. Just because we've discovered, clarified, or affirmed some important insights about life down below doesn't mean our autopilot has actually changed course. If we're not careful, a return to "real life" is simply a return to our default ways of life. We may no longer endorse those ways of life, but our habits are still tuned to them.

Perhaps, for example, our habits still fit with a vision of success that we've come to believe just isn't worth pursuing. If we rush back to "real life," we can fall back into those same habits—and wind up pursuing that same old vision. (Perhaps Jefferson's insights about equality lost just such a battle with his profit-seeking habits.)

This is why so many of the ancient traditions enjoin us to remember. The Potawatomi elders commend their ceremonies as "the way we 'remember to remember.'" In them, you can "start to remember things you didn't know you'd forgotten." The Book of Deuteronomy in the Hebrew Bible instructs the people again and again: *remember*. Remember where you came from. Remember what God has done for you. Especially if and when things start to go well, "remember the LORD your God." Confucius, though called "Master" in the *Analects*, insists of himself, "I transmit rather than innovate; I trust in and love the ancient ways."

We may conclude that it's not God or past traditions that we need to remember. But so long as we believe we've learned something down in the depths, the name of the game for the return journey is to hold on to what we've gained down below so that it can actually change our lives up on the surface.

Unfortunately, just holding on often isn't enough. A new insight or a renovated vision of the good life doesn't just automatically blossom into a changed life. More often than not, change is hard. In the next two chapters, we'll consider (1) the challenge of making changes in our way of life and (2) the challenge of making those changes stick.

Your Turn

1. We're on the way back up to the surface after our deep dive to discern the shape of flourishing life. Let's take stock:
   * What insights do you have into the nature or shape of flourishing life?
   * What insights did you bring with you to this book? What new insights have you had? What new hunches are forming?
   * How have the insights you brought with you been deepened? Challenged? Altered?

2. Which comes more naturally to you: (a) speaking passionately about what you think is right, or (b) acting on what you believe?

3. What practices do you already have in your life that give some of your key values the sort of resilience that Jesus and the rabbis talk about?

4. What insights about the good life have you had for a while that you haven't yet acted on? In what areas of your life are you in danger of growing comfortable in knowing what you should do but refusing to act on that knowledge? (Remember Baldwin's warning.)

FOURTEEN

Change Is Hard

A student came to one of us toward the end of the semester with a problem. She had been rethinking her posture toward her education. Like many of her peers, she had come to Yale profoundly attached to external validation—top scores on exams, glowing comments on her essays, affirmation from peers and mentors alike. Through the course, she had come to see this parade of affirmation in a new light. She had begun to question her obsession with meeting the expectations of others. Eventually, she had decided that she didn't want to live for grades or external validation. She wanted to live for the intrinsic value of the work she was doing and the people she was doing it with. This insight had been life-giving. Conversations with friends were going deeper. Schoolwork felt more meaningful. It was changing her life. And yet . . .

When she got a disappointing grade on a paper for another course, she found herself walking around campus crying. Crying over a grade on a paper. Precisely the sort of thing she thought she didn't—or shouldn't—care so much about anymore. She felt at war with herself. She knew a grade wasn't worthy of being the measure of her life. And yet she was unable to shake this deep feeling of shame and disappointment.

In fact, she said, it was worse than that. On top of the same old shame and disappointment that comes along with attachment to external validation, she now also felt shame and disappointment in herself for having those feelings. They showed that she was still attached to external validation. And she hated it.

Bewildered, the student asked, "When does this change? Why is it like this? I came in ashamed and disappointed whenever I was less than perfect. Now I'm ashamed and disappointed for being so ashamed and disappointed when I know better. Before, I would've just been crushed about the paper. Now I'm crushed about being crushed about the paper. It's a double disappointment. How is this a step toward the good life?"

In short: What gives?

Well, this student was actually trying to do something truly difficult. She was trying to live differently while two crucial things had more or less stayed the same. First, for all her insight, *she* was more or less the same as she was before. Her judgments had changed, but her desires and habits were still the same. Second, the *world* around her was just as it had been before she came to see it differently. She was still under the same pressures—from professors, her family, her peers.

This student had encountered a very real dynamic for any of us who want to change the way we live. We may have come to some meaningful insights. Those insights may even have pointed the way to an entire vision of flourishing life. We have a new understanding of what might be worth living for. So we set out to change our ways. But we ourselves are still very much as we were before having our insights. And the world hasn't been upended either.

This chapter is all about the difficulty of trying to live differently when you and the world are more or less the same as before.

Nudge, Nudge, Nudge

Books by academics don't tend to sell well. But there are times when an academic idea finds its moment. The last decade or so has been that moment for *Nudge: Improving Decisions about Health, Wealth, and Happiness,* by economist Richard H. Thaler and legal scholar Cass R. Sunstein. The book has sold more than two million copies. For many readers, *Nudge* was their first encounter with behavioral economics, a synthesis of psychology and economics that is reshaping the way we think about how people make decisions.

The basic idea is that for centuries economists have been wrong about who and what human beings are. We are not little rational robots who always choose what is best for us. Nor do we even reliably choose what we say we really want. Rather, we are messy, emotive beings who desire all sorts of things—some in our best interests, others not—and choose all sorts of things, often for reasons we ourselves don't understand.

Quite often, we want more than one thing at a time. Even contradictory things. This, Thaler and Sunstein suggest, is how we can think about classic problems of self-control. When we struggle with self-control, what's really going on is that there are two different figures warring within us. There is the farsighted Planner, like Mr. Spock from *Star Trek*—rational, patient, calculating. But there's also a myopic Doer, like TV's bumbling dad Homer Simpson— undisciplined, driven here and there by desire. When you see the donut in the office break room, Homer and Spock pull in two very different directions.

Now, you could say this is simply the battle for virtue. The self-controlled person's Spock simply has Homer pinned. That's not far from how someone like Plato saw it. For him, Spock and Homer are two horses driven by a charioteer. It's like the classic image of the angel and the devil on the shoulders of a cartoon character. Self-control is a matter of resisting the one and following the other. When all goes right, the self sides with Spock against Homer and thereby wins the day. The donut remains uneaten. This is an instance of the "first and best of victories"—the victory over the self.

But that's not always how it goes. The little devil on the shoulder tends to be craftier than the little angel.

And so Thaler and Sunstein recommend a different course of action. Don't try to change yourself. Spock and Homer are never going to stop fighting. There's no final victory for either of them. Don't leave to chance who will end up winning in any given moment. Rather, give Spock the reins in advance. Let him set up the world so that Homer can't help but make the right choice. They give the striking example of a robotic alarm clock. The idea is that the prudent Spock sets the clock at night, when Homer isn't feeling a strong desire to sleep in. Spock picks both the time when the alarm will go off and a cap on how long Homer has to respond. In the morning, when Homer wants just a few more minutes of rest, the clock jumps off the nightstand, making a racket and forcing you to chase it around the bedroom until you're awake enough that even Homer has given up on going back to sleep.

The alarm clock trick is something you could do all by yourself. Some of the most effective "nudges," however, rely on letting Spock enlist other people to help him out. Thaler and Sunstein tell the story of Thaler helping a junior colleague finish his doctoral thesis by setting up a set of incentives for him. The thesis writer gave

Thaler a set of one-hundred-dollar checks to be cashed if ever a draft of a new thesis chapter was not slid under the door by the last day of each month. If a deadline was missed, the money was to be spent on a party to which the thesis writer would not be invited. In the end, no deadlines were missed. A thesis that had gone unfinished far too long was wrapped up in short order. (For what it's worth, one of us put together a scheme very much like this for a friend. The looming threat in that case was a donation to the campaign of a politician the thesis writer despised. The scheme was similarly effective.)

Whether working alone or with others in cahoots, what's being put together is what Thaler and Sunstein call a "choice architecture." The *person* doesn't have to change. Just reconfigure the world around them, and you get the desired behavior.

Thaler and Sunstein go on to describe and propose a wide array of choice architectures that do Spock's work for us, nudging our little Homers without our having to do anything about it. Most of their proposals are in the realms of policy and economics. But the picture they paint of us as human beings and the ways they propose we ought to "manage" ourselves have a self-help strategy built in as well.

Perhaps we think at first about the ways nudges could help us change little things—eat fewer donuts, get up on time, take the stairs more often. But why stop there? Couldn't we set up our world so that we lead our lives well? These sorts of nudges might just be the ticket to changing our whole lives.

The advice to our doubly disappointed Yale student might then be: *Don't try to change yourself. Selves are complex and inevitably conflicted. There will always be a part of you at odds with your own best impulses. Instead, try to find ways to design your world so that it nudges you to behave the way you wish you wanted to.*

Maybe you could start adopting a new way of life with this method. Far be it from us to advise against taking into account empirical insights about human behavior. (Cards on the table: we're not against nudging ourselves in various ways as part of a balanced approach to changing our way of life.) But empirical insights are about what *is*. And when it comes to embarking on a new way of life, we're chasing after a vision of what we believe *ought to be*. And that's at least in part about the exercise of moral agency. At its best, the "nudge" strategy is a way of exercising that agency in advance—setting ourselves up for success.

But notice what happens after the choice architecture is set up. Now we're just rats in the maze. What we do is no longer a function of moral choosing; it's the more or less inevitable result of the choice architecture.

In short, there's a danger that rather than nudging being a mode of exercising your moral agency, you end up treating yourself not as a moral agent but as a research subject in your very own behavioral economics experiment. Even if "lab rat you" succeeds in doing what "choice architect you" believes is right and good—are you really living the life you're after? (Which "you" is *you*?) Or have you just tricked yourself into appearing to do so? If you successfully nudge yourself into spending more time with friends and family, have you succeeded in valuing your prized relationships, or have you exposed yourself as an unrepentant egoist with a remarkable ability to feign relational concern?

But even if we make our peace with this newfangled variation on moral agency, our vision of life may demand changes that just can't be produced with nudges. Repairing a broken relationship. Doing anything genuinely selfless. Changing our career path. It may simply be that there's no way to make the right choice appealing, no matter how many nudges we set up.

Maybe sometimes living well is just difficult. Maybe there's no nudging your way out of it. Maybe being a moral agent means holding yourself accountable to the vision of life you're pursuing. But that brings us right back to our student's problem, because there's still that pesky matter of the unruly self.

Don't Let Your Soul Pull a Fast One

As he later told the story, Abu Hamid al-Ghazali had it made. He was a public intellectual of the first order. Influential at court, he was installed in the sultanate's university in Baghdad. Hundreds of students flocked to his courses. He eventually became the imam of Iraq, the highest-ranking religious figure in the land. The patronage of the powerful aided, no doubt, in his quest for truth—but the prestige itself wasn't exactly a hardship.

Something changed in 1095. Al-Ghazali began to see his interest in status differently. It no longer looked like merely natural ambition or even part and parcel of a desire to be of service to his countrymen. Rather, it was a siren song that pulled him away from what was worthy of his humanity. He began to see his taste for influence as evidence of the weakness of his religious devotion. Even his quest for truth itself was unreliable. "Theory," he confessed, "was easier for me than practice." Easier to talk the talk (or think the thought) than walk the walk.

Unsatisfied with the weakness of his practice and convinced that Baghdad and his distinguished positions there were incompatible with the wholeheartedness he sought, al-Ghazali sold all he had, made arrangements for his family, and left his life of influence.

But taking the man out of Baghdad is easier than taking Baghdad out of the man. Becoming convinced that prestige isn't a worthy aim for one's life isn't the same as no longer desiring it. As our Yale student above could attest, there's something sneaky about such things. We want them even as we want not to want them. Left to our own devices, we're liable to act against what we believe is right. Al-Ghazali's abrupt change of heart may be hard to identify with, but perhaps the problem he was left with is familiar: How can you trust yourself in the process of transformation when the fundamental thing you're trying to change is your *self*?

Al-Ghazali explains the predicament using the metaphor of a savvy businessperson who has a sales associate. That employee, he says, is your soul. There's business to be done, a good profit to be had. But there's also tremendous risk. The associate could just take the money and run. You need to draft a clear contract and then be vigilant in your dealings to make sure you don't get ripped off. After all, this shifty character (which, again, is your soul) may not be trustworthy.

The profit in this metaphor is heavenly joy. Al-Ghazali writes vividly about judgment at the capital-*E* End of all things. He describes a vast set of vaults. In each vault, an hour of one's deeds are stored. At the Judgment, each is opened and one of three things happens: (1) you experience great joy at seeing the splendor of the good works you did during that hour; (2) you experience terror and alarm at seeing an hour spent disobeying God; (3) you experience distress at the emptiness of hours spent sleeping or "absent-minded or preoccupied with something of this world which is merely permissible." Netflix binges might not be *evil*, but in the final accounting, there's something regrettable about hours simply frittered away with no connection to the good we can (and ought to) do.

What you're aiming for is that experience of joy—that's true treasure. But to get that you have to do business with your soul, which, according to al-Ghazali, is an intermediary between you and your body. And that guy is not to be trusted.

So what do you do? Well, you do what any savvy businessperson would do. First, you set the conditions for the relationship. You write the contract and HR manual, so to speak. What are your expectations for this employee? What are you looking for from your soul? Al-Ghazali suggests that we get quite concrete about this. We're looking for our souls to keep our bodies in line—particularly these seven parts: the eye, ear, tongue, stomach, genitals, hands, and feet. The tongue receives special attention, "because it is loose by nature." Created for "invoking [God], remembrance, reiterating knowledge, teaching, guiding the servants of God to His path, reconciling people and other benefits," the tongue can be (and very often is) used for just the opposite. On day one, you have to set the conditions for your soul "that it move the tongue during the day only in invocation [of God]."

Setting expectations is just the first step. Next comes the most important part: vigilance. You gotta make sure your soul keeps up its end of the bargain. Now, that could sound exhausting. At some point, your mind is going to get tired or distracted. Nonstop self-surveillance is draining. But that's not what al-Ghazali means by vigilance. "Know that the reality of vigilance is to be aware of the one watching and to turn attention to him. . . . In other words, vigilance is a state of the heart that results from a kind of knowledge. This state causes the action in the heart and the limbs." Vigilance isn't something you muster up on your own. Vigilance is a natural result of coming to profound knowledge of the fact that God is always watching, able to see not just deeds but the motivations that drive them. Our hearts, al-Ghazali insists, are more visible to God than our faces are to others.

The goal is to impress the knowledge of God's watchful eye upon our minds, and therefore on our hearts, so that our souls can be vigilant. One route to this goal involves overwhelming mystical experiences. When the heart is "crushed by awe . . . it has no room truly to consider another." In such moments, vigilance is absolute and guaranteed.

But flourishing life is not one extended mystical encounter with God. We need to be able to *do* things in the world—and we can't do anything while crushed by awe. So there is a second level at which we can have the sort of knowledge al-Ghazali says is at the heart of vigilance. We can have a healthy "shame" before God that pervades our awareness but does not crowd out other things. This posture drives us to consider before we act: What are our intentions? Are they godly? If not, that's a telltale sign our soul is trying to rip us off and deny us that heavenly reward. If our intentions are godly, perhaps we ought to act. Al-Ghazali emphasizes the importance of this *pause* before action. Each action, after all, is a deal our associate makes on our behalf. And we don't know just how trustworthy our soul happens to be today.

There's much more to al-Ghazali's conception of vigilance. There's vigilance as you act. And after you've acted. There are performance reviews and consequences for noncompliance when your soul gets out of line. But the core of it is this healthy self-suspicion. The pause before we act. All in awareness of the watchful eye of the God who sees our hearts more clearly that we see one another's faces.

We could imagine al-Ghazali's advice to our student: *These involuntary tears over that grade on that paper? They're teaching you a valuable lesson: don't trust yourself. Your soul is fickle. It's not trustworthy. If you want to change so you can live by what is good and right, view yourself as living under God's watchful eye. And take care that you don't fall back into chasing after that which isn't worthy of your pursuit.*

Be Thyself

"To live is the rarest thing in the world. Most people exist, that is all."

With typical flair, Oscar Wilde gets right to the point about how difficult it is to find our way into flourishing life. Not because flourishing is especially complicated. In fact, it's simple. As he sees it, all we really want is *life*. "What man has sought for is, indeed, neither pain nor pleasure, but simply Life. Man has sought to live intensely, fully, perfectly."

For Wilde, living fully has entirely to do with living as an individual. The ancient world, he says, had a mantra: "Know thyself." The "new world"—our world—will have a different slogan: "Be thyself." He could only have been more on the nose had he literally coined "You do you." But "Be thyself" is more apt. "You do you" can be said with a casual or dismissive shrug. "Be thyself" is weighty. It expresses the ethic of authenticity we talked about in chapter 6.

But being yourself is not as easy as it sounds. Even if we buy this ideal of the good life—even if we deeply desire "to live intensely, fully, perfectly" as individuals—more often than we'd care to admit, we just can't pull it off.

How do you learn to be yourself?

To begin with, Wilde says, forget self-suspicion. You naturally want and know how to be you. It's the world and its suspicions that knock you off track. The government wants to hold you under its sway. Society wants to tell you you're living your life wrong. The crowd wants you to fit into one of its boxes. Pushed and pulled by these pressures, you get yourself completely wrong. You give in. You sell out. You conform.

The world *should* be otherwise. Wilde has some ideas about how that ought to go. But it's far from an easy fix. In the meantime, there is a role for suspicion. But it's quite the opposite of self-suspicion. We should be suspicious of the world. We should be suspicious of others' suspicions of us. We should be wary of the ways others' suspicions creep into the words we use as we think about ourselves. For example, Wilde says, "a man is called affected, nowadays, if he dresses as he likes to dress. But in doing that he is acting in a perfectly natural manner. Affectation, in such matters, consists in dressing according to the views of one's neighbour, whose views, as they are the views of the majority, will probably be extremely stupid." To dress as one likes is natural; dressing like everyone else is artificial.

Be that as it may, society has a way of getting its hooks in you. It critiques "affectation," "flamboyance," or "eccentricity," and you start to worry that you might be eccentric, flamboyant, putting on airs. The same goes for selfishness. To live as one wishes to live is not selfish, Wilde insists. Asking others to live a certain way is selfish. But it can be hard to swim against the artificial current—even if doing so actually takes you down nature's stream.

Wilde thinks the best venue for doing this laborious nonwork is *art*. "Art is the most intense mode of Individualism that the world has known." Art is how we express our truest selves. It is "the soul made incarnate."

True, we are not all playwrights of Wilde's caliber. But ideally, for Wilde, each of us will find our own mode of artistic self-expression. The medium doesn't matter. One is a poet, another a woodworker. The aims of both are the same: to make something beautiful. The needs or desires of others—especially the public—don't hold sway over them. A would-be artist who aims to supply what their audience wants reduces themselves to a tradesperson. That is the line between art and commerce.

But if we can resist the pull toward commerce and stick to expression itself, our art serves its purpose: we unveil our true selves. The goal of art is the realization of the authentic self. Ultimately, the work of art we uncover in our medium is *us*.

But that's only if we can cast off the world's demands for conformity and commerce.

If al-Ghazali emphasizes the danger inherent in trying to live differently while we remain unchanged, Wilde has us cast our skeptical eye on the world. For Wilde, the primary threat to realizing our vision of flourishing life is not our self, but rather a world that does not celebrate true individuality. A world that only knows how to value what can be sold. As we awaken to Wilde's vision of flourishing—the actualization of our most authentic selves—our selves are in fact our most reliable guides. At least so long as we can dig them out from under heavy layers of societal expectation.

Wilde's advice to our student, therefore, would be quite different from al-Ghazali's: *You are not your problem. You are finding in your work and in your life the latent possibility of becoming an individual in the truest sense of the word. Your problem is the weight of the world's expectations. That "double disappointment" you feel? That's the true individual within you waking up to the tragedy of living for some-body else's dream. They'll never stop making demands of you. But you can never give in. To live as an individual is to make a promise to disap-point the world rather than disappoint yourself.*

Bearing Fruit

There is a story in the Christian Bible about a rich young man who was searching for flourishing life—or, as he calls it, "eternal life." The man runs up to Jesus and asks him, "What must I do to inherit eternal life?" Jesus answers: You know the rules; follow them. The young man protests. He *has* followed the rules, but it still seems like there's something missing. Jesus lights up. He knows what the young man lacks: he has too much. "You lack one thing; go, sell what you own, and give the money to the poor, and you will have treasure in heaven; then come, follow me." The young man's face falls. "When he heard this, he was shocked and went away griev-ing, for he had many possessions."

This man wouldn't be sad if he didn't think Jesus was right. He wouldn't grieve if he weren't convinced that Jesus had what he was after—and that giving away his possessions was necessary for get-ting it. If he had rejected either premise, he could simply have scoffed and dismissed Jesus's teaching. But he didn't. He walked away sad because he still couldn't imagine selling all he had, even though he was convinced that Jesus had offered the path to what he was after. From the point of view of the story, the rich man *has* insight. He walks away grieving because he can't act on his convic-tion. This is the second-order sadness of our student.

On this Christian account, we can be right about the good

life—we can see it clearly, grasp its contours, and have it offered to us—but still be unwilling to pursue it. Something in us can still resist. And in the case of the rich young man, Jesus can see what it is: his attachment to his wealth.

That attachment to wealth, however, isn't just a feature of this man's individual life. One of Jesus's important insights was that wealth inherently has this distorting power to it. Like the Ring of Power in Tolkien's Middle-earth, it might look inert, but wealth is an active agent. Wealth recruits us even while we believe we own it. It's more like a rival deity than a passive resource to use as we deem fit. "You cannot serve God and wealth," Jesus warns.

Even Jesus's disciples are not immune to wealth's distorting powers. After the young man walks away sad, Jesus warns them, "How hard it will be for those who have wealth to enter the king-dom of God!" Not having fully taken to heart what Jesus taught about the distorting power of wealth, the disciples are perplexed. Jesus doubles down: "Children, how hard it is to enter the kingdom of God!" Jesus makes it clear this isn't *just* about the distorting power of wealth. But wealth is more likely a hindrance than a help. "It is easier for a camel to go through the eye of a needle than for someone who is rich to enter the kingdom of God." The disciples are astounded. "Then who can be saved?" they wonder. Jesus an-swers, "For mortals it is impossible, but not for God; for God all things are possible."

Entering into a new way of life is hard. Entering into truly flourishing life is *really* hard. How hard? Impossible, Jesus says—for humans, at least. It would take divine intervention for us to live the sort of lives truly worthy of our shared humanity.

But Jesus believes that sort of divine intervention is available. The Christian claim is that Jesus *is* divine intervention. The claim is that Jesus has come so that human beings could live toward flourishing life despite the stubbornness of our hearts and our world. In Jesus's presence, individuals and the world itself are being remade.

In the end, the young man may have been off track from the very start. "Good teacher," he says, "what must I *do* to inherit eternal life?" Jesus subtly resists the premise of the man's question by resisting his use of the word *good*. "Why do you call me good? No one is good but God alone." No human being is good. So no human can hope to lay claim to flourishing life like they earned it. There's no job for which the wages are flourishing life. Doing is part of flourishing life, not the ticket in.

All that needs to be done is to admit defeat. Sell what you have. Then come and follow Jesus. Let him do what you cannot.

When it comes down to it, from a Christian point of view, our Yale student simply doesn't have what it takes to live differently. Jesus's advice might be: *Let your sadness be a wake-up call. Even your best intentions to live a worthy life aren't enough. Your stubborn heart is buttressed by a world that in many ways is working against your flourishing. Your best move is to give up your best hopes of making this work on your own and instead come follow me.*

Get Started

Changing a way of life is always difficult. Trying to live differently while we ourselves remain largely as we were is particularly difficult. Maybe, as al-Ghazali says, we just have to admit that as we begin to change, we can't trust ourselves. We need to remain vigilant, mindful that we live under the watchful eye of God.

Trying to live differently while our *circumstances* remain largely as they were is also no easy task. Perhaps, as Wilde says, we have to work hard to resist the world and its pressures. Or maybe Thaler and Sunstein are right: we can control just enough of our circumstances to nudge ourselves in the right direction.

Or maybe, as Jesus says, the whole thing is beyond us. We just don't have what it takes to hold our old instincts in check *and* resist a world that only fans the flames of desires we wish would go out. Perhaps we need God's help if we're going to start living differently. If so, perhaps our efforts are better directed toward seeking God's help.

Because change is hard, we'll need to make a bet on how best to get started. Otherwise, our attempts to live out new insights and live into changed visions of flourishing life are liable to fizzle out before they really get going at all.

Hard as it is to get started, it is equally hard to keep going. That's our challenge for the next chapter: once we start moving, how do we keep moving—and how do we stay on track?

Your Turn

1. How do you want to change your way of life in response to a new or deepened insight about flourishing life?

2. What in you is likely to resist that change?
   * What entrenched desires pull you in the opposite direction of your insight?
   * Which ingrained habits might hold you back from realizing the change you're looking for?

3. What about the world is likely to resist that change?
   * Have some features of the world squelched the potential for significant change in your life in the past?
   * What systems and structures are you personally involved in and connected to that don't accord with your vision of flourishing life?

4. What strategy are you going to adopt to try to overcome the resistance you face from your world and from yourself? Why do you have hope that this strategy will succeed?

FIFTEEN

Making It Stick

Bill W. knew how to quit drinking. He had quit many times. He'd quit quietly, and he'd quit loudly. He'd quit reluctantly, and he'd quit enthusiastically. The trouble was, he was just as good at starting again as he was at quitting—maybe even better. He could quit in the morning and start again by the evening. Sometimes he would stay sober a bit longer. But never for the long haul. The cycles of alcoholism went on for years, tearing his life apart. A successful stockbroker in the 1920s, he lost his job and his fortune. He writes about one morning after a particularly long night:

> I woke up. This had to be stopped. I saw I could not take so much as one drink. I was through forever. Before then, I had written lots of sweet promises, but my wife happily observed that this time I meant business. And so I did.

Problem solved, right?
Not so fast:

> Shortly afterward I came home drunk. There had been no fight. Where had been my high resolve? I simply

didn't know. It hadn't even come to mind. Someone
had pushed a drink my way, and I had taken it.

The cycles of attempts and failures went on for another two
years. He was in and out of the hospital. Finally, in the middle of a
bender, he got a call from an old school friend, who invited himself
over for dinner. The friend, it turns out, had found (Christian)
religion—and a way out of his own alcoholism. He wondered if
Bill wanted out too.

The God talk was a bit of a stumbling block. The friend suggested, "Why don't you choose your own conception of God?" A
way forward began to open up. "It was only a matter of being willing to believe in a Power greater than myself. Nothing more was
required of me to make my beginning," Bill later wrote. He and his
friend made a list of relationships Bill had broken with his drinking. Bill took steps to repair them.

The transformation was so complete that he ended up calling a
doctor friend of his to ask if he had lost his mind. The doctor shook
his head and said, "Something has happened to you I don't understand. But you had better hang on to it."

Beginning a new way of life is difficult. Persisting in a new way
of life can be even harder. Bill W. did hang on. He never had another drink. And along the way, he built Alcoholics Anonymous, a
grassroots organization that has helped millions find and maintain
sobriety.

Among the keys, AA members will tell you, are the twelve
steps. The beginnings of them are right there in Bill W.'s story. He
admitted he was powerless over alcohol (step 1). He came to believe
that a Power greater than himself could restore him to sanity (step

2). He made a searching and fearless moral inventory of himself, made a list of people he had harmed, and made amends (steps 4, 8, and 9).

For those who work the program, these steps aren't just tips and tricks but a way of life. They aren't a one-and-done process either. That whole personal inventory and amends business is ongoing. Step 10 is to continue to take personal inventory and promptly admit it when you're wrong. Same with spiritual awakening. It isn't just a onetime thing either. Step 11 involves prayer and meditation, "to improve our conscious contact with God as we understood Him, praying only for knowledge of His will for us and the power to carry that out." And that bit about helping others along the way wasn't just for Bill W. Nor was it incidental to his ability to keep going. "I soon found that when all other measures failed, work with another alcoholic would save the day."

The steps keep traction in members' lives through regular meetings. Time set aside in the flow of life to return to and work the steps together. Just one alcoholic helping another. And according to a 2020 review study, this peer-to-peer model still matches or beats the best professional interventions in terms of effectiveness.

If we're going to live into visions of life that we take to be worthy of our shared humanity, we'll need strategies not just to get us started, but to help us stay on track for the long haul.

We can think about it as something like an athlete's practice. A soccer player might lift weights or do some cardio (say, triceps pullovers to build strength for throw-ins or agility drills so they can change directions more sharply). They'll also do things in practice that ramp up to look more and more like concentrated versions of what they'll actually do in a game. An agility drill done at first without the ball is now done while dribbling the ball. The triceps pullover turns into actual throw-ins with a weighted medicine ball. Three teammates will practice passing the ball to one another in a small space while a fourth tries to steal it. Perhaps at the end of a practice session the team splits into two full teams of eleven that scrimmage against one another—playing the game more or less exactly as they will on game day. At that point, practice looks the same as playing.

Most traditions commend practices very much like this: concentrated versions of the sort of attention and activity they want us to cultivate for real life. In some cases, these practices become indistinguishable from the way of life itself. The means to sustain a way of life simply *is* the way of life itself.

Some practices build such fundamental skills that they're transferable from one vision of life to another, like how certain forms of strength training might be transferable from one sport to another.

But many are not. Many practices are tuned for the particular vision of life they're commending. In sports, training that will help you run a marathon would wreck your performance in Olympic weight lifting, and vice versa. The two sports want something different from your body. Interference is a real possibility. If we want to learn from across traditions (an admirable desire!), we'll have to keep this in mind.

So how do we stay in a way of life for the long haul? By committing ourselves to practices that are concentrated essences of the way of life we're trying to cultivate. They're more than tips and tricks. They're opportunities to train our attention on what we want to concentrate on. They're opportunities to train our bodies and minds to do what we want to do. They're microcosms of the very way of life we take to be worthy of our shared humanity.

One Cure to Rule Them All

Buddhist practices, the Dalai Lama says, are like a pharmacy full of powerful medicines. You can shop by "symptom." At different times, he notes, we suffer from different counterproductive emotions. Whatever the emotion, chances are there's a practice for that: this meditative practice to counteract envy, that one to counteract hatred, and so on.

But underlying each of the illnesses is a single cause: "ignorance of the true nature of things." Therefore, "practices that teach us how to overcome that ignorance undercut all afflictive emotions. The antidote to ignorance addresses all troubles. This is the extraordinary gift of insight." This insight into the true nature of things is what gets us started on the Buddhist way of life. Returning to it and deepening it in meditation is what keeps us going for the long haul.

What is the true nature of things? That they do not exist in and of themselves. Everything that we perceive as people and things around us are mere "dependent arisings"—temporary and local features of a single cosmic process. (This is the Dalai Lama's language for the idea of non-self, which we've encountered a few times, in chapters 8, 11, and 12. A dependent arising is very much like what Thich Nhat Hanh calls a "manifestation.") Each thing is boundaryless and, in actuality, indistinguishable from the whole. There is an "emptiness" where we might otherwise take inherent existence to be.

Think of the cosmos as an ocean roiling with waves. You may know yourself as the peak of one particular wave, I another. You may even look across the way and see the peak of the adjacent wave which I take myself to be. But at bottom, it's all one ocean. Consciousness creates the illusion that "I" am this particular self-aware wave and "you" are that one. But all that exists is the expanse of water. We are just temporary structures riding this particular piece of the whole, subject to the laws of cause and effect.

We do not usually live with this true nature of things in mind. Left to our own devices, we live in ignorance of how things really are. We treat objects and people and emotions and even insights themselves as if they had inherent existence. We treat them as though they existed independently. Worst of all, we relate to ourselves as if *we* existed independently, as if we existed by and for ourselves. We are beset by the persistent illusions of "I" and "my"— the persistent illusion that we ourselves have inherent existence.

This tenacious ignorance is what traps us in the suffering-filled cycle of death and rebirth (*samsara*; see chapter 8). Liberation from cyclic existence comes when we realize that we, too, are dependent arisings, subject to the laws of cause and effect and part of a single cosmic unfolding process.

Now, just being told about what Buddhists like the Dalai Lama and Thich Nhat Hanh take to be the true nature of things is not the same as achieving what they call insight. Hearing it isn't the same thing as getting it. And even having the insight at one time doesn't guarantee that we'll hold on to it all the time. Our illusions of independent existence are persistent. They tend to crop back up even when we've cut them down.

This is where meditation comes in.

Tibetan Buddhist meditation is the practice of dispelling the persistent illusions that cloud our vision. These illusions give rise to afflictive emotions and counterproductive behavior. They threaten to knock us off course.

The heart of meditation is disciplined attentiveness to the world around us and to our own perception of it. The Dalai Lama says, "All counterproductive emotions are based on and depend upon ignorance of the true nature of persons and things. . . . If we undermine the ignorance that misconceives the nature of ourselves, others, and all things, all destructive emotions are undermined."

With enough practice (and meditation is a lifelong pursuit for those who take it up), a new baseline posture toward the world emerges. It sees all phenomena as mere dependent arisings. Like the ancient Buddhist nun Subha and her monastic sisters, we are no longer even tempted by fleeting pleasures. Subha answers temptation not with steely resolve and heroic willpower, but with matter-of-fact indifference: "What you take as pleasures are not for me." This cultivated nonattachment to the world is a boon for resisting temptations. But that's not all it's good for. It also frees the practitioner to engage others in new, less destructive ways.

Most important, the Dalai Lama says, it cultivates compassion. As we loosen our attachment to ourselves and to cyclic existence, we increase our compassion for the other consciousnesses riding along this single cosmic process. We see that they're also burdened with the persistent illusion of "I" and "my." They, too, struggle with afflictive emotions and counterproductive behaviors. When we really, consistently see the illusion for what it is, we're able to have compassion for all who suffer under its spell: ourselves, those we love, those to whom we are indifferent, and even our enemies.

It takes lifelong meditative practice to allow this insight to do its work. The idea is to return again and again to the core insight, to settle our attention on it and see it clearly. The goal is that after much time in meditation, the insight stays with us even when we're not meditating. The Dalai Lama offers an exhortation and a promise: "Be willing to familiarize yourself with this attitude, taking on yourself the burden of protecting all sentient beings from all problems; do it repeatedly and with regular analysis. Your empathy will be so great that it will suffuse your entire being. Without any desire for reward, your aim will be solely the development of others, never disheartened or discouraged in your task."

The Examen

Iñigo López de Loyola (1491–1556), later known as St. Ignatius of Loyola, hardly seemed like the kind of guy who would found a religious order. For the first part of his life, he was quite at home in the world of swords and chivalry that inspired *Don Quixote*. His confidant, Juan Polanco, readily conceded that early in his life, Ignatius was "especially out of order in regard to gambling, matters pertaining to women, and duelling." In his early days, St. Ignatius was no saint.

He first tried his hand at a military career. It lasted for exactly one battle. After a French cannonball shattered his right leg, Ignatius suffered two painful surgeries that nearly killed him. The second one aimed to recover his debonair good looks—but to no avail.

Religious awakening came during his extended recovery. It was not always clear he would survive. While barely holding on to life, he was letting go of his vision of life. He read spiritual works and had an encounter with the Virgin Mary. From then on, his life would aim at "a different nobility, a different service, a different Lord." His goal was simple but all-encompassing: to help souls.

In this new way of life, Ignatius's considerable skills with a sword were no longer useful. The skill he needed now, he thought, was theology. That required studies he had previously neglected. He boned up on Latin, a thirtysomething studying alongside schoolchildren. Almost a decade later, he became a student of theology in Paris.

Ignatius was almost forty years old, near the average life span for a sixteenth-century European, and his life was about to begin. It was in Paris that he met the friends who would form the core of the Society of Jesus, or the Jesuits. The Jesuits became a powerful force in the world. Within a generation, they were working on five continents and had launched the world's largest education system.

What drove this explosive growth, Jesuits argue, was their commitment to *obedience* to the divine will. As the Jesuit author Jules J. Toner explains, "Obedience issues in an uninterrupted life of heroic deeds and heroic virtues. For one who truly lives under obedience is fully disposed to execute instantly and unhesitatingly whatever is enjoined him, no matter to him whether it be very hard to do." This is what prepared them to take extraordinary risks: traveling to distant continents, serving in foreign courts that had never interacted with Europeans, sometimes at the cost of their lives.

As we've observed in our previous discussion of al-Ghazali, obedience to the divine will is no easy matter, even for those who are striving toward it. Ignatius had two tools to help his compatriots become and remain the sort of people who could live "an uninterrupted life of heroic deeds and heroic virtues." Both are described in his primary work, the *Spiritual Exercises*.

The first tool is a retreat. Traditionally, initiation into the Jesuit order comes by undertaking the exercises through a thirty-day retreat. During this time, you withdraw from the rest of your normal life and commit to silence. You eat only simple meals.

Many of the exercises you go through during the retreat are contemplations, imaginative meditations on Christian scripture or on some scene from life or the tradition's "Big Story." If reading, for example, a story from the life of Jesus, you don't just read, but rather place yourself within the scene. You live it out in your imagination.

In a particularly important contemplation near the end of the *Exercises*, the "Contemplation to Reach Love," Ignatius invites those on retreat to an encounter with God the Giver of good gifts. He writes, "I consider how God dwells in His creatures: in the elements, giving them being; in plants, giving them life; in animals, sensation; in humans, understanding. And so He dwells in me and gives me existence, life, sensation, understanding." Contemplative exercises like this build in the Jesuit a profound love for the vision of life they are committed to pursuing.

The next question is how to sustain this love. As lovely as thirty-day retreats are, they end. And Ignatius was in this for the long haul. What's more, Ignatius and his friends didn't live in a monastery. "Uninterrupted [lives] of heroic deeds" don't happen behind the walls of a cloister or in the secluded spaces of a spiritual retreat. If the "heroic virtues" cultivated through the exercises were to become "uninterrupted [lives] of heroic deeds," something different was needed.

Enter the *examen*, Ignatius's second tool. (That's the original Spanish. English speakers preserve the spelling but generally pronounce it like the English word *examine*.) The examen is a travel-size Ignatian retreat. Through it, practitioners cultivate and maintain an awareness of God's presence and activity in their midst.

The examen is actually part of the full, thirty-day Ignatian exercises. It is one of the first prayers introduced. But it's meant to go with you from the retreat to the road. It's supposed to be part of your daily routine after completing the exercises. As the examen has passed from one generation to the next and made its way around the world, its particulars (mostly, the order of the parts) have changed a bit. But the five fundamental parts remain the same. The outline is largely as follows:

1. Gratitude: Think through your day and give thanks for what you are grateful for.

2. Review: Remember each hour of the day, noticing where you felt God's presence and where you either entered into or turned away from God's activity in your midst.

3. Sorrow: Recall actions for which you are sorry.

4. Forgiveness: Ask for God's forgiveness. Make plans to reconcile with anyone you have hurt and to forgive and reconcile with those who have hurt you.

5. Grace: Ask for God's grace for the coming day and an increased ability to recognize God's presence.

Many other Catholics and Christians of all stripes have made use of the examen over the centuries. Dorothy Day (1897–1980), social activist and cofounder of the Catholic Worker movement, commends the practice in her diaries: "St. Ignatius says never omit 2 examens, 15 minutes each." That's just right for a doer like Day, or the Jesuits Ignatius himself had organized.

The goal of the examen is to learn to notice God's presence in the midst of the comings and goings of regular, busy life. When called to mind in the examen, American Jesuit James Martin argues, "each moment offers a window into where God has been in your day." Some moments, we are speaking and acting in line with what God was up to. In other moments, our path is askew from God's presence and activity. The examen makes space to acknowledge both realities in the particularities of our lives. And it does so regularly. It builds a rhythm. A habit. And hopefully a way of relating to your life not just when you're "examen-ing" it, but as you're living it.

Over time, awareness of the active love of God at work throughout the world becomes a sustained reality. Hour by hour, minute by minute, the Jesuit is supposed to live out of a foundational awareness of God's loving work in their midst. The examen is daily concentrated practice at cultivating this awareness, renewing it when it grows faint, and sustaining it over the course of a life.

Just Wait till I'm Seventy

Yan Hui, Confucius's beloved and diligent student, once asked him about goodness—or *ren* in classical Chinese. (Others translate this term as "humaneness" or "humanity.") *Ren* is perhaps the closest thing we have to Confucius's definition of what it means to lead life well. It is the heart of the way of life Confucius teaches. Edward Slingerland capitalizes his translation of the term ("Goodness") to highlight how important *ren* is for Confucian thought. So when Yan Hui asked about goodness, he was asking a very big question.

Goodness in this holistic sense is about attuning our understanding and action. It is about (a) coming to understand ourselves in relationship to those around us, and (b) acting in accordance with the obligations and responsibilities that attach to those relationships. As attunement grows in one area, it grows in all the others. If we're drawn to Confucius's way of life, we are after *ren*.

That's what Yan Hui was after. He was smart and humble enough to realize that he didn't know how to get there. Knowing the destination is only so helpful if you don't know the way. So he asked. How do we cultivate this alignment of the self? How do we get to Goodness?

Confucius answered, "Restraining yourself and returning to the rites constitutes Goodness. If for one day you managed to restrain yourself and return to the rites, in this way you could lead the entire world back to Goodness."

The precise meaning of the phrase "restraining yourself and returning to the rites" (*ke ji fu li* in Chinese) is obscure and argued over to this day. It doesn't seem to have been clear to Yan Hui either. He was puzzled and politely asked for clarification. "May I inquire as to the specifics?"

Confucius elaborated: "Do not look unless it is in accordance with ritual; do not listen unless it is in accordance with ritual; do not speak unless it is in accordance with ritual; do not move unless it is in accordance with ritual." Yan Hui responds, with characteristic modesty, "Although I am not quick to understand, I ask permission to devote myself to this teaching."

How do we restrain the self? By devoting ourselves to ritual.

Remember, the goal is (a) to cultivate an awareness of our relationships to those around us, and (b) to act in accordance with the obligations and responsibilities that attach to those relationships. What does that have to do with ritual? Well, individual rites provide scripts for how to fulfill our responsibilities in a particular situation. Like the banks of a river, they channel our attention and our energies.

But for Confucius, ritual is much more expansive than just these individual rites. Ritual includes a proper way of doing *everything*. Ritual tells you the proper pairings of inner and outer garments for social occasions, the proper way to greet people of various social standings, what songs to sing and when to sing them, and more. Confucius cared *a lot* about the details. He was a student of the rites. Arriving in a new place, he would ask about every detail of the rites as practiced in that place in ancient times. He would advocate for their preservation and restoration.

It is tempting to see Confucius in this mode as a strict disciplinarian. There are rules, he seems to be saying. Follow them. Try and try again. Live the good life by living the good life. Fake it till you make it.

But Confucius isn't asking us to commit ourselves to the rites like we might take up a New Year's resolution we're doomed to drop. Often, such resolutions fail because no matter how much time we put into whatever "good" behavior we're trying to adopt, we, for whatever reason, never start wanting to do it. But doing the rites, Confucius believes, makes us the sort of people who want to do the rites. Which is perhaps what makes a New Year's resolution succeed if and when it ever does. (Think about the stereotypically insufferable exercise enthusiast. Exercising has made them a person who loves to exercise—and, often enough, to talk about it.) The rites are like a CrossFit that gets *everyone* hooked. They are habits of life so in tune with what it is to be human that the deeper we live in them, the more we desire to live in them. And the result is that eventually, we do whatever we want—and what we want is actually worth doing.

Practicing the particular scripts of these rituals—just as they should be—is a mechanism of tuning your inner self to the Way. Confucius recognized the way the ritual of the everyday forms us. Put your heart, mind, and body through these paces long enough and your whole self will be tuned. Where there are no scripts, you will naturally improvise life according to the Way.

This is precisely the story Confucius tells about his own life, his own journey in the Way over the course of decades: "At fifteen, I set my mind upon learning. At thirty, I took my stand. At forty, I had no doubts. At fifty, I knew the will of Heaven. At sixty, my ear was attuned. At seventy, I follow all the desires of my heart without breaking any rule."

We can line this up with our diving metaphor from chapter 1. Years fifteen through forty describe Confucius's dive into the depths. Age fifty seems to recount an experience of insight at the "bottom" of the dive: knowing "the will of Heaven." Age sixty names part of the return journey, growing in receptivity to the insight he had found. Age seventy encapsulates the ultimate goal: a life where his desire is so attuned to his insight that he lived in perfect harmony with his insight simply by doing whatever he desired. There's an attunement of the self with what Confucius takes to be worth living for and living within: the Way, the Dao, the will of Heaven.

This is why Confucius affirms, "One who knows it is not the equal of one who loves it, and one who loves it is not the equal of one who takes joy in it." Knowing is only half the battle. Our lives inevitably follow what we *love* and what brings us *joy*. If we can fall in love with the good we have found, and if we can tune our inner self to *rejoice* in the Way to flourishing life, we will find ourselves naturally drawn to the good we want to do and be. And that sort of alignment can sustain us for decades.

Stick(y) Together

We need practices to pursue a way of life for the long haul. And those practices have to correspond to the vision of life we're trying to pursue. The journey to the goal is part of the goal. The "thickest" practices will draw on our sense of the really big picture, like how the Dalai Lama's meditation flows from the teaching of no-self, Ignatius's examen depends on belief in the love of God, and Confucian ritual is inseparable from the Confucian Way. In the end, these practices are much more than mere tips or tricks. They are key components of entire ways of life. They are important aspects of flourishing life, or at least life on its way to flourishing.

For many, community is precisely about cultivating ways of life that match practices with values. Now, no community is so homogenous that everyone in it shares the exact same vision of flourishing. We might think about a religious tradition like Christianity, Buddhism, or Islam as commending a unified vision of flourishing life. But from another point of view, each tradition is as much like a sprawling argument over the nature of flourishing life as it is a bastion of consensus. What many individual communities of faith share in common most of all is a set of *practices* that draw on and reinforce the broad strokes of a shared vision of flourishing and their sense of the really big picture.

We can think again of AA meetings and the broader practices of mutual aid that they facilitate. And as much as the Dalai Lama focuses on individual meditative practices, generations of Buddhists have found that over the long haul, one needs the *sangha*, a community of Buddhist practitioners. So also with the Jesuits. Initiation may begin with one person making a retreat. But even this happens in dialogue with a spiritual director, and the life it initiates is one of shared mission and shared practices, like the examen. For Confucius, the connection to community is fundamental. The rituals are essentially communal. They're the thread out of which a communal fabric is woven.

In these various ways, community often provides a context for us to gain access to the best tools a given tradition has to offer. But community is more than simply each tradition's fully stocked toolbox. It doesn't just offer the customized means for a boutique set of ends. Rather, in the formation of particular types of community, means and ends come together. For many, the community organized around a vision is itself an important part of flourishing life. For some, the life of the community simply *is* flourishing life.

We see this in compelling ways in Robin Wall Kimmerer's account of the communal life of her Indigenous nation, the Potawatomi. Kimmerer tells of the long and winding relationship between her people and the various types of *pigan*. While it's the root of the English word *pecan*, *pigan* was used to name the many nuts the Potawatomi encountered on the arduous journey from their original homelands around Lake Michigan to Kansas to Oklahoma. Marched at gunpoint by American soldiers, the Potawatomi lost the hickories, black walnuts, and butternuts of their homeland and discovered pecans.

Nut trees, Kimmerer notes, don't yield a crop every year. Rather, they produce at unpredictable but precisely coordinated intervals: entire groves—indeed, entire species across hundreds of miles—will produce no nuts for years and then suddenly drop an extraordinary yield all in one season. Modern science has yet to fully explain how the trees coordinate this behavior, though it may have something to do with the mycorrhizal (fungal) networks that connect trees to one another belowground. (Trees are amazing.)

However they pull it off, this coordination is integral to the trees' survival. A single tree producing nuts on its own would have its entire crop completely eaten up by the surrounding animal life. No seeds would be left to sprout and grow into new trees. But a whole species in coordination can offer those animals a *more*-than-you-can-eat buffet, leaving enough nuts on the ground to grow new trees. If the trees offered that bounty every year, the animal populations would explode until there were enough of them to eat all the nuts. Hence the unpredictable cycles. There aren't enough boom years in a row for animal populations to swell. Everybody stays at a sustainable level.

In Kimmerer's eyes, this is more than a lesson in systems biology. It yields an insight about the nature of flourishing life itself. Acting as a community, the trees thrive. No lone tree could achieve this on its own. At the same time, pecans produce bumper crops, a joyful delight for human communities and other animal species who come across them. Others thrive too. Pecans' flourishing and humans' and animals' flourishing go together. "All flourishing is mutual." This is the lesson of the pecans.

It's a lesson Kimmerer believes lies at the heart of her nation, recognizable in her description of the Potawatomi Gathering of Nations:

> From the hilltop you can still see pecan groves along the river. At night we dance on the old powwow grounds. The ancient ceremonies greet the sunrise. The smell of corn soup and the sound of drums fill the air as the nine bands of Potawatomi, scattered across the

country by this history of removal, come together again for a few days each year in a search for belonging. . . . There is something like a mycorrhizal network that unites us, an unseen connection of history and family and responsibility to both our ancestors and our children. As a nation, we are beginning to follow the guidance of our elders the pecans by standing together for the benefit of all.

The dances, ceremonies, cuisine, and music speak to practices that weave together the nation and equip each member to live toward the vision of flourishing life that the community commends. But even more, the very way of life woven out of these practices embodies the communally cherished vision: "All flourishing is mutual." Not just Potawatomi life. Not just human life. But all life. For Kimmerer, a truly flourishing community is one whose boundaries extend beyond the human, knitting the people and the trees, animals, and geographies together into an extended network of mutual flourishing.

Means and ends come together. If the end is a holistic world set right, the means will be approximations of that world, to whatever extent is possible here and now. They will be modes of participating in that world's coming to be, learning to play our parts, finding our step in the dance.

Stepping onto the Floor

As we're looking for practices that will help us continue in the vision of flourishing we've discerned, we have at least two important tasks in front of us. First, we ought to adopt practices that help us train in the way of life we're seeking to sustain. Second, we ought to seek out communities where those practices can become a rich way of life—a dance in which we might find our place.

Before (and continuing in the midst of) all this, there is no escaping our responsibility to discern which dance we take to be *worthy* of dancing. That a dance is intricate and deeply communal does not preclude it from being evil or trivial. We can fail as human beings together at least as well as we can alone. But we are especially unlikely to succeed entirely alone. Each of us must choose for ourselves. And then, in hope of the flourishing life we seek together, we join with others on the floor. And we dance.

Your Turn

1. Consider the sorts of practices you want to take up to help you *act* on your vision of flourishing.
   * What one practice can you commit to in order to take an important step toward living as you believe you are responsible to live?
   * Who in your life could help keep you accountable? Perhaps a friend or family member might even want to take up this practice together with you.

2. Consider the sort of community you might need in order to live into your vision of flourishing life.
   * Do you have a community of people who share the most important broad aspects of your vision of flourishing life?
     (i) If you don't, what steps might you take to find or build a community like that?
     (ii) If you do, what practices or rituals regularly bring you together? What sorts of practices might you want to propose you take up together?
   * Who do you talk with about what matters most? Are any of them people you regularly disagree with?
     (i) What intentional steps might you take to go deeper with a friend who has a very different vision of flourishing life?

* If you have two rather distinct groups of friends, some with whom you have greater alignment and some with whom you have less, what might you do to *connect* these two groups? What kinds of conversations would you want to have? How could you create opportunities for these groups to learn from each other? (Maybe reading this book together would be helpful!)

What Matters Most

At semester's end, it's not uncommon for a student or two to seek us out, worried. The gravity of the Question has hit them. Success is not guaranteed. It seems a genuine possibility that they could fall short. They see how they might make one or two little compromises for the sake of expediency or some supposedly important goal. They see how, over time, those compromises might add up or take on a life of their own. And they see how the end result might fall seriously short of their responsibilities, harming the world and letting others down. They see, in other words, that their life could wind up *evil*.

The thing is, they're not entirely wrong to worry. It is not impossible that we might live evil lives. People are known to have lived evil lives, after all. It is not impossible that *you* might live an evil life. If you did, you would fail to live into the worthiness of our shared humanity. It would be a total *betrayal* of what matters most.

But on the whole, our hunch is that you are unlikely to live an evil life of that sort. Much more likely is that you might, despite your best intentions, live a trivial life. Such lives, too, fail to live into the worthiness of our shared humanity. They don't exactly betray what matters most. They just . . . miss it. They lose it in the shuffle. They let it slip by while focusing on other things.

At first glance, it's strange that triviality is a threat at all. Who would want to just fritter away a life? Evil at least has a lurid magnetism. It's always been able to fascinate people and draw some of us in. By comparison, triviality doesn't seem to have much going for it.

But there are at least two centers of gravity that draw us toward triviality. The first dresses up trivialities in impressive trappings and makes them look significant. It's there in advertising and on social media, in politicians' speeches and at PTA meetings, in the college admissions industry and corporate wellness programs. These and other things seduce us into believing trivial things are what matters most. Things like influence, wealth, power, fame—and all these at scale. They claim to matter, and they imply that we can matter, too, if only we invest ourselves in them.

Perhaps any of these in their proper place could contribute meaningfully to a good life. We could say the same of a meaningful career. Such matters can have their place. But on their own they can manage only a cheap imitation of what truly matters most. And lives built on them quickly slide into the sort of triviality celebrated far and wide as "success."

If we get on board and do a good job playing within the system, we can wind up with lives that plenty of people are willing to tell us matter greatly. The world around us can insist that we're succeeding even though we're devoting ourselves to nothing of deep significance. And in a way, we are succeeding. It's just a hollow success. The worst part is we won't have more than the faintest idea how hollow it is unless we've learned to stay in touch with the Question.

Even if we can recognize trivialities for what they are, there's a second center of gravity that encourages us to accept them as the best we can do and the most we deserve. This is the voice that tells us that our lives themselves are trivially small. It takes advantage of the dull ache inside us that worries that we don't, in fact, matter very much at all. The voice that whispers that our lives are insignificant, each of us just a speck of dust on a speck of the universe.

That voice is wrong.

Your life is worth living. It is valuable. In fact, it's beyond valuable. It's *invaluable*. And precisely because it is so truly worth living, your life is worth living well. Your life is too valuable to be guided by anything less than what matters most.

That's not to say that you're the center of the world. It's not to say that you should focus exclusively on yourself. (Your life matters in part because it's not just about you—it matters to and for others!) It's simply to say that how you live, what you devote your life to, how you're treated and how you treat others, what you set your hopes on and how you feel—all this is significant. And this significance can't be stolen or erased. No matter how much the world tries to convince you of your smallness. No matter how often you've accepted triviality in place of what matters most.

The problem is, what matters most will not clamor for your attention. It's rarely loud. It's almost never flashy. It's easy to miss. And it can be hard to hold on to.

Coming to an insight about what matters most is like uncovering a precious, fragile treasure buried in the desert. Unless you mark it and shield it from the wind, the sands of life will blow over the top of it and swallow it back up. Unless you excavate it carefully, it will be lost forever.

So stick with it. Carve out moments of stillness to return to the Question. Early in the morning, before the noise of the day begins. Late in the evening, when the clamor has begun to die down. Right in the middle of the workday, when you can wrest a few minutes from the hands of life's tasks and demands. Whenever and however you can, make space for the Question. Dare to make it a topic of conversation with the people you value most.

If you feel you've found a treasure, return to it again and again—to what matters most. Excavate it. Build your life around it. Become so devoted to it that the thought that your life is meaningless becomes laughable. Become so enamored with it that the trivialities that try to pass as significant appear as empty as they truly are.

Keep pursuing the Question. Live for what matters most. Your life is worth it.

ACKNOWLEDGMENTS

It's a joy to look back and see how much help and support we've received as we've worked on this book. What a gift!

Thank you, first, to our Life Worth Living students, not only at Yale College but at Danbury Federal Correctional Institution, Yale Alumni College, the Yale Office of International Affairs, Laity Lodge, and Grace Farms. We wish we could list you all by name! Our conversations with you have helped teach us how to approach the Question and shaped our visions of a Life Worth Living. Special thanks to Leah Sarna for her always-challenging guest lectures and permission to use a bit of her story in chapter 3.

More than a dozen caring, imaginative graduate student teachers have co-taught Life Worth Living with us at Yale since 2016. Thank you, Orel Beilinson, Kavya Bhat, Joanna Blake-Turner, Jennifer Daigle, Ryan Darr, Max DuBoff, Janna Gonwa, Hugo Havranek, Justin Hawkins, Megann Licskai, Sarah Misgen, Ahmed Nur, Mireille Pardon, Lea Schroeder, and Deborah Streahle. Ben Doolittle has taken up the cause at Yale Medical School; thank you, Dr. Doolittle! Thanks, also, to our many guest lecturers over the years who have so generously shared their lives and their stories with our students. You've shown our students that these questions really do have the power to shape our lives.

From the time when Miroslav and Ryan were first thinking up the class, a string of exceptionally talented and thoughtful student workers have not only helped keep track of the many, many moving pieces but also put their stamp on the course. Thank you, Andrew Schuman, Brendan Kolb, Hilary Vedvig, and Trent Fuenmayor.

We're grateful to the team that has helped take Life Worth Living from Yale to classrooms around the world: Zach Wooten, Meghan Sullivan, Casey Strine, Garrett Potts, Andrea Kasper, Joshua Forstenzer, Daniel Chua, and Abdullah Antepli. Casey, it was your conversations with Matt that first got us thinking about Life Worth Living's potential outside the Yale bubble.

The three of us work together at the Yale Center for Faith & Culture and have benefited immeasurably from our colleagues, past and present: Karin Fransen, Evan Rosa, Julie Davis, Leon Powell, Susan dos Santos, Shivhan Allen, Sarah Farmer, Fallon Thomas, Phil Love, Skip Masback, and Allison Van Rhee. The center's advisory board has been a source of wisdom, encouragement, and the concrete resources that make our work possible. Special thanks to Warner Depuy for his early enthusiasm for Life Worth Living and to the William H. Pitt Foundation for their generous support of the initiative at Yale.

The team at Grace Farms Foundation, led by Sharon Prince, has been a tremendous support in helping us take the spirit of our university course and bring it to broader audiences from middle and high schools to the US Army Chaplaincy to our neighbors in Connecticut and beyond. Lisa Lynne Kirkpatrick was particularly instrumental in getting LWL connected to Grace Farms. Thanks goes also to Kate Parker-Burgard and Mark Davis for their pioneering work with LWL at St. Luke's School and to Rick Branson, Joan Edwards, and Sharon Lauer for their leadership in bringing the LWL approach to the Connecticut Association of Independent Schools. Special thanks to Katie Grosh for her tireless, compassionate, and creative work in bringing LWL to all these audiences.

Thanks also to Chaplain Gerald Connors at Danbury Federal Correctional Institution. And profound thanks to the men in the LWL class there whose insights deeply enriched our own reflections about the nature of the good life.

For a long time we've wanted to share our passion for the Question outside the classroom. But just because something works as a college class doesn't mean it should be a book. There's always the risk that the material will fall flat when moving from the seminar table to the page. We're so grateful to Alice Martell for helping us make the case to publishers that the risk was worth taking, to Meg Leder and Penguin Life for taking that risk, and to Maria Shriver for welcoming us into The Open Field. Meg, Annika Karody, and the rest of their team have done superb work to bring *Life Worth Living* from idea to reality. We hope that work paid off!

Too many people to count have helped shape the thinking behind this work, but we ought to mention a few who helped out with particular pieces of the text. Caleb Maskell gave a careful historian's eye to our discussion of Ida B. Wells. Steven Angle has been a patient teacher of Confucian philosophy. Any infelicities that remain in either case are matters of shoddy execution on our part, not poor instruction on theirs. Dan Ames helped us see the text through the eyes of a sympathetic skeptic. Thank you to Mohamad Hafez for both his amazing guest lecture in Life Worth Living and for taking the time to share some more of his story with us.

Finally, our deep gratitude to Drew Collins and Angela Williams Gorrell. We hope that not only the class but this book reflects the passion, energy, insight, and love you've poured into Life Worth Living over the years.

From Miroslav: To express gratitude adequately, we would need to name all those who contributed to making our lives and projects possible and pleasant—and all the ways in which they have done so. This is, of course, impossible, which to me is a reminder of how much of who I have become and what I have done are not my own achievements. I will mention here only four people, and merely a fraction of what I have received from them. The first two are my co-authors. Both Matt and Ryan are lively intellectuals, superb educators, and wonderful members of the team; without them this book would not have been nearly as good or as thrilling to write. The other two are my spouse, Jessica, and our daughter, Mira. I don't know anybody who thinks about life with as much nuanced insight as well as sensibility for its many beauties and frequent burdens as does Jessica. And nothing brings me as much joy as Mira's inquisitive, affectionate, and playful liveliness.

From Matt: Teaching this course and working with inspiring colleagues to bring these conversations to students at Yale and beyond has brought unity to my personal sense of vocation that I could not previously have fathomed. That has led me to invest time and energy in this work almost without bounds. I am so grateful to my family—my wife, Hannah, and my daughter, Junia—who have supported me as I have invested that time and energy. So often, it seems that we share the costs, but many of the joys come to me (end-of-semester soup and s'mores notwithstanding). It is not a joke, Hannah, when I say that you live a good life while I teach about it; you inspire me every day. Junia, all I want is for you to flourish; forgive me when I have a distorted or narrow picture of what that could be.

From Ryan: I'm ever grateful to the caretakers and educators who've poured their energy, love, and wisdom into my kids' lives over the past four years, navigating the uncertainties, pains, and challenges of pandemic time with skill, commitment, and a surprising amount of good humor. They include Jessica McAnnally-Linz, Linda McAnnally, Janet McAnnally, Ross and Tammy Jutsum, Caitlyn Mack, Laura Carrillo, Abigail Roth, Jess Fressle; all of the wonderful educators at Neighborhood Music School: Vandana Kant, Denise Nutile, Erica Sapp, Amber Canavan, Sharon Moss, Serena Hatch, and Christine Missakian; and the teachers and staff at Beecher Road

ACKNOWLEDGMENTS

School, especially Megan Cofrancesco, Barbara Ahern, Robin Gerber, and Louise Golden. Thank you, Grace and Gabriel, for being so *preposterously* delightful, inquisitive, and caring. So much of what's most meaningful in my life comes from you! And, Heidi, thank you for—well, for everything.

NOTES

All Bible quotations are from the New Revised Standard Version (NRSV) unless otherwise noted.

Introduction: This Book Might Wreck Your Life

xiv **"Like many another":** Ida B. Wells, *Crusade for Justice: The Autobiography of Ida B. Wells*, 2nd ed. (Chicago: University of Chicago Press, 2020), 64.

xiv **When Wells said:** Wells, *Crusade for Justice*, 62.

xvi **Frederick Douglass (1818–1895) read:** Frederick Douglass, *Narrative of the Life of Frederick Douglass, an American Slave, Written by Himself*, critical ed., ed. John R. McKivigan, Peter P. Hinks, and Heather L. Kaufman (New Haven: Yale University Press, 2016), 36–37.

xvii **The one "who agrees":** C. S. Lewis, *The Four Loves* (New York: HarperOne, 2017 [1960]), 84.

xxiv **But to go back:** As Hermann Hesse imagines him, Siddhartha Gautama was, in a very important respect, *like* a rock: "If you toss a stone into water, it takes the swiftest way to the bottom. And Siddhartha is like that when he has a goal, makes a resolve. Siddhartha does nothing, he waits, he thinks, he fasts, but he passes through the things of the world like the stone through the water, never acting, never stirring. He is drawn, he lets himself drop" (*Siddhartha*, trans. Joachim Neugroschel [New York: Penguin Compass, 2003], 56). But even if we hold up being rocklike as an ideal, precisely by *having an ideal*, we show ourselves to be by nature quite different from rocks.

xxv **This is the most:** Confucius says, "One may rob an army of its commander-in-chief; one cannot deprive the humblest man of his free will" (*Analects* 9.26, trans. Simon Leys). Simon Leys notes that Epictetus affirms the same: "The robber of your free will does not exist" (Epictetus II, 22, 105, quoted by Marcus Aurelius, *Meditations*, XI, 36). Leys says, "It is not merely an elite of gentlemen that cannot be deprived of their free will (*zhi*). This irreducible and inalienable privilege of humanity pertains to all, and even to 'the humblest man' (*pifu*)." Simon Leys, *The Analects of Confucius* (New York: Norton, 1997), 163.

xxv **"Do not judge":** Matthew 7:1 (New American Standard Bible [NASB], 1971).

xxvi **He was, as he put:** The quotes from Speer are drawn from his autobiography and from his response to his daughter's question about how it was he could collaborate with Hitler. A discussion of Speer's life and longer excerpts and citations may be found in Stanley Hauerwas, Richard Bondi, and David B. Burrell, *Truthfulness and Tragedy: Further Investigations in Christian Ethics* (Notre Dame, IN: University of Notre Dame Press, 1977), 88–95, and in Miroslav Volf, *Exclusion and Embrace, Revised and Updated: A Theological Exploration of Identity, Otherness, and Reconciliation* (Nashville: Abingdon Press, 2019), 196.

1. What's Worth Wanting?

6 **Socrates's infamous "unexamined life":** Plato, *Apology* 38a5–6, trans. G. M. A. Grube, in *Plato: Complete Works*, ed. John M. Cooper (Indianapolis: Hackett, 1997), 17–36. (There's a standard set of page numbers for Plato's works that will allow you to find a passage in any decent edition. That's what "38a5–6" means here. We'll use those to cite passages from Plato.)

10 **climbing a ladder:** The proverbial ladder leaning against the wrong wall has often been attributed to Stephen Covey or (more recently) Thomas Merton. As far as we can find, the image goes back at least as far as Anne Adalisa Puddicombe's *Garthowen* (1900), published under her pen name, Allen Raine, in which a teacher remarks to his former pupil, "You may get to the top of the ladder, and then find it has not been leaning against the right wall. That would be a poor success . . ." (107). Perhaps more of us ought to worry about the possibility of just this sort of "poor success."

11 **Coates expresses something like this:** Coates, *Between the World and Me* (New York: Spiegel and Grau, 2015).

2. Where Are We Starting From?

19 **now estimated to be worth:** Valuation of the global wellness market from McKinsey & Company (April 8, 2021): Schaun Callaghan, Martin Lösch, Anna Pione, and Warren Teichner, "Feeling Good: The Future of the $1.5 Trillion Wellness Market," April 8, 2021, mckinsey.com/industries/consumer-packaged-goods/our-insights/feeling-good-the-future-of-the-1-5-trillion-wellness-market.

21 **"All men are in search"**: Blaise Pascal, *Pensées* §181, trans. Honor Levi, in *Pensées and Other Writings*, ed. Anthony Levi (Oxford: Oxford University Press, 1995), 51.

25 **"Like anybody, I would like"**: Martin Luther King Jr., "I've Been to the Mountaintop," in *A Call to Conscience: The Landmark Speeches of Dr. Martin Luther King, Jr.*, ed. Clayborne Carson and Kris Shepherd (New York: Grand Central Publishing, 2001), 222–23.

26 **"the melancholy seemed to roll"**: Joseph Wilson Fifer, quoted in Michael Burlingame, *The Inner World of Abraham Lincoln* (Urbana, IL: University of Illinois Press, 1994), 93.

26 **"If there is a worse place"**: Quoted in Burlingame, *Abraham Lincoln*, 105.

27 **Chronic rheumatism had left:** On Constance Lytton's life, see Lyndsey Jenkins, *Constance Lytton: Aristocrat, Suffragette, Martyr* (London: Silvertail Books, 2018), as well as Lytton's autobiographical *Prisons and Prisoners: Some Personal Experiences* (London: William Heinemann, 1914).

3. Who Do We Answer To?

36 **God who gave the Torah:** The word *God* is a bit slippery. On the one hand, it's clear that even among those who believe in just one God (monotheists), there are many different accounts of what God is like. The Abrahamic traditions (Judaism, Christianity, and Islam) each offer their own accounts, as do other religious monotheisms like Sikhism, Hindu monotheisms, and Baha'i traditions. And there are philosophical accounts of God like the one articulated by Plato. Each of these accounts is importantly distinct. But for most of them, part of believing *in* just one God is believing that there *is* only one God, who is the ultimate reality and therefore the source of the values that ought to give shape to human life and the world. And so it doesn't really make sense to monotheists to specify "which" God or even which account of God they have in view. They're interested in understanding who God is and what God is like—in many cases, they are especially interested in understanding the content of God's self-revelation. Most often, when we use the word *God* in this book, we mean God as the person or tradition we're describing understands God. Otherwise, we mean the object of devotion and subject of revelation that many religious and philosophical traditions contend with one another to more or less adequately describe.

36 **forest fire prevention representative:** To the careful reader who recognizes "forest fire prevention representative" as the peculiar phraseology of famed comedian Mitch Hedberg, we say: Well done.

38 **If we both sing:** Note that as the examples turn to the arts, they seem less far-fetched. In the modern world, the fine arts are the primary example of

self-authentication. In fact, as he helped invent the modern ideal of authenticity in the early nineteenth century, Friedrich Schleiermacher (1768–1834) appealed directly to emerging Romantic artistic ideals.

40 **"A man who respects":** *Analects* 1.2 (Leys). All translations of the *Analects* are from *The Analects of Confucius*, trans. Simon Leys (New York: Norton, 1997); *Analects*, trans. Edward Slingerland (Indianapolis: Hackett, 2003); or *The Analects of Confucius*, trans. Burton Watson (New York: Columbia University Press, 2007).

41 **While we may think:** Partly in order to recognize the extent to which Confucius did not see himself as inventing anything new, many contemporary scholars of Confucius and those who came after him use the label *Ruism*, based off the Chinese character *ru*, which ancient scholars who were aligned with Confucius used to describe themselves. (*Confucianism* was a label invented by Western scholars.)

41 **"I transmit rather":** *Analects* 7.1 (Slingerland).

41 **"I simply love antiquity":** *Analects* 7.20 (Slingerland).

41 **We ourselves came to exist:** Much of what we have to say about how Confucius's ideas about tradition might speak to a modern Western audience has been deeply informed by Philip J. Ivanhoe's work, particularly his *Confucian Reflections: Ancient Wisdom for Modern Times* (New York: Routledge, 2013).

42 **It is the root of flourishing:** See *Analects* 14.42.

43 **"Recite in the Name":** Quran 96:1–2. Quotations from the Quran are drawn from *The Study Quran: A New Translation and Commentary*, ed. Sayyed Hossein Nasr et al. (New York: HarperOne, 2015). The story of the Prophet's call, drawn from ancient hadith ("sayings" of the Prophet), is reproduced in *The Study Quran*'s introduction to Surah 96.

43 **"Am I not your Lord?":** Quran 7:172.

44 **What's more, according to:** See the commentary on Quran 7:172 in *The Study Quran*, 466–68.

4. How Does a Good Life Feel?

50 **"Good is pleasure":** Jeremy Bentham, *Codification Proposal*, part I, §3 (London: Robert Heward, 1830), 12.

51 **"Prejudice apart," he said:** Jeremy Bentham, *The Rationale of Reward*, bk. 3, chap. 1 (London: John and H. L. Hunt, 1825), 206.

51 **Rotten Tomatoes audience score:** Film ratings from rottentomatoes.com (as of January 12, 2022). Global box-office draws from boxofficemojo.com.

53 **"The trees are covered":** All quotes are from *Therīgāthā: Poems of the First Buddhist Women*, trans. Charles Hallisey (Cambridge, MA: Harvard University Press, 2015), lines 369–402.

54 **"What you take as pleasures":** For example, *Therīgāthā* lines 188, 195, 203, and 235.

55 **"For Oscar Wilde, posing Somdomite":** The precise wording of Queensberry's card is up to some debate, as the handwriting is quite difficult to read. It may have said "ponce and Somdomite." (*Ponce* referred either to a man who lived off the money of his lover or a pimp. See the *Oxford English Dictionary*, s.v. *ponce* [1].) Queensberry claimed it said "Posing *as a* Somdomite," such that it didn't strictly accuse Wilde of any crime. In any case, *Sodomite* was misspelled but quite clearly the word Queensberry intended to use.

56 **Looking back on:** Oscar Wilde, *De Profundis* (Mineola, NY: Dover, 1996), 45.

56 **"I can resist everything":** Oscar Wilde, *Lady Windermere's Fan*, Act I.

56 **"I wanted to eat":** Wilde, *De Profundis*, 54.

56 **"I filled my life":** Wilde, *De Profundis*, 50.

57 **"I don't regret":** Wilde, *De Profundis*, 69.

57 **He can't contain:** Wilde, *De Profundis*, 89.

57 **"the supreme emotion":** Wilde, *De Profundis*, 52.

58 **"The secret of life":** Wilde, *De Profundis*, 53. Of course, Subha and the Buddha would agree in a certain sense. Life is *duhkha*. That is the truth of the world. But for them, this truth of "ill" should clue us in to something yet more deeply true: *this life* is ill. Wilde is unwilling to look beyond this life in this way. Whereas the Buddha's teaching seeks to cultivate nonattachment to what causes suffering, Wilde rather encourages us to lean into the suffering. The difference in these two lines of thought stems from their assessments of the world itself—their understanding of what we'll call the "really big picture" in chapter 8.

58 **"You came to me":** Wilde, *De Profundis*, 92.

5. What Should We Hope For?

63 **82.5 percent of students:** Ellen Bara Stolzenberg et al., *The American Freshman: National Norms Fall 2017* (Los Angeles: Higher Education Research Institute, 2019), 40.

63 **There's not much that money:** Michael Sandel's excellent *What Money Can't Buy: The Moral Limits of Markets* (New York: Farrar, Straus and

Giroux, 2012) explores the ways that money can now buy things that used to be considered off-limits for market transactions.

63 **The sociologist Hartmut Rosa:** Hartmut Rosa, *Resonance: A Sociology of Our Relationship to the World*, trans. James C. Wagner (Cambridge: Polity, 2019).

64 **the "Triple-A vision":** Rosa, "Available, Accessible, Attainable: The Mindset of Growth and the Resonance Conception of the Good Life," in *The Good Life beyond Growth: New Perspectives*, ed. Hartmut Rosa and Christoph Henning (New York: Routledge, 2018), 39–54.

65 **The Luster of Blessedness:** The title of this section is a near quote from the translation of Aristotle's *Nicomachean Ethics* 1.8, 1099b, by W. D. Ross, revised by J. O. Urmson, in vol. 2 of *The Complete Works of Aristotle: The Revised Oxford Translation*, ed. Jonathan Barnes (Princeton: Princeton University Press, 1984), 1737. We use this translation for all our quotes from the *Nicomachean Ethics*.

65 **He sought out:** We've relied on the dry, admirably meticulous work of Carlo Natali (*Aristotle: His Life and School*, ed. D. S. Hutchinson [Princeton: Princeton University Press, 2013]) for most biographical information on Aristotle.

65 **In the north:** See Thomas R. Martin, *Ancient Greece: From Prehistoric to Hellenistic Times* (New Haven: Yale University Press, 2000), 174–90; Robin Osborne, "The Fourth Century: Political and Military Narrative," in *Classical Greece, 500–323 BC*, ed. Robin Osborne (Oxford: Oxford University Press, 2000), 197–219.

65 **Aristotle, like most Greek philosophers:** *Nicomachean Ethics* 1.6–7, 1097a–b. Lots of English translations render *eudaimonia* as "happiness," which may have made sense in the nineteenth century, but is really unhelpful now, since "happiness" has overwhelmingly emotional connotations, whereas *eudaimonia* doesn't.

66 **Flourishing is fundamentally:** Specifically, he thinks flourishing is an activity of the *soul* in conformity with *virtue*. See *Nicomachean Ethics* 1.7, 1098a.

66 **namely, "external goods":** *Nicomachean Ethics* 1.8, 1099a.

67 **His *eudaimonia* will always:** *Nicomachean Ethics* 1.10, 1100b.

68 **"An impediment (*rāhula*)":** *The Story of Gotama Buddha: The Nidāna-kathā of the Jātakatthakathā* §270, trans. N. A. Jayawickrama (Oxford: Pali Text Society, 1990), 81.

68 **When the invitation:** *Gotama Buddha* §§288–90, 115–17.

69 **"I will make him"**: *Gotama Buddha* §293, 123–24.

70 **The review appeared:** The only reason anybody remembers this is that the now decidedly more well-known writer David Foster Wallace skewered Conroy's essay-mercial in his own classic, *A Supposedly Fun Thing I'll Never Do Again.*

70 **"I realized it had been"**: Quoted in Wallace, *A Supposedly Fun Thing I'll Never Do Again* (New York: Back Bay, 1997), 286.

71 **A typical workday:** Reliable information about labor conditions on cruise ships is difficult to find. The numbers we cite are from Katharina Wolff, Svein Larsen, Einar Marnburg, and Torvald Øgaard, "Worry and Its Correlates Onboard Cruise Ships," *International Maritime Health* 64 (2013): 95.

71 **The median employee:** Mark Matousek, "Carnival and Royal Caribbean Paid Their Median Employee Less Than $20,000 in 2018," *Business Insider*, June 23, 2019, businessinsider.com/carnival-royal-caribbean-norwegian -median-worker-pay-2019-6.

71 **"In order for there"**: Friedrich Nietzsche, "The Greek State," in *The Genealogy of Morality*, rev. student ed., ed. Keith Ansell-Pearson (Cambridge: Cambridge University Press, 2007), 166.

72 **But the Acts of the Apostles:** Acts 9:1–19.

73 **life "with Christ"**: Philippians 1:23.

73 **"I could wish"**: Romans 9:3.

73 **"righteousness, peace, and joy"**: Romans 14:17.

74 **"the genuine solution"**: Karl Marx, "Economic and Philosophical Manuscripts," in *Karl Marx: Selected Writings*, 2nd ed. (Oxford: Oxford University Press, 2000), 97.

74 **"a world in which"**: "Inaugural Address of Harry S. Truman," January 20, 1949, avalon.law.yale.edu/20th_century/truman.asp.

6. How Should We Live?

77 **Before he saw:** We're grateful to Mohamad Hafez for talking with Ryan and Matt and giving us permission to write about his story, as well as for speaking as a guest lecturer to our Yale Life Worth Living class.

78 **Just enough of the beauty:** Brett Sokol, "A Little Piece of Downtown Damascus in New Haven," *The New York Times*, October 12, 2017.

80 **our "moral center"**: James Baldwin, "Notes of a Native Son," in *Collected Essays*, ed. Toni Morrison (New York: Library of America, 1998), 9.

81 "opposite and rival": James Madison, *Federalist,* no. 51.

82 A Western world: We're thinking here, for example, about concerns raised about democratically elected regimes in the United States, Brazil, Hungary, and India.

83 over 2.5 billion tons: National Minerals Information Center, "Iron Ore Statistics and Information," accessed May 18, 2022, usgs.gov/centers/nmic /iron-ore-statistics-and-information.

83 15 billion trees: Justin Worland, "Here's How Many Trees Humans Cut Down Each Year," *Time,* September 2, 2015, time.com/4019277/trees -humans-deforestation.

84 "to live and to be unjust": Nietzsche, "Of the Uses and Disadvantages of History for Life," §3, in *Untimely Meditations,* trans. R. J. Hollingdale (Cambridge: Cambridge University Press, 1997), 76.

84 "injurious, violent, exploitative": Nietzsche, *On the Genealogy of Morality* 2.11, trans. Carol Diethe, rev. student ed. (Cambridge: Cambridge University Press, 2007), 50.

85 "Why this cowardice": Bhagavad Gita, 2.2. Quotes from the Gita are from *The Bhagavad-Gita: Krishna's Counsel in Time of War,* trans. Barbara Stoler Miller (New York: Bantam Books, 1986).

85 "Look to your own duty": Bhagavad Gita, 2.31.

87 doing what the God of Abraham: Perhaps obviously, doing what God says and becoming virtuous aren't mutually exclusive. (God might command you to become virtuous!) But we'll take each option up one at a time in the sections that follow.

87 "The Lord said": Genesis 12:1, 4 (Jewish Study Bible [JSB]).

88 how to treat your enemy's donkey: Exodus 23:4–5.

88 "Give Him what is His": *Pirkei Avot* 3.8, trans. Rabbi Lord Jonathan Sacks (Jerusalem: Koren, 2015). We use this translation for all our quotes from *Pirkei Avot.*

88 "whether all things": Grace Aguilar, *The Spirit of Judaism,* in *Grace Aguilar: Selected Writings,* ed. Michael Galchinsky (Peterborough, Canada: Broadview, 2003), 243.

88 It is said that one: The original saying from Rabbi Hanina (first to second centuries CE) is, "Greater is one who is commanded to do a mitzva and performs it than one who is not commanded to do a mitzva and performs it." *B. Kiddushin* 31a. A mitzva is a righteous act.

88 "Obeying the commandments": 1 Corinthians 7:19.

88 **Your job is to follow:** The Abrahamic traditions are not alone among theistic traditions (that is, ones that include belief in God or gods) in advocating for non-consequentialism. Krishna has just this advice for Arjuna in the Gita: "Be intent on action, not on the fruits of action." The goal is to "be impartial to failure and success." Bhagavad Gita, 2.47, 48.

89 **"Father, for you":** Mark 14:36.

89 **"Take your son":** Genesis 22:2, JSB.

91 **Four sprouts peeked up:** See *Mengzi* 2A6, 6A1, 6A7, trans. Brian W. Van Norden (Indianapolis: Hackett, 2008).

91 **The feeling of compassion:** Our translations for these terms are drawn from a number of scholars, including Irene Bloom, Brian W. Van Norden, and Philip J. Ivanhoe.

95 **"the truths of arithmetic":** John Stuart Mill, *Utilitarianism*, chap. 5, in *On Liberty and Other Essays* (Oxford: Oxford University Press, 1998), 199.

95 **"Maximize goodness impartially":** Peter Singer and Katarina de Lazari-Radek, "The Good Life—a Utilitarian Perspective," in *The Good Life in Comparative Perspective*, ed. Matthew Croasmun and Drew Collins (Waco, TX: Baylor University Press), forthcoming.

96 **Each of us has our own:** See Taylor's *The Ethics of Authenticity* (Cambridge, MA: Harvard University Press, 1991), 28–29. The book is the lightly edited text of lectures he gave on Canadian public radio, of all things.

96 **It's tempting to try:** The popularity of Frederick Buechner's line about vocation has much to do with its promise to resolve the tension between these two responsibilities: "Vocation is the place where our deep gladness meets the world's deep need." *Wishful Thinking: A Seeker's ABC*, rev. ed. (San Francisco: Harper, 1993), 119. The hope is that we happen to live in a universe in which the aims of maximizing our utilitarian responsibility to the world and maximizing our "ethic of authenticity" responsibility to realize ourselves come together. Aside from Buechner's theological grounds, there may not be any particular reason to suppose we live in such a universe.

97 **"Yang Zhu is 'for oneself'":** *Mengzi* 3B9.9, trans. Van Norden.

97 **"Among my people":** *Analects* 13.18 (Slingerland).

98 **Jesus answered with a story:** The parable of the Good Samaritan, as this story is known, is found in Luke 10:25–37.

99 **an undernourished child:** United States Agency for International Development, "Guatemala: Nutrition Profile," June 2014, usaid.gov/sites/default/files/documents/1864/USAID-Guatemala_NCP.pdf.

7. The Recipe Test

107 **Thinkers ranging from:** Aristotle, *Nicomachean Ethics*, bk. 8. Wollstone-craft called friendship "the most holy band of society" and "the most sub-lime of all affections." See *A Vindication of the Rights of Woman*, chaps. 2 and 4, in *A Vindication of the Rights of Men with A Vindication of the Rights of Woman and Hints*, ed. Sylvana Tomaselli (Cambridge: Cambridge University Press, 1995), 98, 151.

108 **Recent research suggests:** See Olga M. Klimecki, "The Plasticity of Social Emotions," *Social Neuroscience* 10 (2015): 466–73.

110 **A vision can be balanced:** Miroslav and Matt have suggested just this about Paul of Tarsus's Christian vision of the good life in *For the Life of the World: Theology That Makes a Difference* (Grand Rapids, MI: Brazos, 2019), 182–85.

110 **The Greek philosopher Chrysippus:** Chrysippus's book was lost, but these words are reported in Diogenes Laertius (180–240), *Lives of Eminent Philosophers* 7.7.189, which can be found in the Loeb Classical Library edition, *Lives of Eminent Philosophers, Books 6–10*, trans. R. D. Hicks (Cambridge, MA: Harvard University Press, 1925), 297.

111 **But Cleanthes sat:** Diogenes Laertius, *Lives of Eminent Philosophers* 7.5.173.

112 **"I was already aware":** Cicero, *Tusculan Disputations* 3.30, quoted in Martha Nussbaum, *The Therapy of Desire: Theory and Practice in Hellenistic Ethics* (Princeton, NJ: Princeton University Press, 1994), 363. Neither Cicero nor Anaxagoras was a Stoic, but Cicero's point here is meant to illustrate a stance that the Stoics admire.

112 **By focusing on the core:** It should be said that over the millennia Stoicism has also found an eager audience among those who have never had to worry about life's circumstances—for example, the Roman imperial elite and the gentry of the colonial European powers. For these, Stoicism offers powerful advice about how not to get caught up in the trivialities of wealth and pleasure in the midst of abundance.

113 **"You will cease":** Seneca the Younger, *Epistles* 5.7, quoted in Nussbaum, *Therapy*, 389.

113 **"Look to the true good":** Seneca the Younger, *Epistles* 23.6, quoted in Nussbaum, *Therapy*, 400.

114 **But for the utilitarian thinkers:** For what it's worth, not all utilitarians elevate pleasure and the absence of pain as defining the good life. Rather, what all utilitarians share is the conviction that (a) there is something in

which all good consists, and (b) right action boils down to maximizing that good without prejudice to where (or for whom) that good comes. "Hedonistic utilitarians" like those we discuss in this book take pleasure and the absence of pain to be this good. "Preference utilitarians," in contrast, think that this good is "desire satisfaction" or "preference fulfillment"—basically, getting what you want. So they worry about making as many people as possible get what they prefer, whatever that happens to be. Preference utilitarians leave a lot more room for circumstances to matter in their own right.

115 **"Would you plug in?"**: The experiment is described in Robert Nozick, *Anarchy, State, and Utopia* (Cambridge, MA: Blackwell, 1974), 42–45; the quoted text is on page 43.

115 **"We learn that something"**: Nozick, *Anarchy*, 44.

117 **The Master said**: *Analects* 3.11 (Watson).

117 **"Do not enter"**: *Analects* 8.13. We've synthesized Slingerland's and Leys's translations.

118 **"A man without humanity"**: *Analects* 4.2 (Leys).

121 **"The humane person"**: *Analects* 15.9 (Watson). Confucius's great interpreter Mencius says something similar by way of a charming analogy with fourth-century-BCE food preferences: "Fish is something I desire; bear's paw is also something I desire. If I cannot have both, I will forsake fish and select bear's paw. Life is something I desire; righteousness is also something I desire. If I cannot have both, I will forsake life and select righteousness. Life is something I desire, but there is something I desire more than life. Hence, I will not do just anything to obtain it. Death is something I hate, but there is something I hate more than death. Hence, there are calamities I do not avoid" (*Mengzi* 6A10.1–2).

122 **All agency, like all ability**: This phrasing is adapted from "All ability is temporary," a favorite slogan of Yale Divinity School student Ben Bond, cochair of DivineAbilities, the school's disability student organization.

8. The Really Big Picture

126 **the idea "that advantage"**: Daniel Markovits, *The Meritocracy Trap: How America's Foundational Myth Feeds Inequality, Dismantles the Middle Class, and Devours the Elite* (New York: Penguin, 2019), ix.

128 **we'll focus for now on two questions**: Norman Wirzba focuses on these two questions to consider what it means to be a creature in *This Sacred Life: Humanity's Place in a Wounded World* (Cambridge: Cambridge University Press, 2021).

129 God "showed a little thing": Julian of Norwich, *Revelations of Divine Love*, Long Text §5, trans. Elizabeth Spearing (New York: Penguin, 1998), 47.

129 "I saw quite certainly": Julian, *Revelations*, Long Text §86.

129 Quoting the Bible: Julian, *Revelations*, Long Text §10, referencing Genesis 1:27.

129 "He who made": Julian, *Revelations*, Long Text §10.

130 "I may make": Julian, *Revelations*, Long Text §31.

130 In our day jobs: For a few recent efforts: Miroslav Volf and Ryan McAnnally-Linz, *The Home of God: A Brief Story of Everything* (Grand Rapids, MI: Brazos, 2022); Miroslav Volf and Matthew Croasmun, *For the Life of the World: Theology That Makes a Difference* (Grand Rapids, MI: Brazos, 2019); Matthew Croasmun and Miroslav Volf, *The Hunger for Home* (Waco, TX: Baylor University Press, 2022).

130 "will be able to separate": Romans 8:39.

130 "Beloved, if God": 1 John 4:11.

131 Even after decades: Information on the pollution at Onondaga Lake from the Environmental Protection Agency, accessed May 18, 2022, cumulis.epa .gov/supercpad/SiteProfiles/index.cfm?fuseaction=second.Healthenv&id =0203382.

131 Some stretches of the shore: Robin Wall Kimmerer, *Braiding Sweetgrass: Indigenous Wisdom, Scientific Knowledge, and the Teachings of Plants* (Minneapolis: Milkweed Editions, 2013), 311.

131 Over several centuries: For background, see David Andrew Nichols, *Peoples of the Inland Sea: Native Americans and Newcomers in the Great Lakes Region, 1600–1870* (Athens, OH: Ohio University Press, 2018); John P. Bowes, *Land Too Good for Indians: Northern Indian Removal* (Norman, OK: University of Oklahoma Press, 2016), 149–81; and R. David Edmunds, *The Potawatomis: Keepers of the Fire* (Norman, OK: University of Oklahoma Press, 1978).

132 "just passing through": Kimmerer, *Braiding Sweetgrass*, 7. Miroslav and Ryan have argued that Christians shouldn't tell the story of everything in ways that lead to this conclusion (Volf and McAnnally-Linz, *Home of God*).

132 Facts like the incredible rate: Jurriaan M. De Vos et al., "Estimating the Normal Background Rate of Species Extinction," *Conservation Biology* 29 (2015): 452–62.

132 **In Haudenosaunee legend:** See Kimmerer's retelling of the story in *Braiding Sweetgrass*, 3–5. She works from Joanne Shenandoah and Douglas M. George's version in *Skywoman: Legends of the Iroquois* (Santa Fe, NM: Clear Light, 1998), 7–14. Other tellings are available from Oneida Nation council member Keller George at oneidaindiannation.com/the-haudenosaunee-creation-story, and in Arthur C. Parker, *Seneca Myths and Folk Tales* (Buffalo, NY: Buffalo Historical Society, 1923), 411–16.

134 **"become indigenous to place":** Kimmerer, *Braiding Sweetgrass*, 210.

134 **"All flourishing is mutual":** Kimmerer, *Braiding Sweetgrass*, 15, 20, 21, 382.

134 **Nanabozho, the mythical First Man:** Kimmerer, *Braiding Sweetgrass*, 207–11.

134 **each creature has a particular gift:** Kimmerer, *Braiding Sweetgrass*, 347.

135 **"Whatever our gift":** Kimmerer, *Braiding Sweetgrass*, 384.

135 **A "pale blue dot":** Carl Sagan, *Pale Blue Dot: A Vision of the Human Future in Space* (New York: Ballantine, 1994).

136 **"On the scale":** Sagan, *Pale Blue Dot*, 3.

136 **"Think of the rivers":** Sagan, *Pale Blue Dot*, 6–7.

138 **"Within groups selfish individuals":** E. O. Wilson, *The Meaning of Human Existence* (New York: Liveright, 2014), 33. Both quotes in this paragraph are from the same source.

138 **One important caveat:** Wilson, *Human Existence*, 25. See also Wilson, *The Social Conquest of Earth* (New York: Liveright, 2012), 290.

138 **"at once saints":** Wilson, *Human Existence*, 27–28.

138 **We are the galaxy:** Wilson, *Social Conquest*, 288.

139 **"to turn Earth":** Wilson, *Human Existence*, 176.

140 **They are emphatic:** "We were created not by a supernatural intelligence but by chance and necessity as one species out of millions of species in Earth's biosphere. . . . We are, it seems, completely alone." Wilson, *Human Existence*, 173.

141 **The inventor Ray Kurzweil:** Ray Kurzweil, *The Singularity Is Near: When Humans Transcend Biology* (New York: Viking, 2005), 14–21.

141 **"the vast knowledge":** Kurzweil, *The Singularity*, 20.

142 **"What we are doing":** Kurzweil, *The Singularity*, 374.

142 **It spells the end:** Kurzweil, *The Singularity*, 8.

142 **What makes us us:** Kurzweil, *The Singularity*, 371.

143 **We grow, we learn:** Kurzweil, *The Singularity*, 382, 386.

143 **"Being human means":** Kurzweil, *The Singularity*, 374.

144 **the fourfold basic insight:** The Buddha presents the Four Noble Truths in what is traditionally regarded as his first sermon. There are various translations available. We have used Deepak Sarma, *Classical Indian Philosophy: A Reader* (New York: Columbia University Press, 2011), 16–19. If you want to find other translations, you can search by the original ancient Pali title (*Dhammacakkappavattana Sutta*) or the Sanskrit translation (*Dharmacakrapravartana Sūtra*).

9. When We (Inevitably) Botch It

153 **Wilde knew the laws:** Wilde, *De Profundis*, 47.

153 **"I am not speaking":** Wilde, *De Profundis*, 3.

153 **"In allowing you":** Wilde, *De Profundis*, 4 (emphasis added).

154 **Wilde, you see:** In addition to *De Profundis*, see his earlier essay "The Soul of Man under Socialism," in *The Complete Works of Oscar Wilde*, ed. Ian Small, vol. 4, *Criticism: Historical Criticism, Intentions, the Soul of Man*, ed. Josephine M. Guy (Oxford: Oxford University Press, 2007), 231–68.

154 **Wilde knew in his bones:** As we will explore in chapter 14, Wilde thought art was *the* mode par excellence for any human being to realize their individuality. But this only intensified his own sense of responsibility to *his* artistic expressions.

158 **When we deny:** We're grateful to Michelle Ting for this way of thinking about the dynamic of denial.

158 **"Don't be cowardly":** Friedrich Nietzsche, *Twilight of the Idols*, "Arrows and Epigrams," §10, trans. Judith Norman, in *The Anti-Christ, Ecce Homo, Twilight of the Idols, and Other Writings* (Cambridge: Cambridge University Press, 2005), 157.

160 **more than 350 million children:** UNICEF, "Child Poverty," accessed May 18, 2022, unicef.org/social-policy/child-poverty.

162 **"a king who":** *Pirkei DeRabbi Eliezer* 3.2 (translation from sefaria.org).

163 **"repentance brings near":** Maimonides, *Mishneh Torah*, bk. 1, sec. 5, §7.6 (translation from sefaria.org).

163 **Indeed, Maimonides says:** Maimonides, *Mishneh Torah*, bk. 1, sec. 5, §2.5.

164 **Maimonides says that God:** Maimonides, *Mishneh Torah*, bk. 1, sec. 5, §2.9.

164 **"confession alone is futile":** *Babylonian Talmud Taanith* 16a (translation from sefaria.org). R. Adda compares confessing sin without changing your ways to holding on to a dead snake while taking a purifying bath. The bath isn't going to purify the impurities you're taking on while in the bath. Confession isn't going to deal with the sin you're unwilling to leave behind.

164 **Close to the human heart:** Classic discussions of the evil impulse in rabbinic thought can be found in Solomon Schechter, *Aspects of Rabbinic Theology* (Woodstock, VT: Jewish Lights, 1993 [1909]), 242–63, and Ephraim E. Urbach, *The Sages: Their Concepts and Beliefs*, trans. Israel Abrahams (Jerusalem: Magnes Press, 1975), 471–83.

165 **"A person's evil inclination":** *Babylonian Talmud Sukkah* 52b (translation from sefaria.org).

165 **"The elemental struggle":** Pema Chödrön, *When Things Fall Apart: Heart Advice for Difficult Times*, 2nd ed. (Boulder, CO: Shambala, 2016), 124.

165 **"You don't confess":** Chödrön, *Start Where You Are: A Guide to Compassionate Living* (Boston: Shambala, 2001), 72.

166 **"When we buy into disapproval":** Chödrön, *When Things Fall Apart*, 27.

166 **"In order to feel":** Chödrön, *When Things Fall Apart*, 93.

166 **"You refrain because":** Chödrön, *Start Where You Are*, 73–74.

167 **Instead, it's taking up:** Chödrön, *Start Where You Are*, 74.

169 **And that might well:** Miroslav has written quite a bit from a Christian perspective about the importance of establishing the truth of harm done in processes of forgiveness and reconciliation: *Free of Charge: Giving and Forgiving in a Culture Stripped of Grace* (Grand Rapids, MI: Zondervan, 2009); *Exclusion and Embrace, Revised and Updated: A Theological Exploration of Identity, Otherness, and Reconciliation* (Nashville: Abingdon Press, 2019).

10. When Life Hurts . . .

172 **"Nature has placed":** Jeremy Bentham, *An Introduction to the Principles of Morals and Legislation*, in *The Collected Works of Jeremy Bentham: An Introduction to the Principles of Morals and Legislation*, ed. J. H. Burns and H. L. A. Hart (Oxford: Clarendon, 1996), 11.

173 **As the psychologist:** Paul Bloom, *The Sweet Spot: The Pleasures of Suffering and the Search for Meaning* (New York: Ecco, 2021), xxiv.

174 **When Julia Wise was young:** Julia Wise's story has been told in more detail, but maybe a bit too dramatically, in Larissa MacFarquhar's *Strangers*

Drowning: Impossible Idealism, Drastic Choices, and the Urge to Help (New York: Penguin, 2015).

174 **Julia is now the community liaison:** centreforeffectivealtruism.org.

175 **"until we reach":** Peter Singer, "Famine, Affluence, and Morality," *Philosophy & Public Affairs* 1 (1972): 241.

177 **"Virtue," she said:** Mary Wollstonecraft, *A Vindication of the Rights of Man*, in *A Vindication of the Rights of Woman and A Vindication of the Rights of Man* (Oxford: Oxford University Press, 1993), 59.

177 **"cunning envious dependents":** Wollstonecraft, *A Vindication of the Rights of Woman*, in *A Vindication of the Rights of Woman and A Vindication of the Rights of Man*, 225.

177 **"hard school of moral discipline":** Wollstonecraft, *Rights of Man*, 57.

177 **"preposterous distinctions of rank":** Wollstonecraft, *Rights of Woman*, 225.

177 **"the galling yoke":** Wollstonecraft, *Rights of Woman*, 101.

178 **"It is justice":** Wollstonecraft, *Rights of Woman*, 143.

178 **"quickly become wise":** Wollstonecraft, *Rights of Woman*, 262.

179 **With the exception:** "If wealth is fairly distributed, there should be no poverty; if your state or house is in harmony, there should be no scarcity; and if your people are content, there should be no instability." *Analects* 16.1 (Slingerland).

179 **"If you could just":** *Analects* 12.18 (Slingerland).

180 **"it has never happened":** *Mengzi* 6B5.4.

180 **"When the world is drowning":** *Mengzi* 4A17.3.

180 **"I would rectify":** *Analects* 13.3 (Watson).

180 **"Let the ruler":** *Analects* 12.11 (Watson).

180 **"If a true king":** *Analects* 13.12 (Slingerland).

180 **"To 'govern' means":** *Analects* 12.17 (Slingerland).

181 **Things like distributing:** See *Mengzi* 1A3; 1A7; 3A3.13–20; 7A22.

181 **"In being a filial son":** *Analects* 2.21 (Slingerland).

182 **"Evil," he remarked:** Baldwin, "This Nettle, Danger . . . ," in *Collected Essays*, 687.

182 **"it goes without saying":** Baldwin, "Notes of a Native Son," in *Collected Essays*, 84.

183 **"One must never":** Baldwin, "Notes of a Native Son," 84.

183 **"Life is tragic, and, *therefore*"**: Baldwin, "The Creative Process," in *Collected Essays*, 671 (emphasis original).

184 **"Whoever debases others"**: Baldwin, *The Fire Next Time*, in *Collected Essays*, 334.

184 **"the political institutions"**: Baldwin, *The Fire Next Time*, 337.

184 **"Not everything that is faced"**: Baldwin, "As Much Truth as One Can Bear," in *The Cross of Redemption*, ed. Randall Kenan (New York: Vintage International, 2011), 42.

185 **"It has always seemed"**: Baldwin, "Nothing Personal," in *Collected Essays*, 698.

185 **"each of us, helplessly"**: Baldwin, "Freaks and the American Ideal of Manhood," in *Collected Essays*, 828.

185 **"The sea rises"**: Baldwin, "Nothing Personal," 706.

11. . . . And There's No Fixing It

188 **"He grieved greatly"**: Aśvaghoṣa, *The Life of the Buddha* 5.5–6, trans. Patrick Olivelle (New York: New York University Press and JJC Foundation, 2008), 127–29.

188 **"[1] My life shall"**: Aśvaghoṣa, *Life of the Buddha* 5.35.

188 **"If that's not possible"**: Aśvaghoṣa, *Life of the Buddha* 5.37.

188 **"Both in the past"**: *Dhammacakkappavattana Sutta*, quoted in Damien Keown, *Buddhism: A Very Short Introduction*, 2nd ed. (Oxford: Oxford University Press, 2013), 48.

191 **Psychologists Paul Bloom**: Paul Bloom and Konika Banerjee, "Why Did This Happen to Me? Religious Believers' and Non-believers' Teleological Reasoning about Life Events," *Cognition* 133 (2014): 282, cited in Bloom, *The Sweet Spot*, 182.

191 **"there is no agent"**: Al-Ghazali, *Faith in Divine Unity and Trust in Divine Providence, Book XXXV of the Revival of the Religious Sciences*, trans. David B. Burrell (Louisville, KY: Fons Vitae, 2001), 15.

192 **Among the ninety-nine**: In Arabic, these names are: *Al-Raḥmān, Al-Raḥīm, Al-'Adl, Al-Laṭīf, Al-Ḥakīm*, and *Al-Barr*. We use David Burrell and Nazih Daher's translations from al-Ghazālī, *The Ninety-Nine Beautiful Names of God* (Cambridge: Islamic Texts Society, 1995), 49–51.

192 **"Everything which God"**: Al-Ghazali, *Faith in Divine Unity*, 45–46.

193 **"if there were no"**: Al-Ghazali, *Faith in Divine Unity*, 46.

193 **"under all circumstances"**: Al-Ghazali, *On Patience and Thankfulness, Book XXXII of the Revival of the Religious Sciences*, trans. H. T. Littlejohn (Cambridge: Islamic Texts Society, 2011), 67.

193 **He then lost:** Nasrin Rouzati, "Evil and Human Suffering in Islamic Thought—Towards a Mystical Theodicy," *Religions* 9 (2018): 4, mdpi .com/2077-1444/9/2/47/htm; Brannon M. Wheeler, *Prophets in the Quran: An Introduction to the Quran and Muslim Exegesis* (London: Continuum, 2002), 157–60.

193 **He says to the faithful:** Al-Ghazali, *Faith in Divine Unity*, 47.

194 **"What doesn't kill me"**: Nietzsche, *Twilight of the Idols*, "Arrows and Epigrams," §8.

195 **"We invented happiness"**: Nietzsche, *Thus Spoke Zarathustra*, ed. Adrian Del Castro and Robert Pippin (Cambridge: Cambridge University Press, 2006), bk. 1, "Zarathustra's Prologue," §5.

195 **"the religion of compassion"**: Nietzsche, *The Gay Science* §338, trans. Josefine Nauckhoff (Cambridge: Cambridge University Press, 2001), 191.

195 **Life, for Nietzsche:** "I consider life itself to be an instinct for growth, for endurance, for the accumulation of force, for power: when there is no will to power, there is decline." Nietzsche, *The Anti-Christ: A Curse on Christianity* §6, trans. Judith Norman, in *The Anti-Christ, Ecce Homo, Twilight of the Idols, and Other Writings*, 6.

195 **"The discipline of suffering"**: Nietzsche, *Beyond Good and Evil* §225, trans. Judith Norman (Cambridge: Cambridge University Press, 2002), 116.

196 **"not wanting to help"**: These words belong to a character in Nietzsche's *Thus Spoke Zarathustra*, but they accord with his negative evaluation of pity throughout his works. Nietzsche, *Thus Spoke Zarathustra*, pt. 4, "The Ugliest Human Being."

196 **"this monstrous sum"**: Nietzsche, *The Gay Science* §337.

196 **"Have you ever said Yes"**: Nietzsche, *Thus Spoke Zarathustra*, pt. 4, "The Sleepwalker Song," §10.

197 **his "abysmal thought"**: *Thus Spoke Zarathustra*, pt. 3, "On the Vision and the Riddle," §2, and *Ecce Homo*, "Why I Am So Wise," §3.

198 **The story we get:** Muslim theologies offer an explanation for these differences. Over time, they say, God's revelations to the prophets before Muhammad were corrupted. God revealed those corruptions to Muhammad, with the Quran offering the definitive truth with regard to Job and also to figures like Moses and Jesus.

198 **"blameless and upright"**: Job 1:1, JSB.

200 **"I am incensed"**: Job 42:7, JSB.

200 **"restored Job's fortunes"**: Job 42:10, JSB.

202 **Another's suffering is:** Nietzsche observes, "What we most deeply and personally suffer from is incomprehensible and inaccessible to nearly everyone else; here we are hidden from our nearest, even if we eat from the same pot." *The Gay Science* §338.

202 **"I opened the passenger"**: Angela Williams Gorrell, *The Gravity of Joy: A Story of Being Lost and Found* (Grand Rapids, MI: Eerdmans, 2021), 6.

203 **"I hope you have a vision"**: Angela Williams Gorrell, Life Worth Living class lecture, Yale College, April 25, 2019.

12. When It Ends

208 **"Crito, we owe"**: Plato, *Phaedo* 118a, trans. G. M. A. Grube, in *Plato: Complete Works*. It is quite unlikely that Plato's *Phaedo* is a strictly accurate account of Socrates's jailhouse conversations and death. The work seems to put a good deal of Plato's own views on his teacher's lips. Two other works by Plato, the *Apology* and *Crito*, are also set on the days of Socrates's trial and death. They paint a slightly different but overlapping view.

209 **"life is a disease"**: Nietzsche, *The Gay Science* §340.

209 **The best life:** See Plato, *Phaedo* 82d.

210 **"escape the contamination"**: Plato, *Phaedo* 67a.

210 **"live in complete"**: Plato, *Gorgias* 523b, trans. Donald J. Zeyl, in Plato, *Complete Works*, 865.

210 **"training for death"**: Plato, *Phaedo* 81a.

211 **"The cloud," Nhat Hanh says:** Thich Nhat Hanh, *No Death, No Fear: Comforting Wisdom for Life* (New York: Riverhead, 2002), 25.

211 **"There is no real"**: Nhat Hanh, *No Death, No Fear*, 26.

211 **"Our true nature"**: Nhat Hanh, *No Death, No Fear*, 7.

211 **"nothing remains the same"**: Nhat Hanh, *No Death, No Fear*, 39.

212 **"the cream of enlightened wisdom"**: Nhat Hanh, *No Death, No Fear*, 14.

212 **"We can enjoy life"**: Nhat Hanh, *No Death, No Fear*, 5.

212 **"reality is free"**: Nhat Hanh, *No Death, No Fear*, 5.

212 **Shakespeare's Hamlet famously:** William Shakespeare, *Hamlet*, 3.1. In *The Oxford Shakespeare: The Complete Works*, 2nd ed., ed. Stanley Wells and Gary Taylor (Oxford: Clarendon, 2005), 697.

212 **Nhat Hanh imagines:** Nhat Hanh, *No Death, No Fear*, 13; see also 47.

212 **"instead of birth":** Nhat Hanh, *No Death, No Fear*, 71.

213 **"If your practice":** Nhat Hanh, *No Death, No Fear*, 83.

213 **"the conditions for happiness":** Nhat Hanh, *No Death, No Fear*, 100.

213 **philosopher Martha Nussbaum:** Martha Nussbaum, *The Therapy of Desire: Theory and Practice in Hellenistic Ethics* (Princeton, NJ: Princeton University Press, 1994), 206.

214 **"intrudes upon the value":** Nussbaum, *Therapy*, 209.

214 **"It is hard to have":** C. S. Lewis, *A Grief Observed* (San Francisco: HarperOne, 2004 [1961]), 15.

214 **"an eternal life":** Martin Hägglund, *This Life: Secular Faith and Spiritual Freedom* (New York: Anchor, 2020), 4.

215 **"Any life worth":** Hägglund, *This Life*, 6.

215 **"Caring about someone":** Hägglund, *This Life*, 10.

215 **"Eternal activity does not":** Hägglund, *This Life*, 5.

215 **"If I believed":** Hägglund, *This Life*, 5.

215 **"What I do":** Hägglund, *This Life*, 5.

216 **"Being invulnerable to":** Hägglund, *Dying for Time: Proust, Woolf, Nabakov* (Cambridge, MA: Harvard University Press, 2012), 11.

216 **It cuts our ties:** Hägglund, *This Life*, 9.

216 **"Such an ideal":** Hägglund, *This Life*, 207.

217 **"state of death":** Ignatius of Antioch, *Epistle to the Romans* 6, in *The Apostolic Fathers: Greek Texts and English Translations*, 3rd ed., ed. Michael Holmes (Grand Rapids, MI: Baker Academic, 2007), 233. The other quote from Ignatius in this paragraph is from the same location.

217 **Paul writes of death:** 1 Corinthians 15:26.

218 **"put on imperishability":** 1 Corinthians 15:53.

218 **suffer "utter bereavement":** This is how Hägglund describes the proper response to loss of loved ones. *This Life*, 62.

218 **They should mourn, Paul writes:** 1 Thessalonians 4:13.

218 **neither seeing death:** This is how the sixteenth-century theologian John Calvin interprets Paul in his commentary on 1 Thessalonians 4:13.

218 **Jesus Christ is "life-giving"**: 1 Corinthians 15:45.

218 **God's life-giving**: Quoting the Hebrew scriptures, Paul affirms, "The earth and its fullness are the Lord's." 1 Corinthians 10:26, quoting Psalm 24:1.

221 **An ancient Christian text**: As with many ancient texts, the historical accuracy of *The Passion of Perpetua and Felicity* has been doubted. Whether or not its particular story is true, it is incontestable that those who wrote the story and ordinary people throughout history and across the world thought it was the noblest of things to give their lives rather than betray their vision of the good life.

13. It Turns Out We Have Some Work to Do

228 **"Jefferson began to"**: Henry Wiencek, "The Dark Side of Thomas Jefferson," *Smithsonian Magazine*, October 2012.

229 **"in the course of"**: Andrew Levy, *The First Emancipator: The Forgotten Story of Robert Carter, the Founding Father Who Freed His Slaves* (New York: Random House, 2005), 93.

229 **As Levy describes Carter**: Levy, *First Emancipator*, 144.

230 **"In this instance"**: Peter Singer, "Famine, Affluence, and Morality," 242.

230 **"We are all bound"**: Kimmerer, *Braiding Sweetgrass*, 383.

231 **"The moral covenant"**: Kimmerer, *Braiding Sweetgrass*, 384.

231 **"We are inquiring"**: Aristotle, *Nicomachean Ethics* 2.2, 1103b.

231 **"All my life I grew"**: *Pirkei Avot* 1:17.

231 **"For one whose good deeds"**: *Pirkei Avot* 3.12.

232 **"To what may one whose wisdom"**: *Pirkei Avot* 3:22.

232 **"Why do you call me 'Lord'"**: Luke 6:46–49.

233 **"I can talk all day"**: *Analects* 2.9 (Leys).

233 **"People are always"**: Baldwin, "White Racism or World Community?" in *Collected Essays*, 752.

238 **The Potawatomi elders**: Kimmerer, *Braiding Sweetgrass*, 5.

239 **"remember the Lord"**: Deuteronomy 8:18.

239 **"I transmit rather"**: *Analects* 7:1 (Slingerland).

14. Change Is Hard

243 **When you see**: Richard H. Thaler and Cass R. Sunstein, *Nudge: The Final Edition* (New Haven, CT: Yale University Press, 2021), 52.

244 **two horses driven:** The allegory of the chariot is found in Plato's *Phaedrus* 246a–254e.

244 **"first and best":** Plato, *Laws* 626e, trans. Trevor J. Saunders, in *Plato: Complete Works*.

244 **They give the striking example:** The example of Clocky the robotic alarm clock is described in Thaler and Sunstein, *Nudge*, 53–54.

245 **A thesis that:** Thaler and Sunstein, *Nudge*, 54–55.

247 **As he later:** Al-Ghazali narrated his story of transformation some twelve years after the fact in his spiritual autobiography, *Deliverance from Error*. For the traditional account of al-Ghazali's crisis and transformation, see Eric Ormsby's *Ghazali: The Revival of Islam* (London: Oneworld Publications, 2008), 29–33, 106–10. Of course, the lives we live and the stories we tell ourselves about them later may be two different things. Kenneth Garden's recent book, *The First Islamic Reviver: Abu Hamid al-Ghazali and His Revival of the Religious Sciences* (New York: Oxford University Press, 2013), raises the question of whether the story al-Ghazali tells in *Deliverance* is the best way to understand what happened to him in 1095. The fact that the story of al-Ghazali's radical departure from Baghdad persists is a good reminder that the stories we tell are sometimes more enduring than our lives themselves; we should take care with the stories we tell—especially the ones we tell ourselves.

247 **"Theory," he confessed:** *Al-Ghazali's Path to Sufism: His Deliverance from Error*, trans. R. J. McCarthy (Louisville, KY: Fons Vitae, 2000), 51.

248 **The associate could:** "Whenever . . . the intellect neglects the soul it will find nothing but disloyalty in it and the loss of capital—just like the disloyal servant who, left at liberty, may abscond with the money." *Al-Ghazali on Vigilance and Self-Examination*, trans. Anthony F. Shaker (Cambridge: Islamic Text Society, 2015), 5.

248 **"absent-minded or preoccupied":** *Al-Ghazali on Vigilance*, 7.

249 **"because it is loose":** *Al-Ghazali on Vigilance*, 9. The other quotes in this paragraph are from the same source.

249 **"Know that the reality":** *Al-Ghazali on Vigilance*, 17.

250 **"crushed by awe":** *Al-Ghazali on Vigilance*, 18.

251 **"To live is the rarest":** Oscar Wilde, "Soul of Man," 239.

251 **"What man has sought":** Wilde, "Soul of Man," 267.

251 **The ancient world:** Wilde, "Soul of Man," 240.

252 **But it's far from:** Wilde was an advocate for a type of anarchic socialism, which is the central concern of his essay "The Soul of Man under Socialism." Wilde's hope was that without an overbearing government (the anarchic part) and with all of our basic needs provided for (the socialism part), all of us would be free to realize our most authentic selves in unencumbered artistic expression.

252 **"a man is called":** Wilde, "Soul of Man," 263.

252 **"Art is the most":** Wilde, "Soul of Man," 248.

253 **"the soul made incarnate":** Oscar Wilde, *De Profundis*, 52.

254 **There is a story:** Mark 10:17–22.

255 **"You cannot serve":** Luke 16:13.

255 **"How hard it will be":** Mark 10:23.

255 **"Children, how hard":** Mark 10:24.

255 **"It is easier":** Mark 10:25.

255 **"Then who can":** Mark 10:26.

255 **"For mortals it is":** Mark 10:27.

256 **"Why do you call me good?":** Mark 10:18.

15. Making It Stick

259 **"I woke up":** *Alcoholics Anonymous: The Story of How Many Thousands of Men and Women Have Recovered from Alcoholism*, 4th ed. (New York: Alcoholics Anonymous World Services, 2001), 5.

259 **"Shortly afterward I":** *Alcoholics Anonymous*, 5.

260 **"Why don't you":** *Alcoholics Anonymous*, 12.

260 **"Something has happened":** *Alcoholics Anonymous*, 14.

261 **"I soon found":** *Alcoholics Anonymous*, 15, 16.

261 **And according to a 2020:** John F. Kelly, Keith Humphreys, and Marica Ferri, "Alcoholics Anonymous and Other 12-Step Programs for Alcohol Use Disorder," *Cochrane Database of Systematic Reviews*, no. 3 (2020), CD012880, https://doi.org/10.1002/14651858.CD012880.

263 **"ignorance of the true nature":** Dalai Lama, *How to See Yourself as You Really Are*, trans. and ed. Jeffrey Hopkins (New York: Atria Books, 2006), 28.

264 **We are beset:** For one discussion of the illusion of "my" and "I," see *How to See Yourself*, 32–38. The illusion of "I" is a subtle thing in Buddhist thought. The Dalai Lama strains language (perhaps helpfully!) to capture

this nuance by insisting, "It is not that phenomena *are* illusions; rather, they are *like* illusions." *How to See Yourself,* 176.

265 "**All counterproductive emotions**": *How to See Yourself,* 31.

265 "**What you take as pleasures**": See chapter 4 in this book.

266 "**Be willing to familiarize**": Dalai Lama, *How to See Yourself,* 236.

266 "**especially out of order**": Joseph de Guibert, *The Jesuits: Their Spiritual Doctrine and Practice, a Historical Study,* ed. George E. Ganss, trans. William J. Young (Chicago: Institute of Jesuit Sources, 1964), 23, cited in Christ Lowney, *Heroic Leadership* (Chicago: Loyola Press, 2003), 40.

266 "**a different nobility**": Joseph A. Tetlow, *The Spiritual Exercises of Ignatius Loyola: With Commentary* (New York: Crossroad, 2009), 14.

267 "**Obedience issues in**": Jules J. Toner, trans., "Deliberation of Our First Fathers," *Woodstock Letters: A Historical Journal of Jesuit Educational and Missionary Activities* 95 (1966): 328, in Lowney, *Heroic Leadership,* 49.

267 **Both are described:** We should be careful to point out that the *Exercises* are hardly a literary classic. They are the notes of a practitioner urgently preparing laborers for divine orders. Much more than a book (the *Exercises*), what has come down to us are the practices themselves (the exercises).

268 **You live it:** Ignatius, *Spiritual Exercises* §112. The number given indicates the paragraph number in Ignatius's text, not the page number in Tetlow's translation.

268 "**I consider how**": *Spiritual Exercises,* §235.

269 **The outline is:** Adapted from James Martin, *The Jesuit Guide to (Almost) Everything: A Spirituality for Real Life* (New York: HarperCollins, 2010), 97.

269 "**St. Ignatius says**": Dorothy Day, *Duty of Delight: The Diaries of Dorothy Day* (Milwaukee: Marquette University Press, 2008), 129.

270 "**each moment offers**": Martin, *Jesuit Guide,* 91.

271 "**Restraining yourself and returning**": This exchange between Yan Hui and Confucius is found in *Analects* 12.1. We are quoting from Edward Slingerland's translation. There is some controversy about how to understand the relationship between restraining the self and returning to the rites, on the one hand, and goodness, on the other. Slingerland makes it sound like the former are simply the substance of the latter. There are good reasons to think the relationship may be more like that of instrumental means to an end. Roger Ames and Henry Rosemont Jr., in their philosophical translation of the *Analects* (New York: Ballantine, 1998), translate, "Through self-discipline and observing ritual propriety one be-

comes authoritative in one's conduct [*ren*]." Self-discipline and ritual propriety are the means by which one establishes one's *ren*.

273 **"At fifteen, I set"**: *Analects* 2.4 (Leys).

273 **Age seventy encapsulates**: There is some resonance on this point between Confucius and the Christian theologian Augustine of Hippo, who wrote, "Love, and do what you want" (*Homilies on the First Epistle of John* 7.4.8, trans. Boniface Ramsey [Hyde Park, NY: New City Press, 2008], 110). The idea is that desires proceeding from true, ordered love produce good, loving action.

273 **"One who knows"**: *Analects* 6.20 (Slingerland).

276 **"From the hilltop"**: Kimmerer, *Braiding Sweetgrass*, 21.